Study Guide

for use with

Fundamental Financial Accounting Concepts

Fifth Edition

Thomas P. Edmonds
Cindy D. Edmonds
Both of University of Alabama -- Birmingham

Frances M. McNair
Mississippi State University

Philip R. Olds
Virginia Commonwealth University

Prepared by
Philip R. Olds
Virginia Commonwealth University

**McGraw-Hill
Irwin**

Boston   Burr Ridge, IL   Dubuque, IA   Madison, WI   New York   San Francisco   St. Louis
Bangkok   Bogotá   Caracas   Kuala Lumpur   Lisbon   London   Madrid   Mexico City
Milan   Montreal   New Delhi   Santiago   Seoul   Singapore   Sydney   Taipei   Toronto

McGraw-Hill
Irwin

Study Guide for use with
FUNDAMENTAL FINANCIAL ACCOUNTING CONCEPTS
Thomas P. Edmonds, Cindy D. Edmonds, Frances M. McNair, Philip R. Olds

Published by McGraw-Hill/Irwin, an imprint of The McGraw-Hill Companies, Inc., 1221 Avenue of the
Americas, New York, NY 10020. Copyright © 2006, 2003, 2000, 1998, 1996 by The McGraw-Hill Companies,
Inc. All rights reserved.

1 2 3 4 5 6 7 8 9 0 QPD/QPD 0 9 8 7 6 5 4

ISBN 0-07-298945-9

www.mhhe.com

Introduction

How to Use This Study Guide

There are at least three different ways this study guide can be used to supplement the textbook. **First**, some students should find it helpful if used immediately after reading a given chapter in the text. The articulation problems, explained below, will especially be useful to help you determine if you have learned the basic concepts in a chapter.

Second, some students will find this guide helpful if used after a given chapter has been covered in class. Students often make mistakes working assigned homework problems and would like additional, similar problems to work for which they have solutions. The "exercise-type problems" in this guide provide that opportunity. Not only are the solutions provided, but they were written with students, not accounting instructors, in mind. This means that solutions are not simply presented, they are explained. Forms for answering these exercise-type problems are provided in this book. This not only saves you time, but also gives a little help if you are having trouble getting started on a problem.

Third, this study guide contains multiple-choice problems (with solutions) similar to those used by many accounting instructors on exams. Working the multiple choice problems is a good way to review for exams. Even if your instructor does not use multiple-choice questions, you will find these are a good way to review many different concepts from a chapter in a relatively short length of time.

As you can see, the study guide is not just for students who are having difficulty understanding accounting. However, regardless of why you are using this study guide, **you will get the best results if you do NOT look at the solutions before you make a serious effort to solve the problems on your own.**

How to Study for This Accounting Course

If accounting instructors throughout the country were asked "What one thing can students do to improve their grade in the first accounting course?" their answer would be, **KEEP UP!** Unlike some disciplines, accounting is not a subject for which you can cram the night before an exam.

What should you do to keep up in this course?

First: **Read** the chapter thoroughly **before** it is covered in **class**. As you read the material be sure to **study the examples and illustrations in the text carefully**. Students often skip these because they take a considerable time to analyze, but understanding the examples included in each chapter is essential to being able to work assigned homework problems.

Second: **Work** assigned homework **problems before** they are reviewed in **class**. You will learn much more by attempting to work a problem on your own, even if you do not work it correctly, than you will learn by reviewing the instructor's solution to a problem that you have not attempted in advance.

Finally: Some students need to work more problems than are assigned as homework. If you do not understand the material in a chapter after the two steps described above, **work more problems!** This study guide can be helpful for this purpose.

Many students find it helpful to work in study groups. When you try to explain an accounting concept to another student, you often learn more than the student that you are trying to help. Study groups work best if each person studies some on their own before the group meeting.

If you are making a serious effort in this course, but continue to have difficulties, **talk to your instructor.** As instructors, we often have students talk to us after they have gotten too far behind to be helped. If you do not understand Chapter 3, for example, you cannot understand Chapter 4. Ask for help as soon as you have a problem.

What is an Articulation Problem?

One of the first and easiest things to learn in accounting is that there are four basic financial statements. As explained in Chapter 1, these statements are the:

> Balance Sheet
> Income Statement
> Statement of Cash Flows
> Statement of Changes in Stockholders' Equity

Each of these financial statements is based on a relatively simple model, which you might think of as an equation or format. Learning the basic format of each statement also is relatively simple.

One of the most difficult things for most students to learn, however, is the way the different financial statements interrelate. When an event occurs in a business, very seldom does that event affect only one of the statements; often all four are affected. For example, every event that affects the income statement also affects the balance sheet.

Accounting theorists refer to this interrelated characteristic as articulation. Accountants in the real world seldom use the term articulation, but they must constantly deal with the concept.

Accounting instructors sometimes ask non-accounting instructors, such as those who teach finance courses, "What accounting concept important to your course do students have the most trouble understanding?" They often answer, "Students do not understand how the financial statements relate to each other." Understanding the concept of articulation is important to all business majors, not just accounting majors.

The text being used in your accounting course places great emphasis on the concept of articulation. In the textbook, this concept is usually presented in the context of the **horizontal model.** Most chapters in this study guide provide a series of articulation questions which will help you understand concepts related to the horizontal model presented in the text. You should study these questions early in your review of each chapter. If you do not understand most of the articulation questions presented, then you do not understand the concepts in that chapter as well as you should. Please take the time to review these questions carefully.

What is a Multiple True-False Problem?

Multiple true-false (MTF) problems can be thought of as a cross between a traditional multiple-choice question and a traditional true-false question. Sometimes, a MTF item will present a set of facts (like a multiple-choice question). Next, four or five statements related to those facts will be presented and you are asked to indicate if **each** of these statements is true or false. Unlike a multiple-choice question in which one and only one choice is true, for a MTF item any number of the "choices" can be true or false.

This study guide also uses a second form of the MTF item. This form simply presents four or five statements about a common topic, and asks you to indicate if **each** item is true or false. Again, any number of the statements can be true or false. An advantage of MTF items is that they allow you to assess your understanding of many different facts and concepts about a topic more quickly than if a series of multiple-choice items were used. Even if your instructor does not use MTF items on his or her exams, you should find them helpful in studying for other types of exam questions.

Good luck in your course!

Philip R. Olds

Comments and suggestions about this Study Guide are welcome and may be sent to:

Prof. Philip R. Olds
Box 844000
Richmond, Virginia, 23284-4000
or
E-mail to:
prolds@vcu.edu

Table of Contents

Chapter One
Elements of Financial Statements

Learning Objectives for the Chapter

After completing this chapter you should be able to:

1. Explain the role of accounting in society.
2. Distinguish among the different accounting entities involved in business events.
3. Name and define the major elements of financial statements.
4. Describe the relationships expressed in the accounting equation.
5. Record business events in general ledger accounts organized under the accounting equation.
6. Explain how the historical cost and reliability concepts affect amounts reported in financial statements.
7. Classify business events as asset source, use, or exchange transactions.
8. Use the general ledger account information to prepare four financial statements.
9. Record business events using a horizontal financial statements model.
10. Explain how to use the price-earnings ratio and growth percentage analysis to assess the market value of common stock.
11. Identify three types of business organizations and some of the technical terms they use in their real world financial reports.

Brief Explanation of the Learning Objectives

1.   Explain the role of accounting in society.

Many decisions made by individuals, businesses, not-for-profit entities, and governments are based on financial information. Accounting is the profession responsible for developing much of that financial information.

2.   Distinguish among the different accounting entities involved in business events.

One important principle of accounting is the separate entity assumption. Among other things, this means that accountants consider the business entity to be separate from its owners. It is also important to remember that business events always involve at least two entities. Be sure you understand which entity's financial statements you are being asked about. For example, if Smith Company provides tax advice to Jones Company, Smith will recognize revenue, but Jones will recognize an expense.

3.   Name and define the major elements of financial statements.

There are nine elements of financial statements discussed in this chapter: *assets, liabilities, equity,* (which is subdivided into *common stock* and *retained earnings*), *revenues, expenses, net income, and distributions.* Below is a brief explanation of these elements.

Assets: Things with future economic value to the business.

Liabilities: Claims against assets made by non-owners.

Stockholders' Equity: *Common stock* is that portion of equity resulting from direct investment by the owners. *Retained earnings* is that portion of owners' equity resulting from *net income* the business has earned but has <u>not</u> distributed to the owners.

Revenues: An increase in assets that results from the business providing services (or selling goods) to customers. (In Chapter 3 it will be shown that revenues can result in a reduction of liabilities as well as an increase in assets.)

Expenses: A reduction in assets that the business incurred in the hopes of producing revenues. (In Chapter 2 it will be shown that expenses can result in increased liabilities as well as a reduction in assets.)

Net Income Revenues - expenses = net income. A positive net income increases retained earnings. A negative net income, called a net loss, decreases retained earnings.

Distributions When a business has earned net income it may choose to keep these earnings in the business, or to pay out part or all of the earnings to the owners of the business. If the business is a corporation, the distributions are called dividends. Because the payment of distributions is not expected to generate revenue for the business entity, they are not considered expenses, but the do reduce retained earnings.

4.   Describe the relationships expressed in the accounting equation.

The most common way of stating the accounting equation is:

Assets   =   Liabilities   +   Equity

Equity refers to the owners' claims against assets. Generically, equity is often referred to as *owners' equity*, but in a corporation the term most commonly used is *stockholders' equity*, and this is the term used throughout this course. The relationships that exist among the three variables in the accounting equation are like those of any other algebraic equation. If the amount on one side of the equation are increased or decreased, the amounts on the other side must increase or decrease by the same amount.

5.   **Record business events in general ledger accounts organized under an accounting equation.**

This is done with the use of the self-study problems presented below. The articulation problems are especially intended to help you accomplish this objective, but remember, the articulation problems focus on broad account types such as assets. The general ledger accounts are more detailed, and include numerous different types of asset, liability, and stockholders' equity accounts.

6.   **Explain how the historical cost and reliability concepts affect amounts reported in financial statements.**

Historical cost refers the amount that was paid for something when it was originally purchased. Fair market-value, or current value, refers to what something is worth today. Accounting in the United States reports most assets and liabilities at their historical costs, not their current value. Decision makers would usually prefer to know an asset's current value rather than its historical cost, but determining current value can be expensive and inaccurate. Since accounting places great importance in reporting reliable information, historical cost, which is easily verified and thus more reliable, is reported in most situations.

7.   **Classify business events as asset source, use, or exchange transactions.**

Asset source: An event that causes total assets to increase. There will be a corresponding increase in liabilities and/or stockholders' equity.

Asset use: An event that causes total assets to decrease. There will be a corresponding decrease in liabilities and/or stockholders' equity.

Asset exchange: An event that causes one asset to increase and another asset to decrease by the same amount. It is possible that more than two assets will be involved in such an event, but the net effect on assets will be that total assets do not change.

8.   **Use the general ledger account information to prepare four financial statements.**

The four financial statements are:

Balance Sheet: A listing of the *assets, liabilities*, and components of *stockholders' equity* of a business <u>as of a particular date</u>.

Income Statement: A comparison of the *revenues* earned and *expenses* incurred by a business <u>for a particular period</u>, usually one year.

Statement of Changes in Stockholders' Equity:	A detailed explanation of the stockholders' equity section of the balance sheet. This statement provides more explanation about why the balances changed for *common stock* and *retained earnings* <u>during a particular period</u> than is provided on the balance sheet.
Statement of Cash Flows:	A detailed explanation of how the business obtained and used cash <u>during a particular period</u>, usually a year. This statement is divided into three sections: *operating activities, investing activities*, and *financing activities*.

The two exercise-type self-study problems are intended to help you accomplish this objective more completely.

9.   **Record business events using a horizontal financial statements model.**

This is accomplished with the use of the self-study problems presented below. The articulation problems are especially intended to help you accomplish this objective.

10.   **Explain how to use the price-earnings ratio and growth percentage analysis to assess the market value of common stock.**

The *price-earnings ratio* (P/E ratio) is computed by dividing the market price of one share of a company's stock by the company's *earnings per share* (EPS). If a company's P/E ratio is 15, this means that on a given day, investors were willing to pay $15 for each $1 of earnings the company produced in its last accounting period. The higher a company's P/E ratio, the more optimistic investors are about its future earnings potential. This optimism often is based on the fact that a particular company has experienced a higher growth rate in its earnings than the average company in its industry.

11.   **Identify three types of business organizations and some of the technical terms they use in their real world financial reports.**

Most businesses can be classified as being engaged in service activities, merchandising activities, or manufacturing activities. Service entities generally do not sell things to others, but provide some form of service, such as legal advice. Merchandising entities, such as Wal-Mart, sell things to customers that other entities made. Manufacturing entities make the items they sell, and they often do not sell directly to the ultimate user of the goods, but rather to merchandising entities. For example, Norelco manufactures electric shavers and sells them to Costco, a merchandiser, who sells them to the final customer. Different types of entities often use slightly different terminology to describe similar accounting events. For example, in a service entity, revenue may be called *service revenue*, but in merchandising and manufacturing entities revenue is often called *sales*.

Self-Study Problems

Articulation Problems

For each situation below, indicate its effects on the accounting elements shown on the accompanying chart. Use the following letters to indicate your answer (you do not need to enter amounts):

Increase = **I**   Decrease = **D**   No effect = **N**

1. Derek Co. acquired cash from the owners to begin business operations.

Assets	Liabilities	Equity	Revenues	Expenses	Net Income	Cash

2. Ergo Co. provided services to its customers for cash.

Assets	Liabilities	Equity	Revenues	Expenses	Net Income	Cash

3. Freight Co. borrowed cash from the Local Bank.

Assets	Liabilities	Equity	Revenues	Expenses	Net Income	Cash

4. Galaxy Co. incurred operating expenses and paid cash.

Assets	Liabilities	Equity	Revenues	Expenses	Net Income	Cash

5. Halley Co. purchased land for cash.

Assets	Liabilities	Equity	Revenues	Expenses	Net Income	Cash

6.   Iris Co. made a cash distribution to its owners

Assets	Liabilities	Equity	Revenues	Expenses	Net Income	Cash

Multiple-Choice Problems

1.   The Jersey Company provided services to a customer for $1,000 cash. Which of the following statements related to this transaction are <u>false</u>?
    a.   Total assets would increase.
    b.   Total liabilities would not be affected.
    c.   Retained earnings would not be affected.
    d.   Cash flow from *operating* activities would increase.

2.   The following amounts were drawn from the records of Kansas Co.: Total Assets = $1,100; Common stock = $300; Retained Earnings = $200. Based on this information, total liabilities must be equal to:
    a. $300
    b. $600
    c. $800
    d. $900

3.   During 2005 the following events occurred at Lance Co.: owners invested $10,000 of cash; revenue of $20,000 was earned; the company borrowed $4,000 from the bank; expenses of $13,000 were incurred; and $2,000 cash was distributed to the owners. What was Lance's net income for 2005?
    a. $ 1,000
    b. $ 5,000
    c. $ 7,000
    d. $11,000

4.   Mars Co. borrowed $8,000 cash. As a result of this event:
    a.   Assets increased.
    b.   Expenses increased.
    c.   Stockholders' equity increased.
    d.   Revenue increased.

5.   Nevada Co. purchased land for $2,000 cash. As a result of this event:
 a.   Cash flow from *operating* activities would decrease.
 b.   Cash flow from *investing* activities would increase.
 c.   Cash flow from *financing* activities would decrease.
 d.   Cash flow from *investing* activities would decrease.

The following information applies to Questions 6 - 10.

At the <u>beginning</u> of 2006 Oslo Co. had the following account balances:

Assets	$10,000
Liabilities	6,000
Common stock	3,000
Retained Earnings	1,000

During 2006 the following cash events occurred:

a.   Provided services to customers for $8,000.
b.   Repaid $2,000 of debt.
c.   Owners invested an additional $3,000 in the business.
d.   Incurred operating expenses of $5,000.
e.   Dividends amounted to $1,000.

6.   Oslo's net income for 2006 was:
 a. $1,000
 b. $2,000
 c. $3,000
 d. $4,000

7.   Total assets at the end of 2006 are:
 a. $ 3,000
 b. $13,000
 c. $15,000
 d. $18,000

8.   Total liabilities at the end of 2006 are:
 a. $ 0
 b. $4,000
 c. $6,000
 d. $8,000

9. Common stock at the end of 2006 is:
   a. $3,000
   b. $4,000
   c. $5,000
   d. $6,000

10. Retained earnings at the end of 2006 are:
    a. $1,000
    b. $2,000
    c. $3,000
    d. $4,000

11. The following information is available for Plano Co. for 2009:

Sales	$5,500,000
Net Earnings	400,000
Stockholders' Equity	2,000,000
EPS	2.00
Current stock price	37.00
Number of shares outstanding	200,000

    What is Plano Company's P/E ratio?
    a. 2.8 times
    b. 5.0
    c. 5.5
    d. 18.5

12. Razor Co. borrowed $1,000 from the Town & Country Bank. Which of the following elements of financial statements would <u>not</u> be immediately affected by this event?
    a. Assets
    b. Liabilities
    c. Revenues
    d. Cash

13. Which of the following statements is true?
    a. Net income is an account on the balance sheet.
    b. Cash flow from operating activities appears on the income statement.
    c. Beginning and ending cash balances appear on the statement of changes in stockholders' equity.
    d. Retained earnings is an account that appears on both the balance sheet and the statement of changes in stockholders' equity.

14. Which of the following statements is true?
    a. An increase in net income will always cause *stockholders' equity* on the balance sheet to increase.
    b. An increase in assets is always the result of revenues earned.
    c. A decrease in liabilities will be reflected in the *investing* section of the statement of cash flows.
    d. A distribution will decrease *common stock* on the balance sheet.

15. Which of the following would appear in the *investing* section of the statement of cash flows?
    a. A stock-brokerage firm earns revenue by providing investment advice.
    b. A business purchases land on which to build an office.
    c. The owners of a company invest cash in the business.
    d. A company repays money it had borrowed from the local bank.

16. Based on the P/E ratios provided for the following companies, determine which company investors seem to be <u>least</u> optimistic about regarding its potential for future growth.

Company:	**Nedra**	**Porter**	**Tully**	**Wall**
P/E Ratio:	12.3	16.8	17.9	25.4

    a. Nedra
    b. Porter
    c. Tully
    d. Wall

17. Sterling Co. provided services to customers and received cash. Which of the following choices reflects how this event would affect the company's financial statements?

	Assets	=	Liab.	+	Equity	Rev	−	Exp.	=	Net Inc.	Cash Flow
a.	I		N		N	I		N		N	I
b.	I		N		I	I		N		I	I
c.	N		N		I	I		N		I	I
d.	N		N		N	I		N		I	I

18.   Texas Co. incurred operating expenses and paid cash. Which of the following choices reflects how this event would affect the company's financial statements?

	Assets	=	Liab.	+	Equity	Rev	–	Exp.	=	Net Inc.	Cash Flow
a.	D		N		D	D		N		D	D
b.	N		D		D	N		I		D	D
c.	D		D		N	N		N		N	D
d.	D		N		D	N		I		D	D

19.   Utah Co. borrowed cash from the Corner Bank. Which of the following choices reflects how this event would affect the company's financial statements?

	Assets	=	Liab.	+	Equity	Rev.	–	Exp.	=	Net Inc.	Cash Flow
a.	I		I		N	N		N		N	I
b.	I		I		I	I		N		I	I
c.	I		I		N	N		I		D	I
d.	N		I		D	N		I		D	I

Multiple True-False Problems

1.   Indicate if each of the following statements about the statement of cash flows (SCF) is true or false.
    a.   When a business acquires cash from the owners, it is reported in the *investing activities* section of the SCF.
    b.   When a business buys land for cash, it is reported in the *operating activities* section of the SCF.
    c.   When a business makes a distribution to its owners, it is reported in the *financing activities* section of the SCF.
    d.   When a company repays a bank loan, it is reported in the *financing activities* section of the SCF.
    e.   When a company incurs cash expenses, it is reported in the *operating activities* section of the SCF.

2.   Indicate if each of the following statements about the balance sheet is true or false.
    a.   The accounting equation may be expressed as: Assets – Liabilities = Equity.
    b.   One purpose of the balance sheet is to explain how a company obtained its cash.
    c.   A liability account or an equity account must decrease if the cash account decreases.
    d.   If a company owned land, its balance sheet would report the land at the amount at which it was purchased originally, not at its current market value.
    e.   If a company paid cash for advertising expense but forgot to record this transaction, the company's balance sheet would not balance.

3. The following information relates to the Vending Co. for its first year of operations. All transactions were in cash.

> Acquired $20,000 from its owners.
> Paid $4,000 for salaries.
> Purchased land for $15,000
> Earned $12,000 of revenue.
> Made a $2,000 distribution to the owners.

Indicate if each of the following statements is true or false.
   a. At the end of the year total assets were $11,000.
   b. Net income for the year was $6,000.
   c. Net cash flows from *financing activities* was $18,000.
   d. The balance in Retained Earnings at the end of the year was $6,000.
   e. The balance in the cash account at the end of the year was $11,000.

4. Indicate if each of the following statements about the closing process is true or false.
   a. The Common Stock account is closed at the end of each year.
   b. Liability accounts are closed at the end of each year.
   c. Revenue accounts are closed at the end of each year.
   d. Expense accounts are closed at the end of each year.
   e. Accounts that are closed always begin the following year with a $-0- balance.

Exercise-Type Problems

P-1. Wyoming Co. began its operations on January 1, 2005. During 2005 it had the following cash transactions.

a. The owners invested $10,000 in the business.
b. Provided services to customers for $6,000.
c. Borrowed $5,000 from the Local Bank.
d. Incurred $2,500 in expenses.
e. Made a $1,500 distribution to the owners.

Required:
1. Explain how each of these transactions would affect Wyoming's accounting equation using the form provided below. Use brackets, ( ), to indicate amounts being subtracted. The first transaction has been done as an example.
2. Prepare an income statement, statement of changes in stockholders' equity, balance sheet, and statement of cash flows. Use the forms provided below.

Form for requirement 1

| | | | | | Stockholders' Equity | | |
Event	Assets	=	Liabilities	+	Common Stock	+	Retained Earnings
a.	10,000				10,000		
b.							
c.							
d.							
e.							
Totals							

Forms for requirement 2

Wyoming Company
Income Statement
For the Year Ended December 31, 2005

Revenues	$
Expenses	
Net income	$

Wyoming Company
Statement of Changes in Stockholders' Equity
For the Year Ended December 31, 2005

Beginning Common stock	$	
Plus: Investments		
Ending Common stock		$
Beginning Retained Earnings	$	
Plus: Net Income		
Less: Dividends		
Ending Retained Earnings		
Total Stockholders' Equity		$

Wyoming Company
Balance Sheet
As of December 31, 2005

Assets:
     Cash $ _____
Total Assets $ _____

Liabilities:
     Note payable $
Total Liabilities

Stockholders' Equity:
     Common stock $
     Retained Earnings   _____
Total Stockholders' Equity   _____

Total Liabilities and Stockholders' Equity $ _____

Wyoming Company
Statement of Cash Flows
For the Year Ended December 31, 2005

Cash Flows from Operating Activities:
    Cash Receipts from Revenue $
    Cash Payments for Expenses   _____
Net Cash Flow from Operating Activities $

Cash Flow from Investing Activities:

Cash Flows from Financing Activities:
    Cash Receipts from Owners' Investments
    Cash Receipts from Borrowed Funds
    Cash Payments for Dividends   _____
Net Cash Flow from Financing Activities

Net Increase in Cash $_____

P-2   Wyoming Co., which began operations in 2005 (see P-1 above), continued in business during 2006. Assume the account balances at January 1, 2006, were:

Assets	$17,000	Common stock	$10,000
Liabilities	5,000	Retained Earnings	2,000

Wyoming had the following cash transactions during 2006:

a.   Purchased land for $8,000.
b.   Provided service to customers for $10,000.
c.   Owners invested $6,000 in the business.
d.   Wyoming repaid the $5,000 borrowed from the Local Bank in 2005. (Assume no interest charges).
e.   Incurred $4,500 in expenses.
f.   Made a $2,000 distribution to the owners.

Required:
1.   Explain how each of these transactions would affect Wyoming's accounting equation using the form provided on the following page. Use brackets, ( ), to indicate amounts being subtracted. The first transaction has been done as an example.
2.   Prepare an income statement, statement of changes in stockholders' equity, balance sheet, and statement of cash flows. Prepare these statements using your own paper, but use the format shown in P-1 or in the textbook as your guide.

Form for requirement 1

					Stockholders' Equity		
Event	Assets	=	Liabilities	+	Common Stock	+	Retained Earnings
Beg. Bal.	17,000		5,000		10,000		2,000
a.	8,000 land (8,000)						
b.							
c.							
d.							
e.							
f.							
Totals							

Solutions to Self-Study Problems

Articulation Problems

1.   Derek Co. acquired cash from the owners to begin business operations.

Assets	Liabilities	Equity	Revenues	Expenses	Net Income	Cash
I	N	I	N	N	N	I

Cash, an asset increased, and common stock, a part of stockholders' equity, increased.

2.   Ergo Co. provided services to its customers for cash.

Assets	Liabilities	Equity	Revenues	Expenses	Net Income	Cash
I	N	I	I	N	I	I

Cash, an asset increased. The company earned revenues, which caused net income to increase. An increase in net income causes retained earnings, a part of stockholders' equity, to increase.

3.   Freight Co. borrowed cash from the Local Bank.

Assets	Liabilities	Equity	Revenues	Expenses	Net Income	Cash
I	I	N	N	N	N	I

Cash, an asset increased. Because the borrowed money will have to be repaid to the bank, liabilities also increased. This cash was not earned. Therefore, it is not revenue.

4.   Galaxy Co. incurred operating expenses and paid cash.

Assets	Liabilities	Equity	Revenues	Expenses	Net Income	Cash
D	N	D	N	I	D	D

Cash, an asset, decreased. Because the cash was spent in the hopes of producing revenue, this is an expense. The increase in expense caused net income to decrease, which caused retained earnings, a part of stockholders' equity, to decrease.

5.   Halley Co. purchased land for cash.

Assets	Liabilities	Equity	Revenues	Expenses	Net Income	Cash
N	N	N	N	N	N	D

One asset, cash, decreased while another asset, land, increased by the same amount. Therefore, there was no change in total assets. This expenditure was not an expense because the company received land, an asset that the company can sell if it wishes.

6.   Iris Co. made a cash distribution to its owners.

Assets	Liabilities	Equity	Revenues	Expenses	Net Income	Cash
D	N	D	N	N	N	D

Cash, an asset, decreased while retained earnings, a part of stockholders' equity, decreased. This payment of cash was not an expense because the money was not spent in the expectation that it would produce revenues.

Multiple-Choice Problems

1.   c.   Revenues increase, causing net income to increase, causing retained earnings to increase.

2.   b.

Assets	$ 1,100
less: Common stock	300
Retained Earnings	200
equals: Liabilities	**$ 600**

3.   c.

Revenue	$20,000
less: Expenses	13,000
Net Income	**$ 7,000**

4.   a.   Cash is an asset. (Liabilities also increased.)

5.   d.   Purchasing land is an *investing* activity. The purchase of land caused cash to decrease.

6.   c.

Revenue	$ 8,000
less: Expenses	5,000
Net Income	**$ 3,000**

7.   b.

Beginning balance	$10,000
Transaction a	8,000
Transaction b	(2,000)
Transaction c	3,000
Transaction d	(5,000)
Transaction e	(1,000)
Ending balance	**$13,000**

8.   b.

Beginning balance	$ 6,000
Transaction b	(2,000)
Ending balance	**$ 4,000**

9.   d.

Beginning balance	$ 3,000
Transaction c	3,000
Ending balance	**$ 6,000**

10.   c.

Beginning balance	$ 1,000
Transaction a	8,000
Transaction d	(5,000)
Transaction e	(1,000)
Ending balance	**$ 3,000**

11.   d. $37 ÷ $2.00 = **18.5 times**

12.   c.

13.   d.

14.   a.

15.   b.

16.   a.   Nedra Co. has the lowest P/E ratio, suggesting investors are the least optimistic about its potential for future growth.

17.   b.   See articulation problem No. 2 for an explanation of the correct answer.

18.   d.   See articulation problem No. 4 for an explanation of the correct answer.

19.   a.   See articulation problem No. 3 for an explanation of the correct answer.

Multiple True-False Problems

1.   a.   **False**, this is a financing activity.
      b.   **False**, this is an investing activity.
      c.   **True**.
      d.   **True**.
      e.   **True**.

2.   a.   **True**, Assets - Liabilities = Equity is the algebraic equivalent of Assets = Liabilities + Equity.
      b.   **False**, the statement of cash flows explains how a company got its cash. The balance sheet does show how much cash a company has at year-end, but it does not provide much information as to how the cash was obtained.
      c.   **False**, cash could decrease and another asset account, such as land, could increase and the balance sheet would still balance.
      d.   **True**, this is referred to as the historical cost principle, and is explained more formally in Chapter 2.
      e.   **False**, because the company forgot to record the transaction, its cash (and thus assets) would be overstated. However, the error would also understate its expenses, which would cause retained earnings (an equity account) to be overstated. Because both assets and equity are overstated by the same amount, the balance sheet would still balance, although the balances are incorrect.

3.   a.   **False**, total assets are $26,000 ($20,000 − 4,000 − 15,000 + 15,000 + 12,000 − 2,000 = $26,000)
      b.   **False**, net income is $8,000 ($12,000 − 4,000 = $8,000) Dividends are not expenses.
      c.   **True**, ($20,000 − 2,000 = $18,000)
      d.   **True**, ($12,000 − 4,000 − 2,000 = $6,000) Dividends are not expenses, but they do reduce retained earnings.
      e.   **True**, ($20,000 − 4,000 − 15,000 + 12,000 − 2,000 = $11,000)

4. a. **False**, accounts that appear on the balance sheet are <u>not</u> closed at the end of the year.
    b. **False**, accounts that appear on the balance sheet are <u>not</u> closed at the end of the year.
    c. **True**, accounts that appear on the income statement are closed at the end of the year.
    d. **True**, accounts that appear on the income statement are closed at the end of the year.
    e. **True**, closing an account reduces its balance to $-0-.

Exercise-Type Problems

P-1 Solution for requirement 1

					Stockholders' Equity		
Event	**Assets**	**=**	**Liabilities**	**+**	**Common Stock**	**+**	**Retained Earnings**
a.	10,000				10,000		
b.	6,000						6,000
c.	5,000		5,000				
d.	(2,500)						(2,500)
e.	(1,500)						(1,500)
Totals	<u>17,000</u>		<u>5,000</u>		<u>10,000</u>		<u>2,000</u>

Solution for requirement 2

Wyoming Company
Income Statement
For the Year Ended December 31, 2005

Revenues	$ 6,000
Expenses	2,500
Net income	$ 3,500

Wyoming Company
Statement of Changes in Stockholders' Equity
For the Year Ended December 31, 2005

Beginning Common stock	$ 0	
Plus: Investments	10,000	
Ending Common stock		$10,000
Beginning Retained Earnings	0	
Plus: Net Income	3,500	
Less: Dividends	(1,500)	
Ending Retained Earnings		2,000
Total Stockholders' Equity		$12,000

Wyoming Company
Balance Sheet
As of December 31, 2005

Assets:

Cash		$17,000
Total Assets		$17,000

Liabilities:

Note payable	$ 5,000	
Total Liabilities		$ 5,000

Stockholders' Equity:

Common stock	10,000	
Retained Earnings	2,000	
Total Stockholders' Equity		12,000
Total Liabilities and Stockholders' Equity		$17,000

Wyoming Company
Statement of Cash Flows
For the Year Ended December 31, 2005

Cash Flows from Operating Activities:

Cash Receipts from Revenue	$ 6,000	
Cash Payments for Expenses	(2,500)	
Net Cash Flow from Operating Activities		$ 3,500

Cash Flow from Investing Activities:

		0

Cash Flows from Financing Activities:

Cash Receipts from Owners' Investments	10,000	
Cash Receipts from Borrowed Funds	5,000	
Cash Payments for Dividends	(1,500)	
Net Cash Flow from Financing Activities		13,500
Net Increase in Cash		$17,000

P-2

Solution for requirement 1

					Stockholders' Equity		
Event	Assets	=	Liabilities	+	Common Stock	+	Retained Earnings
Beg. Bal.	17,000		5,000		10,000		2,000
a.	8,000 land (8,000)						
b.	10,000						10,000
c.	6,000				6,000		
d.	(5,000)		(5,000)				
e.	(4,500)						(4,500)
g.	(2,000)						(2,000)
Totals	21,500		0		16,000		5,500

Solution for requirement 2

Wyoming Company
Income Statement
For the Year Ended December 31, 2006

Revenues	$10,000
Expenses	4,500
Net income	$ 5,500

Wyoming Company
Statement of Changes in Stockholders' Equity
For the Year Ended December 31, 2006

Beginning Common stock	$10,000	
Plus: Investments	6,000	
Ending Common stock		$16,000
Beginning Retained Earnings	2,000	
Plus: Net Income	5,500	
Less: Dividends	(2,000)	
Ending Retained Earnings		5,500
Total Stockholders' Equity		$21,500

Wyoming Company
Balance Sheet
As of December 31, 2006

Assets:

Cash	$13,500	
Land	8,000	
Total Assets		$21,500

Liabilities:		$ 0

Stockholders' Equity:

Common stock	$16,000	
Retained Earnings	5,500	
Total Stockholders' Equity		21,500
Total Liabilities and Stockholders' Equity		$21,500

Wyoming Company
Statement of Cash Flows
For the Year Ended December 31, 2006

Cash Flows from Operating Activities:

Cash Receipts from Revenue	$10,000	
Cash Payments for Expenses	(4,500)	
Net Cash Flow from Operating Activities		$ 5,500

Cash Flow from Investing Activities:

Payment for Purchase of Land	(8,000)	
Net Cash Flow from Investing Activities		(8,000)

Cash Flows from Financing Activities:

Cash Receipts from Owners' Investments	6,000	
Repayment of Borrowed Funds	(5,000)	
Cash Payments for Dividends	(2,000)	
Net Cash Flow from Financing Activities		(1,000)

Net Decrease in Cash   (3,500)

Add: Beginning Cash Balance		17,000
Cash Balance at December 31, 2006		$13,500

Chapter Two
Accounting for Accruals

Learning Objectives for the Chapter

After completing this chapter you should be able to:

1. Record basic accrual events in a horizontal financial statements model.
2. Organize general ledger accounts under an accounting equation.
3. Prepare financial statements based on accrual accounting.
4. Describe the matching concept, the accounting cycle, and the closing process.
5. Record business events involving interest-bearing receivables and payables in a horizontal financial statements model.
6. Prepare a vertical statements model.
7. Explain how business events affect financial statements over multiple accounting cycles.
8. Describe the auditor's role in financial reporting.
9. Describe the articles of the AICPA's code of professional conduct and identify the major factors that lead to unethical conduct.
10. Classify accounting events into one of four categories:
    a. asset source transactions.
    b. asset use transactions.
    c. asset exchange transactions.
    d. claims exchange transactions.

Brief Explanation of the Learning Objectives

1.   Record basic accrual events in a horizontal financial statements model.

Cash accounting only recognizes events when cash is either received or paid by a business. Accrual accounting recognizes significant events in the period in which the event occurs regardless of whether or not cash was exchanged in that event. An accrual-type event is one in which a significant business transaction or adjusting activity occurred *before* cash is exchanged. (Accrual accounting includes both accrual-type events as explained in Chapter 2 and deferral-type events that will be explained in Chapter 3.)

The basic approach for recording accrual events in a horizontal financial statements model is the same as for cash events, but additional accounts are involved. This learning objective is examined further through the use of the self-study problems. The articulation problems are especially intended to help you achieve this objective.

2.   Organize general ledger accounts under an accounting equation.

The development of this skill was begun in Chapter 1, but no accrual events or accounts were involved. Chapter 2 continues this objective with accrual events, primarily receivables and payables. This learning objective is examined further through the use of the self-study problems. The articulation problems are especially intended to help you achieve this objective.

3.   Prepare financial statements based on accrual accounting.

This learning objective is also examined through the use of the self-study problems. The exercise-type problems are especially intended to help you achieve this objective.

4.   Describe the matching concept, the accounting cycle, and the closing process.

The accrual system has as its basis the *matching principle*. The matching principle is a two step process. First, revenues are recognized in the accounting period in which they are earned. This is often called the revenue recognition principle. Revenues are said to be earned when an exchange takes place. Exchanging services today for a promise to be paid cash later qualifies as an exchange. Second, the costs that were necessary to produce those revenues are recognized as expenses in that same period. Thus, accountants say that expenses are matched with revenues in order to measure a company's net earnings under the accrual basis of accounting.

Adhering to the accrual basis of accounting requires companies to make adjusting entries. Additionally, because we want to match expenses and revenues on a period by period basis, it is necessary to close those accounts at the end of each accounting period. The closing process results in revenue and expense accounts having zero balances at the beginning of the each accounting period.

5.   Record business events involving interest-bearing receivables and payables in a horizontal financial statements model.

This learning objective is also examined further through the use of the self-study problems, but as a reminder, interest expense and interest revenue are computed as follows:

Principle x Annual interest rate x Portion of the year involved

6.   Prepare a vertical statements model.

The textbook uses the vertical statements models to focus your attention on the cumulative effects of all of the accounting events for a given accounting period, usually a year. In contrast, the horizontal model focuses attention on the effects on the financial statements of a single accounting event. Vertical statements models are really just informal financial statements; income statements, statements of changes in equity, balance sheets, and statements of cash flows.

If you understand how to prepare the formal financial statements, you should understand how to prepare a vertical statements model, and vice versa. The exercise-type self-study problems are intended to help you practice this skill.

7.   Explain how business events affect financial statements over multiple accounting cycles.

The key to understanding how business events affect multiple accounting periods is knowing that the balances for accounts that appear on the balance sheet continue from one year to the next, while those appearing on the income statement do not. Revenue and expense accounts start with a zero balance at the beginning of each year.

This learning objective is examined further through the use of the self-study problems. The two exercise-type problems are especially intended to help you achieve this objective.

8.   Describe the auditor's role in financial reporting.

The primary role of the independent auditor is to verify that a company's financial statements have been prepared in accordance with GAAP, and that they are free from material error.

9.   Describe the articles of the AICPA's code of professional conduct and identify the major factors that lead to unethical conduct.

Independent auditors are hired and paid by the company whose financial statements they are auditing. The primary purpose of the audit, however, is to give some assurance to "third-parties" (parties not closely associated with the business) that the financial statements have been properly prepared. Because of this responsibility to parties other than their clients, auditors are said to "serve the public interest." The essence of the AICPA's code of ethics for independent auditors is to insure they fulfill their responsibilities to the third-party users, even though they are paid by the company they audit. Although there are many facets to the code of ethics, none is more important than those devoted to establishing an appropriate degree of independence of the auditor from the company. The textbook discusses some of these rules in more detail.

10.   Classify accounting events into one of four categories:

Asset source: An event that causes total assets to increase. There will be a corresponding increase in liabilities and/or stockholders' equity.

Asset use: An event that causes total assets to decrease. There will be a corresponding decrease in liabilities and/or stockholders' equity.

Asset exchange: An event that causes one asset to increase and another asset to decrease by the same amount. It is possible that more than two assets will be involved in such an event, but the net effect on assets will be that total assets do not change.

Claims exchange: An event that does not involve assets. One claims-type account is increased while another decreases by the same amount. Events of this type usually involve either an increase in liabilities and an increase in expenses (which decreases retained earnings) *or* a decrease in liabilities and an increase in revenues (which increases retained earnings).

Self-Study Problems

Articulation Problems

For each situation below, indicate its effects on the accounting elements shown on the accompanying chart. Use the following letters to indicate your answer (you do not need to enter amounts):

Increase = **I**   Decrease = **D**   No effect = **N**

1.   Larkin Co. acquired cash from the owners to start the business.

Assets	Liabilities	Equity	Revenues	Expenses	Net Income	Cash

2.   Munich Co. provided services to its customers for cash.

Assets	Liabilities	Equity	Revenues	Expenses	Net Income	Cash

3.   Nassau Co. provided services to a customer on account.

Assets	Liabilities	Equity	Revenues	Expenses	Net Income	Cash

4.   Nassau Co. collected cash from accounts receivable.

Assets	Liabilities	Equity	Revenues	Expenses	Net Income	Cash

5.   Page Co. incurred cash operating expenses.

Assets	Liabilities	Equity	Revenues	Expenses	Net Income	Cash

6.   Quito Co. incurred operating expenses on account.

Assets	Liabilities	Equity	Revenues	Expenses	Net Income	Cash

7.   Quito Co. paid accounts payable.

Assets	Liabilities	Equity	Revenues	Expenses	Net Income	Cash

8.   Reston Co. purchased a certificate of deposit from the Local Bank.

Assets	Liabilities	Equity	Revenues	Expenses	Net Income	Cash

9.   Stealth Co. borrowed cash from the National Bank.

Assets	Liabilities	Equity	Revenues	Expenses	Net Income	Cash

10.   Train Co. distributed cash to its owners.

Assets	Liabilities	Equity	Revenues	Expenses	Net Income	Cash

11.   Nguyen Co. made an adjustment for accrued salaries of employees at the end of the accounting period.

Assets	Liabilities	Equity	Revenues	Expenses	Net Income	Cash

12.   At the end of the accounting period Reston Co. accrued interest related to the certificate of deposit it purchased in transaction 8.

Assets	Liabilities	Equity	Revenues	Expenses	Net Income	Cash

13.   At the end of the accounting period Stealth Co. accrued interest on the money it borrowed in transaction 9.

Assets	Liabilities	Equity	Revenues	Expenses	Net Income	Cash

Multiple-Choice Questions

The following information applies to questions 1 and 2.

Yoga Co. had the following events in 2005:

a.   Provided services to customers for $10,000 on account.
b.   Incurred operating expenses of $ 7,000 on account.
c.   Paid $5,000 on accounts payable.
d.   Made a cash distribution of $1,000.
e.   Received $6,000 cash from accounts receivable.
f.   Borrowed $2,000 from the bank.

1.   What was net income for Yoga in 2006?
    a. $1,000
    b. $2,000
    c. $3,000
    d. $7,000

2.   What was net cash flow from operating activities for Yoga?
        a. $1,000
        b. $2,000
        c. $3,000
        d. $4,000

The following information applies to questions 3 - 6.

The following account balances were drawn from the records of Atlanta Co. on December 31, 2007.

Notes Payable	$10,000	Expenses	$25,000
Revenue	30,000	Accounts Receivable	10,000
Accounts Payable	2,000	Common Stock	11,000
Land	8,000	Dividends	2,000
Cash	12,000		

3.   Total assets on Atlanta's balance sheet would be:
        a. $28,000
        b. $30,000
        c. $35,000
        d. $60,000

4.   Total liabilities on Atlanta's balance sheet would be:
        a. $ 2,000
        b. $12,000
        c. $22,000
        d. $32,000

5.   For 2007, net income for Atlanta would be:
        a. $ 3,000
        b. $ 5,000
        c. $13,000
        d. $15,000

6.   Retained earnings on Atlanta's balance sheet would be:
        a. $18,000
        b. $ 9,000
        c. $ 7,000
        d. $ 3,000

7.   Which of the following is an asset <u>source</u> transaction?
   a.   Borrowed money from the bank.
   b.   Purchased land for cash.
   c.   Incurred operating expenses on account.
   d.   Incurred cash operating expenses.

8.   Which of the following is an asset <u>use</u> transaction?
   a.   Borrowed money from the bank.
   b.   Owners invested land in the business.
   c.   Incurred operating expenses on account.
   d.   Made cash distribution to owners.

9.   Which of the following is an asset <u>exchange</u> transaction?
   a.   Repaid a bank loan.
   b.   Owners invested land in the business.
   c.   Collected accounts receivable.
   d.   Incurred operating expenses on account.

10.   On October 1, 2006, Boston Co. borrowed $10,000 from Merchants' Bank. The loan carried a 12% interest rate and a one-year term. Which of the following statements related to this event are true?
   a.   Boston Co. would show a $10,000 cash inflow in the *investing* section of its 2006 statement of cash flows?
   b.   On Boston's 2006 balance sheet, total liabilities related to this loan would be $10,000.
   c.   On Boston's <u>2007</u> income statement there would be interest expense of $1,200.
   d.   On Boston's 2006 income statement there would be interest expense of $300.

11.   Seattle Co. incurred expenses on account. This event would:
   a.   Decrease total assets.
   b.   Decrease retained earnings.
   c.   Decrease net cash flows from operating activities.
   d.   Have no effect on Seattle Co.'s financial statements.

12. The following information was taken from the records of Cairo Co. on December 31, 2009.

Total Assets	$50,000	Dividends	$ 5,000
Total Liabilities	30,000	Retained Earnings	8,000
Common Stock	12,000	Net Income	10,000

What was the balance in Cairo's retained earnings account on <u>January 1, 2009</u>?
  a. $(7,000)
  b. $ 0
  c. $ 2,000
  d. $ 3,000

13. On October 1, 2006, Davis Co. borrowed $10,000 from Big Bank. The loan carried a 12% interest rate and a one-year term. The loan was repaid, along with the proper amount of interest, in 2007. Which of the following statements related to these events is <u>false</u>?
  a.   Davis Co. would show a $10,000 cash <u>outflow</u> in the *financing* section of its <u>2007</u> statement of cash flows?
  b.   Davis's assets increase $10,000 in 2006.
  c.   Davis's assets will decrease $10,000 in <u>2007</u>.
  d.   Neither the borrowing nor repayment of this loan will have any effect on the *investing* section of Davis's statement of cash flows.

14. If a company incurs an expense on account:
  a.   Cash flows from operating are decreased.
  b.   Cash flows from operating are increased.
  c.   Total assets decrease.
  d.   Total assets are not affected.

15. When prepared on the accrual accounting basis, the income statement is most closely related to which of the following accounting concepts or principles?
  a.   Matching principle
  b.   Materiality concept
  c.   Historical cost principle
  d.   Entity concept

16. Europe Co. provided services to customers on account. Which of the following choices reflects how this event would affect the company's financial statements?

	Assets	=	Liab.	+	Equity	Rev.	–	Exp.	=	Net Inc.	Cash Flow
a.	N		I		I	I		N		I	N
b.	N		N		N	N		N		N	N
c.	I		N		I	I		N		I	N
d.	N		N		N	I		N		I	N

17. Fairbanks Co. incurred operating expenses on account. Which of the following choices reflects how this event would affect the company's financial statements?

	Assets	=	Liab.	+	Equity	Rev.	–	Exp.	=	Net Inc.	Cash Flow
a.	D		N		D	N		I		D	N
b.	N		I		D	N		I		D	N
c.	D		N		D	D		N		D	N
d.	N		I		D	N		D		D	N

18. Giant Co. repaid the principal of a note payable. Which of the following choices reflects how this event would affect the company's financial statements?

	Assets	=	Liab.	+	Equity	Rev.	–	Exp.	=	Net Inc.	Cash Flow
a.	D		D		D	N		I		D	D
b.	D		D		N	N		N		N	N
c.	D		D		N	N		N		N	D
d.	N		N		N	N		N		N	D

19. On December 31, 2005, the Hugo Co. accrued the interest on a note payable. Which of the following choices reflects how this event would affect the company's financial statements?

	Assets	=	Liab.	+	Equity	Rev.	–	Exp.	=	Net Inc.	Cash Flow
a.	D		D		D	N		I		D	D
b.	D		D		N	N		N		N	D
c.	N		I		D	N		I		D	N
d.	N		I		D	N		N		N	N

Multiple True-False Problems

1. Consider the following four events that occurred at Juan Co.

    Earned $10,000 of revenue, on account.
    Incurred $6,000 of expenses on account.
    Collected $8,000 of accounts receivable.
    Paid $5,000 of the accounts payable.

    Based only on the four transactions above, indicate if each of the following statements is true or false.
    a.   Juan's net income is $3,000.
    b.   The balance in accounts receivable is $2,000.
    c.   Juan's cash flows from operating activities is $3,000.
    d.   The balance in accounts payable is $5,000.
    e.   Juan's total assets are $5,000.

2. On September 1, 2005, Kentucky Co. borrowed $5,000 from the City Bank. The loan had a one-year term and carried an interest rate of 9%. Based on this information, indicate if each of the following statements is true or false.
    a.   Kentucky should report $150 of interest expense on its **2005** income statement.
    b.   Kentucky's December 31, **2005**, balance sheet should report total liabilities of $5,000 related to this loan.
    c.   Net cash flows from *operating activities* related to this loan would be ($450) for **2006.**
    d.   Kentucky should report $450 of interest expense on its **2006** income statement.
    e.   Net cash flows from *financing activities* related to this loan would be ($5,000) for **2006.**

3. Indicate if each of the following statements related to financial audits is true or false.
    a.   A company would prefer **not** to receive a *qualified* audit opinion.
    b.   If a company's auditors certify that its financial statements were prepared in accordance with GAAP, investors can assume that any money they have invested in the company is safe.
    c.   A company's books may be audited by a CPA who owns stock in the company provided the auditor owns only an immaterial amount of the company's stock.
    d.   A company can "fire" its auditor if the auditor does not agree with the company's accounting methods.
    e.   If an auditor is called on to testify in court about a company he or she audits, the auditor can refuse to do so under the "rule of confidentiality."

Exercise-Type Problems

P-1.   Largo Co. began its operations on January 1, 2005. During 2005 the following events occurred.

a.   Owners invested $20,000 in the business.
b.   On May 1, 2005, Largo borrowed $5,000 from the Local Bank by giving the bank a note payable. The note is due to be repaid in one year along with 9% interest.
c.   Provided services to customers for $15,000 on account.
d.   Purchased land for $7,000 cash.
e.   Incurred cash expenses of $2,000.
f.   Collected $9,000 from accounts receivable.
g.   Incurred operating expenses of $7,000 on account.
h.   Dividends amounted to $1,000.
i.   Paid $4,000 on accounts payable.
j.   At the end of the year, recorded accrued interest on the bank note. (See transaction (b).

Required:
1.   Explain how each of these events would affect Largo's accounting equation using the form provided below. Use ( ) to indicate amounts being subtracted. The first transaction has been done as an example.
2.   Prepare an income statement, a statement of changes in stockholders' equity, a balance sheet, and a statement of cash flows. Use the forms provided on the following pages.

Form for requirement 1

					Stockholders' Equity		
Event	Assets	=	Liabilities	+	Common Stock	+	Retained Earnings
a.	20,000				20,000		
b.							
c.							
d.							
e.							
f.							
g.							
h.							
i.							
j.							
Totals							

Forms for requirement 2

Largo Co.
Income Statement
For the Year Ended December 31, 2005

Revenues $
Expenses
Net income $

Largo Co.
Statement of Changes in Stockholders' Equity
For the Year Ended December 31, 2005

Beginning Common Stock $ _____

   Plus: Investments   _____

Ending Common Stock $ _____

Beginning Retained Earnings

   Plus: Net Income

   Less: Dividends   _____

Ending Retained Earnings   _____

Total Stockholders' Equity $ _____

Largo Co.
Balance Sheet
As of December 31, 2005

Assets:

   Cash $ _____

   Accounts Receivable

   Land   _____

Total Assets $ _____

Liabilities:

   Accounts Payable $ _____

   Interest Payable

   Note payable   _____

Total Liabilities $ _____

Stockholders' Equity:

   Common Stock

   Retained Earnings   _____

Total Stockholders' Equity

Total Liabilities and Stockholders' Equity $ _____

Largo Co.
Statement of Cash Flows
For the Year Ended December 31, 2005

Cash Flows from Operating Activities:
    Cash Receipts from Revenue $
    Cash Payments for Expenses   _____
Net Cash Flow from Operating Activities $

Cash Flow from Investing Activities:
    Cash Payment for Purchase of Land   _____
Net Cash Flow from Investing Activities

Cash Flows from Financing Activities:
    Cash Receipts from Owners' Investments
    Cash Receipts from Borrowed Funds
    Cash Payments for Dividends   _____
Net Cash Flow from Financing Activities   _____

Net Increase in Cash $_____

P-2   Largo Co., which began operations in 2005 (see P-1), continued in business during 2006. Assume the account balances at January 1, 2006, were:

Cash	$20,000	Interest Payable	$ 300
Accounts Receivable	6,000	Notes Payable	5,000
Land	7,000	Common Stock	20,000
Accounts Payable	3,000	Retained Earnings	4,700

The following events occurred during 2006:

a.   Incurred $6,000 of expenses in cash.
b.   Provided services to customers for $12,000 on account.
c.   On April 30, 2006, Largo repaid money, including interest, which was borrowed on May 1, 2005, from the Local Bank. (See P-1.) Largo had borrowed $5,000 for one year with a 9% interest rate.
d.   Incurred expenses of $3,000 on account.
e.   Collected $11,000 from accounts receivable.
f.   Paid $4,000 on accounts payable.
g.   Accrued wages of $500 were owed to employees at the end of the year.

Required:

1.   Explain how each of these transactions would affect Largo's accounting equation using the form provided below. Use ( ) to indicate amounts being subtracted. The first transaction has been done as an example.

2.   Prepare an income statement, statement of changes in stockholders' equity, balance sheet, and statement of cash flows. Prepare these statements using your own paper, but use the format shown in P-1, or in the textbook, as your guide.

Form for requirement 1

					Stockholders' Equity		
Event	**Assets**	=	**Liabilities**	+	**Common Stock**	+	**Retained Earnings**
Beg. Bal.	33,000		8,300		20,000		4,700
a.	(6,000)						(6,000)
b.							
c.							
d.							
e.							
f.							
g.							
Totals							

Solutions to Self-Study Problems

Articulation Problems

1.   Larkin Co. acquired cash from the owners to start the business.

Assets	Liabilities	Equity	Revenues	Expenses	Net Income	Cash
I	N	I	N	N	N	I

Cash, an asset, increased, and common stock, a part of stockholders' equity, increased.

2.   Munich Co. provided services to its customers for cash.

Assets	Liabilities	Equity	Revenues	Expenses	Net Income	Cash
I	N	I	I	N	I	I

Cash, an asset, increased. The company earned revenues, which caused net income to increase. An increase in net income causes retained earnings, a part of stockholders' equity, to increase.

3.   Nassau Co. provided services to a customer on account.

Assets	Liabilities	Equity	Revenues	Expenses	Net Income	Cash
I	N	I	I	N	I	N

Accounts receivable, an asset, increased. The company earned revenues, which caused net income to increase. An increase in net income causes retained earnings, a part of stockholders' equity, to increase.

4.   Nassau Co. collected cash from accounts receivable.

Assets	Liabilities	Equity	Revenues	Expenses	Net Income	Cash
N	N	N	N	N	N	I

One asset, cash, increased while another asset, accounts receivable, decreased by the same amount.

5.   Page Co. incurred cash operating expenses.

Assets	Liabilities	Equity	Revenues	Expenses	Net Income	Cash
D	N	D	N	I	D	D

Cash, an asset, decreased. Because the cash was spent in the hopes of producing revenue, this is an expense. The increase in expense caused net income to decrease, which caused retained earnings, a part of stockholders' equity, to decrease.

6.   Quito Co. incurred operating expenses on account.

Assets	Liabilities	Equity	Revenues	Expenses	Net Income	Cash
N	I	D	N	I	D	N

A cost was incurred but was not paid; this increased liabilities. Because the cost was incurred in the hopes of producing revenue, this is an expense. The increase in expense caused net income to decrease, which caused retained earnings, a part of stockholders' equity, to decrease.

7.   Quito Co. paid accounts payable.

Assets	Liabilities	Equity	Revenues	Expenses	Net Income	Cash
D	D	N	N	N	N	D

Cash decreased because liabilities were paid (reduced).

8.   Reston Co. purchased a certificate of deposit from the Local Bank.

Assets	Liabilities	Equity	Revenues	Expenses	Net Income	Cash
N	N	N	N	N	N	D

One asset, the certificate of deposit, increased while another asset, cash, decreased by the same amount.

9.   Stealth Co. borrowed cash from National Bank.

Assets	Liabilities	Equity	Revenues	Expenses	Net Income	Cash
I	I	N	N	N	N	I

Cash, an asset, increased. Because the borrowed money will have to be repaid to the bank, liabilities also increased. This cash was not earned. Therefore, it is not revenue.

10.   Train Co. distributed cash to its owners.

Assets	Liabilities	Equity	Revenues	Expenses	Net Income	Cash
D	N	D	N	N	N	D

Cash, an asset, decreased while retained earnings, a part of stockholders' equity, decreased. This payment of cash was not an expense because the money was not spent in the expectation that it would produce revenues.

11.   Nguyen Co. made an adjustment for accrued salaries of employees at the end of the accounting period.

Assets	Liabilities	Equity	Revenues	Expenses	Net Income	Cash
N	I	D	N	I	D	N

A cost was incurred but was not paid; this increased wages payable, a liability. Because the cost was incurred in the hopes of producing revenue, this is an expense. The increase in expense caused net income to decrease, which caused retained earnings, a part of stockholders' equity, to decrease.

12. At the end of the accounting period Reston Co. accrued interest related to the certificate of deposit it purchased in transaction 8.

Assets	Liabilities	Equity	Revenues	Expenses	Net Income	Cash
I	N	I	I	N	I	N

The company is owed interest on the CD; this increases interest receivable, an asset. This increase in assets occurred because the company earned interest revenue, which caused net income to increase. An increase in net income causes retained earnings, a part of stockholders' equity, to increase.

13. At the end of the accounting period Stealth Co. accrued interest on the money it borrowed in transaction 9.

Assets	Liabilities	Equity	Revenues	Expenses	Net Income	Cash
N	I	D	N	I	D	N

The company owes the bank a fee for the money it borrowed; thus its liabilities (interest payable) have increased. Because this cost was incurred in the hopes of producing revenues, it is an expense. The increase in expense caused net income to decrease, which caused retained earnings, a part of stockholders' equity, to decrease.

Multiple-Choice Problems

1. c.
Revenue	$10,000
less: Expenses	7,000
Net Income	**$ 3,000**

2. a.
Cash collected from accounts receivable	$ 6,000
Cash paid on accounts payable	(5,000)
Cash flow from operating activities	**$ 1,000**

3. b.
Cash	$12,000
Accounts receivable	10,000
Land	8,000
Total assets	**$30,000**

4. b.
Accounts payable	$ 2,000
Notes payable	10,000
Total liabilities	**$12,000**

5. b.
Revenue	$30,000
less: Expenses	25,000
Net Income	**$ 5,000**

6. c.
Total assets (No. 3 above)	$30,000
less: Total liabilities (No. 4 above)	12,000
equals: Total stockholders' equity	18,000
less: Common stock	11,000
equals: Retained earnings	**$ 7,000**

7.   a.   Total assets increased; thus (a) was an asset source transaction. (Total liabilities also increased.)

8.   d.   Total assets decreased, thus (d) is an asset use transaction. (Total stockholders' equity also decreased.)

9.   c.   In choice (c) cash increased and accounts receivable decreased; thus total assets do not change.

10.   d.   Boston has three months of interest expense in 2006. This amounts to $300, computed as follows: [($10,000 x .09) x 3/12] = $300.

11.   b.   Expenses increased causing net income to decrease causing retained earnings to decrease.

12.   d.

Beginning retained earnings	$?
add: Net income	10,000
less: Dividends	5,000
equals: Ending retained earnings	$ 8,000

By plugging for the missing amount beginning retained earnings can be determined to be **$3,000.**

13.   c.   In 2007 Davis must repay the $10,000 originally borrowed plus interest. The interest for one year on $10,000 at 12% is $1,200. Thus, the total amount of cash Davis must give to the bank in 2007 is $11,200, not $10,000.

14.   d.   Liabilities are increased and stockholders' equity is decreased, but neither cash nor any other assets are affected.

15.   a.   The matching principle calls for expenses to be matched with revenues to compute net earnings.

16.   c.   See articulation problem 3 for an explanation of the correct answer.

17.   b.   See articulation problem 6 for an explanation of the correct answer.

18.   c.   Assets decrease because cash was paid out to reduce the liability, notes payable.

19.   c.   See articulation problem 13 for an explanation of the correct answer.

Multiple True-False Problems

1.   a.   **False**, net income is $4,000 ($10,000 – $6,000).
      b.   **True**, accounts receivable total $10,000 – $8,000.
      c.   **True**, cash flows total $8,000 – $5,000.
      d.   **False**, accounts payable total $1,000 ($6,000 – $5,000).
      e.   **True**:   The balance in cash is (see item c.) $3,000
                        The balance in accounts receivable is (see item b.)   2,000
                        Total assets are $5,000

2. a. **True**, ($5,000 x .09 x 4/12 = $150)
    b. **False**, Kentucky's liabilities should total $5,150 ($5,000 for Notes Payable and $150 for Interest Payable).
    c. **True**, cash paid for interest was $450 ($5,000 x .09 x 12/12).
    d. **False**, even though the company paid $450 of interest in cash during 2006 (see c. above) only $300 of this would be reported as interest expense in 2006 ($5,000 x .09 x 8/12).
    e. **True**, the repayment of $5,000 principal should be classified as a *financing* activity.

3. a. **True**, a *qualified* opinion means something about a company's financial statements is not fully in accordance with GAAP. Companies want to receive *unqualified* audit opinions.
    b. **False**, even a company that is in financial difficulty can prepare its financial statements according to the rules of GAAP.
    c. **False**, neither auditors nor members of their immediate family should own **any** stock or have any other financial interest in companies they audit.
    d. **True**, companies can fire their auditors for any reason, or for no reason at all. However, auditors are permitted to publicly disclose why they think the company fired them.
    e. **False**, the rules that require auditors to keep confidential information about companies they audit, do not apply to court testimony.

Exercise-Type Problems

P-1   **Solution for Requirement 1**

					Stockholders' Equity		
Event	Assets	=	Liabilities	+	Common Stock	+	Retained Earnings
a.	20,000				20,000		
b.	5,000		5,000				
c.	15,000						15,000
d.	(7,000) 7,000 land						
e.	(2,000)						(2,000)
f.	(9,000) A/R 9,000						
g.			7,000				(7,000)
h.	(1,000)						(1,000)
i.	(4,000)		(4,000)				
j.			300 [(5,000x.09)x8/12]				(300)
Totals	33,000		8,300		20,000		4,700

Note: A/R = Accounts Receivable

Solution for requirement 2

Largo Co.
Income Statement
For the Year Ended December 31, 2005

Revenues	$15,000
Expenses	9,300
Net income	$ 5,700

Largo Co.
Statement of Changes in Stockholders' Equity
For the Year Ended December 31, 2005

Beginning Common Stock	$ 0	
Plus: Investments	20,000	
Ending Common Stock		$20,000
Beginning Retained Earnings	0	
Plus: Net Income	5,700	
Less: Dividends	(1,000)	
Ending Retained Earnings		4,700
Total Stockholders' Equity		$24,700

Largo Co.
Balance Sheet
As of December 31, 2005

Assets:		
Cash	$20,000	
Accounts Receivable	6,000	
Land	7,000	
Total Assets		$33,000
Liabilities:		
Accounts Payable	$ 3,000	
Interest Payable	300	
Note payable	5,000	
Total Liabilities		$ 8,300
Stockholders' Equity:		
Common Stock	20,000	
Retained Earnings	4,700	
Total Stockholders' Equity		24,700
Total Liabilities and Stockholders' Equity		$33,000

Largo Co.
Statement of Cash Flows
For the Year Ended December 31, 2005

Cash Flows from Operating Activities:

Cash Receipts from Revenue	$ 9,000	
Cash Payments for Expenses	(6,000)	
Net Cash Flow from Operating Activities		$ 3,000

Cash Flows from Investing Activities:

Cash Payments for Purchase of Land	(7,000)	
Net Cash Flow from Investing Activities:		(7,000)

Cash Flows from Financing Activities:

Cash Receipts from Owners' Investments	20,000	
Cash Receipts from Borrowed Funds	5,000	
Cash Payments for Dividends	(1,000)	
Net Cash Flow from Financing Activities		24,000
Net Increase in Cash		$20,000

P-2

Solution for requirement 1

						Stockholders' Equity		
Event	**Assets**	=	**Liabilities**	+		**Common Stock**	+	**Retained Earnings**
Beg. Bal.	33,000		8,300			20,000		4,700
a.	(6,000)							(6,000)
b.	12,000 A/R							12,000
c.	(5,450)		(5,000) N/P					
			(300) I/P					(150) **(5,000x.09)x4/12]**
d.			3,000					(3,000)
e.	(11,000) A/R							
	11,000							
f.	(4,000)		(4,000)					
g.			500 W/P					(500)
Totals	29,550		2,500			20,000		7,050

Note: A/R = Accounts Receivable; N/P = Notes Payable; I/P = Interest Payable; W/P = Wages Payable

Solution for requirement 2

Largo Co.
Income Statement
For the Year Ended December 31, 2006

Revenues	$12,000
Expenses [6,000 + 150 + 3,000 + 500]	9,650
Net income	$ 2,350

Largo Co.
Statement of Changes in Stockholders' Equity
For the Year Ended December 31, 2006

Beginning Common Stock	$20,000	
Plus: Investments	0	
Ending Common Stock		$20,000
Beginning Retained Earnings	4,700	
Plus: Net Income	2,350	
Ending Retained Earnings		7,050
Total Stockholders' Equity		$27,050

Largo Co.
Balance Sheet
As of December 31, 2006

Assets:		
Cash	$15,550	
Accounts Receivable	7,000	
Land	7,000	
Total Assets		$29,550
Liabilities:		
Accounts Payable	$ 2,000	
Wages Payable	500	
Total Liabilities		$ 2,500
Stockholders' Equity:		
Common Stock	20,000	
Retained Earnings	7,050	
Total Stockholders' Equity		27,050
Total Liabilities and Stockholders' Equity		$29,550

Largo Co.
Statement of Cash Flows
For the Year Ended December 31, 2006

Cash Flows from Operating Activities:		
Cash Receipts from Revenue	$11,000	
Cash Payments for Expenses	(10,450)	
Net Cash Flow from Operating Activities		$ 550
Cash Flow from Investing Activities:		0
Cash Flows from Financing Activities:		
Cash Repayment Borrowed Funds	(5,000)	
Net Cash Flow from Financing Activities		(5,000)
Net Decrease in Cash		(4,450)
Add: Beginning Cash Balance		20,000
Cash Balance at December 31, 2006		$15,550

Chapter Three
Accounting for Deferrals

Learning Objectives for the Chapter

After completing this chapter you should be able to:

1. Provide a more complete explanation of the accrual accounting system.
2. Identify business events that involve deferrals.
3. Record deferral events under an accounting equation.
4. Prepare financial statements that include cash, accrual, and deferral events.
5. Explain how deferral events affect the financial statements.
6. Explain the effects of end-of-period adjustments related to deferrals.
7. Distinguish between a cost that is an asset and a cost that is an expense.
8. Distinguish gains and losses from revenue and expenses.
9. Analyze financial statements and make meaningful comparisons between companies by using a debt-to-assets ratio, a return-on-assets ratio, and a return-on-equity ratio.
10. Record deferral events in a financial statements model.

Brief Explanation of the Learning Objectives

1.   Provide a more complete explanation of the accrual accounting system.

In Chapter 2 you learned that *accrual accounting* recognizes significant events in the period in which an event occurs regardless of whether or not cash was exchanged at the time of that event. In Chapter 2 the only noncash events that occurred were accrual events. An *accrual type* event was defined as one in which a significant business transaction or adjusting activity occurs *before* cash is exchanged. You now know that a *deferral type* event is one in which the business transaction or adjusting activity occurs *after* cash is exchanged.

After completing Chapter 3 you should understand that the accrual accounting system involves cash transactions, accrual transactions (and related year-end adjustments), and deferral transactions (and related year-end adjustments).

2.   Identify business events that involve deferrals.

A *deferral type* event is one in which a significant business transaction or adjusting activity occurs **after** cash is exchanged. The following diagrams may help to keep accruals and deferrals clear in your mind.

ACCRUAL: Business Action → (followed by) → Cash Exchange

DEFERRAL: Cash Exchange → (followed by) → Business Action

3.   Record deferral events under an accounting equation.

This learning objective is examined further through the use of the self-study problems presented below. The articulation problems are especially intended to help you achieve this objective.

4.   Prepare financial statements that include cash, accrual, and deferral events.

This learning objective is examined further through the use of the self-study problems presented below. The exercise-type problem is especially intended to help you achieve this objective.

5.   Explain how deferral events affect the financial statements.

This learning objective is examined further through the use of the self-study problems presented below. The articulation problems are especially intended to help you achieve this objective. Pay particular attention to the effects of deferral events on *inventory* accounts, *prepaid asset* accounts, and *unearned revenue* accounts.

6.   Explain the effects of end-of-period adjustments related to deferrals.

As a general rule, deferral adjustments affect either *assets and expenses* or *liabilities and revenues*.
This learning objective is examined further through the use of the self-study problems presented below. The articulation problems are especially intended to help you achieve this objective.

7.   Distinguish between a cost that is an asset and a cost that is an expense.

Unless a liability is being paid, when a company spends money it incurs a cost. This cost can result in the company obtaining an asset or incurring an expense. If the expenditure results in the company obtaining something with "future economic value to the business," then an asset has been obtained. If no asset was obtained, but the money was spent (or obligated to be spent in the future) in anticipation of producing revenue, the cost was an expense. If a cost is incurred that does not result in an asset and is not expected to produce revenue, either directly or indirectly, then that cost probably should be labeled a *loss*.

8.   Distinguish gains and losses from revenue and expenses.

Revenues and gains have similar effects on a company's financial statements, as do expenses and losses. The difference between these related terms often results from the objectives of a business. Revenue is the term of choice for activities that are related to a company's primary business operations. However, when a company has earnings related to an activity not within the scope of its primary operations, they are often referred to as *gains*. Furthermore, in this situation gains are often used to describe the net amount earned. Consider this example. A firm of attorneys provides services to its clients and is paid; this would be revenue. Suppose the same firm sells land for $10,000 that it had purchased for $6,000. The net amount of $4,000 the firm earned would be called a *gain*, because buying and selling land is not the primary purpose of the firm. If the business buying and selling the land had been a real estate firm, then it would report revenue of $10,000 and an expense of $6,000, resulting in a profit of $4,000.

Losses are related to expenses in the same way as gains are to revenues, but the term loss is used in another context as well. If a cost is incurred that is not reasonably related to the production of revenue, the cost is called a loss. For example, if a flood damages a company's store, and the damage is not covered by insurance, it would be deemed a loss, not an expense. There is no reasonable expectation that the flood damage will produce revenue for the business.

9.   **Analyze financial statements and make meaningful comparisons between companies by using a debt-to-assets ratio, a return-on-assets ratio, and a return-on-equity ratio.**

The debt-to-assets ratio reveals what percentage of a company's assets is financed with borrowed money. The higher the debt-to-assets ratio is, the greater its financial risks, other things being equal. The debt-to-assets ratio is defined as:

$$\frac{\text{Total debt}}{\text{Total assets}}$$

The return-on-assets ratio (ROA) helps measure how well a company is using the assets available to it. The more earnings that can be generated for a given amount of assets, the better the company is performing. The ROA ratio is defined as:

$$\frac{\text{Net income}}{\text{Total assets}}$$

The return-on-equity ratio (ROE) helps to measure how much the owners of a company are earning on the money they have invested in the business. The higher the return, the better it is for the owners. The ROE is defined as:

$$\frac{\text{Net income}}{\text{Equity}}$$

10.   **Record deferral events in a financial statements model.**

This learning objective is examined further through the use of the self-study problems presented below. The articulation problems are especially intended to help you achieve this objective.

Self-Study Problems

Articulation Problems

For each situation below, indicate its effects on the accounting elements shown on the accompanying chart. Use the following letters to indicate your answer (you do not need to enter amounts):

Increase = **I**   Decrease = **D**   No effect = **N**

1. Alaska Co. provided services to customers for cash.

Assets	Liabilities	Equity	Revenues	Expenses	Net Income	Cash

2. Bedford Co. provided services to its customers on account.

Assets	Liabilities	Equity	Revenues	Expenses	Net Income	Cash

3. Carolina Co. collected cash from customers for services that Carolina agreed to perform in the future.

Assets	Liabilities	Equity	Revenues	Expenses	Net Income	Cash

4. Bedford Co. collected cash from accounts receivable.

Assets	Liabilities	Equity	Revenues	Expenses	Net Income	Cash

5.   Carolina Co. provided services to its customers who had previously given it cash (see transaction 3).

Assets	Liabilities	Equity	Revenues	Expenses	Net Income	Cash

6.   Dijon Co. purchased equipment for cash.

Assets	Liabilities	Equity	Revenues	Expenses	Net Income	Cash

7.   Finn Co. made a cash distribution to its owners.

Assets	Liabilities	Equity	Revenues	Expenses	Net Income	Cash

8.   Georgia Co. purchased land using a note payable.

Assets	Liabilities	Equity	Revenues	Expenses	Net Income	Cash

9.   Huston Co. purchased $1,000 of office supplies for cash.

Assets	Liabilities	Equity	Revenues	Expenses	Net Income	Cash

10.   Georgia Co. paid off the note payable it had used to purchase land (see transaction 8).

Assets	Liabilities	Equity	Revenues	Expenses	Net Income	Cash

11.   Islay Co. paid cash in advance for a three-year lease of office space.

Assets	Liabilities	Equity	Revenues	Expenses	Net Income	Cash

12.   Georgia Co. sold land for $8,000. The land had originally been purchased for $6,000. Show the "net" effects.

Assets	Liabilities	Equity	Revenues	Expenses	Net Income	Cash

13.   Dijon Co. made a year-end adjustment to record depreciation on the equipment it purchased in transaction 6.

Assets	Liabilities	Equity	Revenues	Expenses	Net Income	Cash

14.   Islay Co. made a year-end adjustment related to the prepaid lease of office space that occurred in transaction 11.

Assets	Liabilities	Equity	Revenues	Expenses	Net Income	Cash

15.   Huston Co. made a year-end adjustment after it determined that only $300 of the office supplies purchased in transaction 9 were still on hand.

Assets	Liabilities	Equity	Revenues	Expenses	Net Income	Cash

Multiple-Choice Problems

1.   Jager Co. paid three years of rent in advance. This event would be classified as an/a:
    a.   Asset source transaction.
    b.   Asset use transaction.
    c.   Asset exchange transaction.
    d.   Claims exchange transaction.

2.   On January 1, 2005, Kistler Co. received $3,000 for three years' rent in advance. On December 31, 2005, Kistler made an adjustment to reflect the fact that one year of rent revenue had been earned. This <u>adjustment</u> is an example of an/a:
    a.   Asset source transaction.
    b.   Asset use transaction.
    c.   Asset exchange transaction.
    d.   Claims exchange transaction.

3.   At the beginning of 2009 Logan Co. had $1,000 of supplies. During the year it purchased an additional $4,000 of supplies on account. Later, Logan paid $3,000 on accounts payable related to the supplies. A count of supplies at the end of 2009 showed that supplies worth $500 were still on hand. Pertaining to supplies, how much *expense* and *cash flow from operating activities* would be shown on Logan's 2009 financial statements?

	Expense	Cash Flow
a.	$ 4,500	$ 3,000
b.	$ 3,000	$ 3,000
c.	$ 3,000	$ 4,000
d.	$ 4,500	$ 4,000

4.   When a company incurs expenses:
    a.   Assets may increase.
    b.   Liabilities may increase.
    c.   Cash may increase.
    d.   Common Stock may decrease.

5.   On January 1, 2005, Moss Co. purchased equipment that cost $10,000 and had an expected life of four years and estimated salvage value of $2,000. For 2005, the amount of expense that should be shown on Moss' income statement, and cash flow from *investing* activities that should be shown on its statement of cash flows would be:

	Expense	Cash Flow
a.	$ 2,500	$ 0
b.	$ 2,500	$10,000
c.	$ 2,000	$ 0
d.	$ 2,000	$10,000

6.   On January 1, 2005, Nectar Co. purchased equipment that cost $18,000 and had an expected life of six years and estimated salvage value of $3,000. For 2006, the amount of expense that should be shown on Nectar's income statement and accumulated depreciation that should be shown on its balance sheet would be:

	Expense	Accumulated Depreciation
a.	$ 3,000	$ 3,000
b.	$ 3,000	$ 6,000
c.	$ 2,500	$ 2,500
d.	$ 2,500	$ 5,000

7.   On January 1, 2005, Orchid Co. purchased equipment that cost $25,000 and had an expected life of five years and estimated salvage value of $5,000. At the end of 2006, what would be the amount of accumulated depreciation and book value that would be shown on Orchid's balance sheet?

	Accumulated Depreciation	Book Value
a.	$ 8,000	$12,000
b.	$ 8,000	$17,000
c.	$10,000	$10,000
d.	$10,000	$15,000

8.   Which of the following is <u>not</u> an example of a deferral type item?
      a.   Supplies inventory
      b.   Prepaid rent
      c.   Unearned revenue
      d.   Interest expense

9.   Which of the following items would <u>not</u> appear in the *investing* activities section of the statement of cash flows?
   a.   Cash inflow from interest revenue.
   b.   Cash outflow for the purchase of a certificate of deposit.
   c.   Cash outflow for the purchase of land.
   d.   Cash inflow from the sale of land.

10.   Which of the following would appear on the income statement?
   a.   Accumulated Depreciation
   b.   Gain on Sale of Land
   c.   Prepaid Rent
   d.   Dividends

11.   Which of the following statements is true?
   a.   An accrual event occurs when a company receives cash before it is earned.
   b.   Wages payable is an example of a deferral.
   c.   A deferral event occurs when a company receives cash before it is earned.
   d.   A company that properly records *accrued interest payable* also will recognize interest revenue.

12.   On January 1, 2005, the Moss Co. prepaid $3,000 on a three-year insurance policy. At the end of the year Moss made the proper adjustment related to the prepaid policy. What is the net effect of these two events on Moss' assets for 2005?
   a.   No effect.
   b. $ 2,000 increase.
   c. $ 1,000 decrease.
   d. $ 3,000 decrease.

13.   Peach Co. purchased office supplies for cash. Which of the following choices reflects how this event would affect the company's financial statements?

	Assets	=	Liab.	+	Equity	Rev.	−	Exp.	=	Net Inc.	Cash Flow
a.	D		N		D	N		I		D	D
b.	N		N		N	N		I		D	D
c.	D		N		D	N		N		N	D
d.	N		N		N	N		N		N	D

14. Quick Co. recorded depreciation on its equipment. Which of the following choices reflects how this event would affect the company's financial statements?

	Assets	=	Liab.	+	Equity	Rev.	-	Exp.	=	Net Inc.	Cash Flow
a.	D	=	N	+	D	N	-	I	=	D	D
b.	N	=	N	+	N	N	-	I	=	D	N
c.	D	=	N	+	D	N	-	I	=	D	N
d.	N	=	N	+	D	N	-	N	=	N	D

15. Rose Co. received cash from customers for services that Dylan promised to provide in the future. Which of the following choices reflects how this event would affect the company's financial statements?

	Assets	=	Liab.	+	Equity	Rev.	-	Exp.	=	Net Inc.	Cash Flow
a.	I	=	N	+	I	I	-	N	=	I	I
b.	I	=	I	+	N	N	-	N	=	N	I
c.	N	=	I	+	I	I	-	N	=	I	I
d.	N	=	N	+	N	N	-	N	=	N	I

The following information applies to questions 16 through 19.

The following account balances are available for Salvia Co.:

Assets	$10,000	Revenue	$ 7,500
Liabilities	7,000	Expenses	6,000
Common Stock	1,000	Net Earnings	1,500
Retained Earnings	2,000		

16. What is Salvia's debt-to-asset ratio?
    a.   30%
    b.   43%
    c.   60%
    d.   70%

17. What is Salvia's return-on-equity ratio?
    a.   50%
    b.   75%
    c.   150%
    d.   250%

18.   What is Salvia's return-on-assets ratio?
         a.   15%
         b.   50%
         c.   70%
         d.   75%

19.   If Salvia borrows $3,000 from the Local Bank, what will its new debt-to-assets ratio be?
         a.   54%
         b.   77%
         c.   100%
         d.   130%

Multiple True-False Problems

1.   Indicate if each of the following statements related to accruals and deferrals is true or false.
         a.   The expense a company incurs for electric utilities is a deferral event.
         b.   Assume Forest Co. pays its workers on Friday of each week. If 2008 end on a Wednesday, Forest Co. will have an accrual related to wages.
         c.   Unpaid interest on a loan is a deferral event.
         d.   Accrual events affect the income statement before the statement of cash flows.
         e.   Deferral events affect the income statement before the statement of cash flows.

2.   The following events occurred at Tomato Co. during 2009.

             Earned $20,000 of cash revenues.
             Paid $3,600 on November 1, to rent office space for one-year.
             Paid $8,000 for wages.
             On December 31, $500 of wages expense was accrued.

         Based only on the events above, indicate if each of the following statements is true or false.
         a.   Net income is $10,900.
         b.   The amount of net cash flows from operating activities is $12,000.
         c.   The amount of liabilities that should be reported on Tomato's balance sheet is $0.
         d.   The amount of assets that should be reported on Tomato's balance sheet is $12,000.
         e.   The amount of net cash flows from investing activities is $0.

3.   On April 1, 2005 Urn Co. Urn purchased a new delivery truck for cash. The truck cost $30,000. It has an expected useful life of 5 years, and an estimated salvage value of $7,500. Assuming Urn uses the straight-line method of depreciation, indicate if each of the following statements is true or false.
   a.   Urn's depreciation expense for **2005** should be $3,375.
   b.   Urn's depreciation expense for **2006** should be $4,500.
   c.   The balance in accumulated depreciation on Urn's **2006** balance sheet should be $4,500.
   d.   The purchase of the truck had the immediate effect of causing Urn's debt-to-assets ratio to increase.
   e.   When Urn recorded depreciation on the truck for **2005**, it caused the company's debt-to-asset ratio to increase.

Exercise-Type Problem

P-1   Vessel Co. began operations on January 1, 2005. On January 1, 2006, the company records showed the following account balances:

Cash	$10,000	Accounts Payable	$ 3,500
Accounts Receivable	5,000	Wages Payable	500
Supplies	1,000	Common Stock	8,000
		Retained Earnings	4,000

The following events occurred during 2006:

a.   Paid the Wages Payable of $500.
b.   Purchased supplies of $3,000 with cash.
c.   Provided services of $12,000 on account.
d.   Purchased office equipment for $5,000 with cash. The equipment has an expected life of four years and expected salvage value of $1,000.
e.   A customer gave Vessel $6,000 for services that Vessel agreed to perform in the future.
f.   Incurred expenses of $7,000 on account.
g.   Collected $11,000 from Accounts Receivable.
h.   Paid $8,500 on Accounts Payable.
i.   Made a $2,000 distribution to the owners.
j.   A count of the supplies revealed that $1,500 remained on hand. (Adjustment required.)
k.   A review of the contract with the customer that gave Vessel the cash advance (transaction e) revealed that Vessel had completed one-third of the promised work. (Adjustment required.)
l.   Vessel determined that a full-year of depreciation should be recognized on the equipment purchased in transaction (d). (Adjustment required.)

Required:

1.   Explain how each of these events would affect Vessel's accounting equation using the form provided on the next page. Notice that this form has a separate column for each account. Use ( ) to indicate amounts being subtracted.

2.   Prepare an income statement, a statement of changes in stockholders' equity, a balance sheet, and a statement of cash flows. Use the forms provided on the following pages.

Form for requirement 1

Event	Assets					Liabilities			Equity	
	Cash	Accounts Receivable	Supplies	Equip-ment	Accum. Deprec.	Accounts Payable	Wages Payable	Unearned Revenue	Common Stock	Retained Earnings
Beg. Bal.	10,000	5,000	1,000			3,500	500		8,000	4,000
a										
b										
c										
d										
e										
f										
g										
h										
i										
j										
k										
l										
Totals										

Forms for requirement 2

Vessel Co.
Income Statement
For the Year Ended December 31, 2006

Revenues	$
Expenses	
Net Income	$

Vessel Co.
Statement of Changes in Stockholders' Equity
For the Year Ended December 31, 2006

Beginning Common Stock	$	
Plus: Investments		
Ending Common Stock		$
Beginning Retained Earnings		
Plus: Net Income		
Less: Dividends		
Ending Retained Earnings		
Total Equity		$

Vessel Co.
Balance Sheet
As of December 31, 2006

Assets:

Cash		$	
Accounts Receivable			
Supplies			
Office Equipment	$		
Less: Accum. Depreciation			
Total Assets			$

Liabilities:

Accounts Payable	$	
Unearned Revenue		
Total Liabilities		$

Equity:

Common Stock		
Retained Earnings		
Total Equity		
Total Liabilities and Equity		$

Vessel Co.
Statement of Cash Flows
For the Year Ended December 31, 2006

Cash Flows from Operating Activities:
 Inflows from Customers $
 Outflows for Expenses   _____
Net Cash Flow from Operating Activities $

Cash Flow from Investing Activities:
 Outflows for Equipment
Net Cash Flow from Investing Activities

Cash Flows from Financing Activities:
 Outflows for Dividends
Net Cash Flow from Financing Activities

Net Decrease in Cash
Add: Beginning Cash Balance   _____

Cash Balance at December 31, 2006 $_____

Solutions to Self-Study Problems

Articulation Problems

1.   Alaska Co. provided services to customers for cash.

Assets	Liabilities	Equity	Revenues	Expenses	Net Income	Cash
I	N	I	I	N	I	I

Cash, an asset, increased. The company earned revenues, which caused net income to increase. An increase in net income causes retained earnings, a part of owners' equity, to increase.

2.   Bedford Co. provided services to its customers on account.

Assets	Liabilities	Equity	Revenues	Expenses	Net Income	Cash
I	N	I	I	N	I	N

Accounts receivable, an asset, increased. The company earned revenues, which caused net income to increase. An increase in net income causes retained earnings, a part of owners' equity, to increase.

3.   Carolina Co. collected cash from customers for services that Carolina agreed to perform in the future.

Assets	Liabilities	Equity	Revenues	Expenses	Net Income	Cash
I	I	N	N	N	N	I

Cash increased, but the cash has not yet been earned. Therefore, the company has a liability to the customer. The company must either perform the services or return the cash. (Legally, the company may not have the option of simply returning the cash.)

4.   Bedford Co. collected cash from accounts receivable.

Assets	Liabilities	Equity	Revenues	Expenses	Net Income	Cash
N	N	N	N	N	N	I

One asset, cash, increased while another asset, accounts receivable, decreased by the same amount.

5.   Carolina Co. provided services to its customers who had previously given it cash (see transaction 3).

Assets	Liabilities	Equity	Revenues	Expenses	Net Income	Cash
N	D	I	I	N	I	N

Although the company did not receive any assets, it has *earned* the cash it was given in transaction 3. Thus, it no longer has the obligation (liability) to provide services to the customer that gave it the cash. Because the company earned revenues, net income increased. An increase in net income causes retained earnings, a part of owners' equity, to increase.

6.   Dijon Co. purchased equipment for cash.

Assets	Liabilities	Equity	Revenues	Expenses	Net Income	Cash
N	N	N	N	N	N	D

One asset, equipment, increased while another asset, cash, decreased by the same amount. The purchase of equipment was not an immediate expense because the equipment has future value and will be used to help produce revenue in future periods. Therefore, it would understate net income for this period to recognize the full cost as an expense for this period. Over time, the cost of the equipment will become an expense as it is depreciated.

7.   Finn Co. made a cash distribution to its owners.

Assets	Liabilities	Equity	Revenues	Expenses	Net Income	Cash
D	N	D	N	N	N	D

Cash, an asset, decreased while retained earnings, a part of owners' equity, decreased. This payment of cash was not an expense because the money was not spent in the expectation that it would produce revenues.

8.   Georgia Co. purchased land using a note payable.

Assets	Liabilities	Equity	Revenues	Expenses	Net Income	Cash
I	I	N	N	N	N	N

Land, an asset, increased and notes payable, a liability, also increased.

9.   Huston Co. purchased $1,000 of office supplies for cash.

Assets	Liabilities	Equity	Revenues	Expenses	Net Income	Cash
N	N	N	N	N	N	D

One asset, supplies inventory, increased while another asset, cash, decreased by the same amount. The purchase of supplies inventory was not an immediate expense because the supplies have future value and will be used to help produce revenue in the future. The cost of the supplies will become an expense as they are consumed (i.e., used to produce revenue).

10.   Georgia Co. paid off the note payable it had used to purchase land (see transaction 8).

Assets	Liabilities	Equity	Revenues	Expenses	Net Income	Cash
D	D	N	N	N	N	D

Cash decreased because liabilities were paid (reduced).

11.   Islay Co. paid cash in advance for a three-year lease of office space.

Assets	Liabilities	Equity	Revenues	Expenses	Net Income	Cash
N	N	N	N	N	N	D

The right to use office space in the future is something of value (an asset) to a business. Therefore, one asset, prepaid rent, increased while another asset, cash, decreased by the same amount. The prepayment of rent was not an immediate expense because the future rent has value and will be used to help produce revenue in the future. The cost of the rent will become an expense as the rent contract expires (i.e., is used to produce revenue).

12.   Georgia Co. sold land for $8,000. The land had originally been purchased for $6,000. Show the "net" effects.

Assets	Liabilities	Equity	Revenues	Expenses	Net Income	Cash
I	N	I	I	N	I	I

One asset, land, decreased by $6,000, but another, cash, increased by $8,000, causing total assets to increase by $2,000. Because the land was sold for more than it originally cost the company, a gain was made on the sale. Although a gain is not exactly the same as a revenue account, it has the same effect on net income, retained earnings, and total equity. Therefore, the solution here shows the gain as an increase in revenues.

13.   Dijon Co. made a year-end adjustment to record depreciation on the equipment it purchased in transaction 6.

Assets	Liabilities	Equity	Revenues	Expenses	Net Income	Cash
D	N	D	N	I	D	N

Because equipment does not last forever a portion of it is removed from assets each accounting period. Because the equipment is used to produce revenues, the portion expiring that period is recognized as an expense. The increase in expenses causes net income to decrease, which causes retained earnings, a part of equity, to decrease.

14.   Islay Co. made a year-end adjustment related to the prepaid lease of office space that occurred in transaction 11.

Assets	Liabilities	Equity	Revenues	Expenses	Net Income	Cash
D	N	D	N	I	D	N

Because the prepaid rent contract had only a three-year life, one-third of it is removed from assets each accounting period. Because the office space is used to produce revenues, the portion of prepaid rent that expires that period is recognized as an expense. The increase in expenses causes net income to decrease, which causes retained earnings, a part of equity, to decrease.

15.   Huston Co. made a year-end adjustment after it determined that only $300 of the office supplies purchased in transaction 9 were still on-hand.

Assets	Liabilities	Equity	Revenues	Expenses	Net Income	Cash
D	N	D	N	I	D	N

If no adjustment was made to the supplies inventory account, the balance would still be the $1,000 amount that was purchased in transaction 9. This would cause an overstatement of assets because only $300 of the supplies remains. Therefore, assets must be decreased (by $700). Because the supplies were used to produce revenues, the portion that was used this period is recognized as an expense. The increase in expenses causes net income to decrease, which causes retained earnings, a part of equity, to decrease.

Multiple Choice Questions

1.   c.   Cash decreases and Prepaid Rent, an asset, increases by the same amount.

2.   d.   Unearned Rent Revenue, a liability, decreased, and Equity increased (because of the rent revenue that was earned).

3.   a.   Expense:

Beginning supplies	$1,000		Cash Flows are affected only by
Purchases	4,000		the cash payment of **$3,000.**
	5,000		
−Supplies on hand	500		
Supplies expense	**$4,500**		

4.   b.   An example would be incurred expenses on account.

5.   d.   Dep. Exp: $\dfrac{\$10,000 - \$2,000}{4 \text{ years}}$ =   **$2,000**

Cash Flow: Purchase of equipment   =   **$10,000**

6.   d.   Dep. Exp: $\dfrac{\$18,000 - \$3,000}{6 \text{ years}}$ = $2,500

Accum. Depr. $2,500 x 2 years   =   **$5,000**

7.   b.   Dep. Exp: $\dfrac{\$25,000 - \$5,000}{5 \text{ years}}$ = $4,000

Accum. Depr. $4,000 x 2 years   = $8,000

	Cost	Accum. Depr.	Book Value
Book Value:	$25,000 −	$8,000 =	**$17,000**

8.   d.

9.   a.   Interest revenue would appear in the *Operating Activities* section of the cash statement assuming it was collected.

10. b.

11. c.

12. c.   The January 1, transaction had no effect on total assets because Cash decreased and Prepaid Insurance, another asset, increased by the same amount. However, the end of the year adjustment decreased Prepaid Insurance by $1,000 and increased expenses by $1,000.

13. d.   See articulation problem 9 for an explanation of the correct answer.

14. c.   See articulation problem 13 for an explanation of the correct answer.

15. b.   See articulation problem 3 for an explanation of the correct answer.

16. d.

Total Debt	÷	**Total Assets**	=	**%**
$7,000	÷	$10,000	=	70%

17. a.

Net Earnings	÷	**Equity**	=	**%**
$1,500	÷	$1,000 + $2,000	=	50%

18. a.

Net Earnings	÷	**Total Assets**	=	**%**
$1,500	÷	$10,000	=	15%

19. b.

Ratio	Before Borrowing		Effect of Borrowing		After Borrowing		
Total Debt	$7,000	+	$3,000	=	$10,000		
Total Assets	$10,000	+	$3,000	=	$13,000	=	76.9%

Multiple-False Problems

1.   a.   **False**, because the expense is incurred before the cash is paid, electric utilities usually are accrual events.
     b.   **True**, Forest Co. will owe its workers for three days of accrued wages.
     c.   **False**, when expenses are incurred before the cash is paid, an accrual event is created.
     d.   **True**, see a. and c. above.
     e.   **False**, deferral events occur when cash is paid (or received) before the expense (or revenue) is incurred.

2.   a.   **True**: ($20,000 - $8,000 - $500 - $600* = $10,900)
                     *($3,600 ÷ 12 months) x 2 months = $600)
     b.   **False**, net cash flows from operating activities are $8,400. ($20,000 - $3,600 - $8,000)
     c.   **False**, Tomato would have $500 of Wages Payable.
     d.   **False**, assets should total $11,400. (*Cash* is **$8,400**, see b. above; *Prepaid Rent* is **$3,000** [$3,600 - $600]) (Total assets are: $8,400 + $3,000 = $11,400)
     e.   **True**, the cash paid to acquire the asset Prepaid Rent is classified as an *operating activity*, not an *investing activity*.

3.   a.   **True:**   ($30,000 – $7,500) ÷ 5 years = $4,500 per year. However, for 2005, only 9 months of depreciation expense should be recorded. $4,500 x 9/12 = $3,375)

   b.   **True**, see the computations in a.

   c.   **False**, Accumulated Depreciation as of December 31, 2006 is equal to the depreciation expense for 2005 and 2006. ($3,375 + $4,500 = **$7,875**)

   d.   **False**, the cash purchase of the truck is an asset exchange. Since neither total assets nor total debt was affected, the debt-to-assets ratio would not be affected.

   e.   **True**, as Accumulated Depreciation, a contra-asset account, increases, total assets decrease. If total assets decrease and total debt remains the same, the debt-to-assets ratio will increase.

Exercise-Type Problem

Solution for requirement 2   (Solution for requirement 1 follows.)

Vessel Co.
Income Statement
For the Year Ended December 31, 2006

Revenues	(12,000 + 2,000)	$14,000
Expenses	(7,000 + 2,500 + 1,000)	10,500
Net Income		$ 3,500

Vessel Co.
Statement of Changes in Stockholders' Equity
For the Year Ended December 31, 2006

Beginning Common Stock	$ 8,000	
Plus: Investments	0	
Ending Common Stock		$ 8,000
Beginning Retained Earnings	4,000	
Plus: Net Income	3,500	
Less: Dividends	(2,000)	
Ending Retained Earnings		5,500
Total Equity		$13,500

Vessel Co.
Balance Sheet
As of December 31, 2006

Assets:

Cash		$ 8,000	
Accounts Receivable		6,000	
Supplies		1,500	
Office Equipment	$5,000		
Less: Accum. Depreciation	1,000	4,000	
Total Assets			$19,500

Liabilities:

Accounts Payable	$ 2,000	
Unearned Revenue	4,000	
Total Liabilities		$ 6,000

Equity:

Common Stock	8,000	
Retained Earnings	5,500	
Total Equity		13,500
Total Liabilities and Equity		$19,500

Vessel Co.
Statement of Cash Flows
For the Year Ended December 31, 2006

Cash Flows from Operating Activities:

Inflows from Customers	$17,000	
Outflows for Expenses	(12,000)	
Net Cash Flow from Operating Activities		$ 5,000

Cash Flows from Investing Activities:

Outflows for Equipment	(5,000)	
Net Cash Flow from Investing Activities		(5,000)

Cash Flows from Financing Activities:

Outflows for Dividends	(2,000)	
Net Cash Flow from Financing Activities		(2,000)

Net Decrease in Cash		(2,000)
Add: Beginning Cash Balance		10,000
Cash Balance at December 31, 2006		$ 8,000

Solution for requirement 1

Event	Assets					Liabilities			Equity	
	Cash	Accounts Receivable	Supplies	Equipment	Accum. Deprec.	Accounts Payable	Wages Payable	Unearned Revenue	Common Stock	Retained Earnings
Beg. Bal.	10,000	5,000	1,000			3,500	500		8,000	4,000
a	(500)						(500)			
b	(3,000)		3,000							
c		12,000								12,000
d	(5,000)			5,000						
e	6,000							6,000		
f						7,000				(7,000)
g	11,000	(11,000)								
h	(8,500)					(8,500)				
i.	(2,000)									(2,000)
j			(2,500)							(2,500)
k								(2,000)		2,000
l					1,000					(1,000)
Totals	8,000	6,000	1,500	5,000	1,000	2,000	0	4,000	8,000	5,500

Chapter Four
The Double-Entry Accounting System

Learning Objectives for the Chapter

After completing this chapter you should be able to:

1. Explain the fundamental concepts associated with double-entry accounting systems.
2. Describe business events using debit/credit terminology.
3. Record transactions in T-accounts.
4. Identify events that need adjusting entries and record them.
5. State the need for, and record, closing entries.
6. Prepare and interpret a trial balance.
7. Record transactions using the general journal format.
8. Describe the components of an annual report including the management, discussion and analysis section (MD&A) and the footnotes to financial statements.
9. Describe the role of the Securities and Exchange Commission (SEC) in financial reporting.

Brief Explanation of the Learning Objectives

1.   Explain the fundamental concepts associated with double-entry accounting systems.

The system presented in Chapter 4 is simply a new way of solving the accounting problems presented in the preceding chapters. All of the accounting concepts you learned in Chapters 1, 2, and 3 are essential to understanding the double-entry system. (Do not make the mistake of trying to memorize journal entries. Rather, realize that journal entries are simply another way of expressing the effects of a business event on a company's assets, liabilities, equity, revenues, and expenses.)

The debit-credit system is based on the following rules:
- Assets = liabilities + equity.
- Debits = credits.
- Debit means the left side and credit means the right side of an account.
- Asset accounts are increased with debits and decreased with credits.
- Liability accounts are increased with credits and decreased with debits.
- Equity is increased by credits to equity accounts and decreased by debits to equity accounts. Expense accounts require special attention. Expense accounts are **increased with debits**, but increasing expenses cause equity to decrease.

2.   **Describe business events using debit/credit terminology.**

This learning objective is examined further through the use of the self-study problems presented below.

3.   **Record transactions in T-accounts.**

The use of T-accounts: T-accounts are used as instructional tools to help organize the effects of journal entries. Rather than formally recording journal entries and then posting the entries to the general ledger, we can often replace these two procedures with T-accounts. Some accounting instructors allow this and others do not; ask your instructor what he or she prefers.

This learning objective is examined further through the use of the self-study problems presented below. The exercise-type problems are especially intended to help you achieve this objective.

4.   **Identify events that need adjusting entries and record them.**

Adjusting journal entries are used to make the end of period adjustments for accruals (Chapter 2) and deferrals (Chapter 3). If adjusting entries are not made, many of the account balances shown on the financial statements will be incorrect.

5.   **State the need for, and record, closing entries.**

Closing entries are made at the end of the accounting period and accomplish two basic tasks. First, they eliminate the balances in the revenue and expense accounts (after the income statement has been prepared) so that the business can start over accumulating revenues and expenses for the next period. Second, closing entries get the correct balance in the Retained Earnings account so that the balance sheet can be prepared.

6.   **Prepare and interpret a trial balance.**

Before financial statements are prepared the trial balance is used to insure that total debits equal total credits. If the trial balance does not balance, the balance sheet will not balance and the earnings statement probably will report an erroneous net earnings.

7.   **Record transactions using the general journal format.**

Journal entries are used to record an accounting event initially. Their use makes it easy to insure that debits = credits. This learning objective is examined further through the use of the self-study problems.

8.   **Describe the components of an annual report including the management, discussion and analysis (MD&A) section and the footnotes to financial statements.**

The major components of the annual reports for public companies are:

Financial statements, which were described above.

Footnotes to the financial statements, which help explain how the statements were prepared. The footnotes also provide details about some of the information that is summarized in the financial statements. Technically, the footnotes are considered a part of the financial statements.

Management's discussion and analysis, which presents a candid view of how a company's management thinks the business is doing compared to past results and future opportunities. This section also usually identifies the company's major competitors. One might expect a company's management to present an overly optimistic view of the company's situation in the MD&A, but this is not usually the case. Management can be held liable for misleading information presented in the MD&A.

The **independent auditor's report** (often called the auditor's opinion), which states whether or not the company's financial statements were prepared in accordance with GAAP.

9.   **Describe the role of the Securities and Exchange Commission (SEC) in financial reporting.**

The Securities and Exchange Commission (SEC) is a governmental agency charged with the responsibility for regulating financial reporting and the trading of financial securities (stocks and bonds) of larger corporations in the United States. Although the SEC has the ultimate power to establish the accounting rules these companies must follow, it allows the private accounting profession to establish most accounting standards (GAAP). The primary rule-making body in the private accounting profession is the Financial Accounting Standards Board (FASB).

Self-Study Problems

Articulation Problems

For each situation below, do two things:

First, prepare a journal entry to record the event in debit-credit form in the space provided. See the textbook for the proper form.

Second, indicate the effects of the event on the accounting elements shown on the accompanying chart. Use the following letters to indicate your answer (you do not need to enter amounts):

Increase = **I**   Decrease = **D**   No effect = **N**

1. The owners of Dover Co. began their business by investing $10,000 of cash.

_____   _____

_____   _____

Assets	Liabilities	Equity	Revenues	Expenses	Net Income	Cash

2. Epstein Co. provided services to customers for $15,000 cash.

_____   _____

_____   _____

Assets	Liabilities	Equity	Revenues	Expenses	Net Income	Cash

3. Epstein Co. provided services to its customers for $20,000 on account.

_____   _____

_____   _____

Assets	Liabilities	Equity	Revenues	Expenses	Net Income	Cash

4.   Foutz Co. collected $8,000 cash from customers for services that Foutz agreed to perform
      in the future.

_____   _____   _____

_____   _____   _____

Assets	Liabilities	Equity	Revenues	Expenses	Net Income	Cash

5.   Epstein Co. collected $13,000 cash from accounts receivable.

_____   _____   _____

_____   _____   _____

Assets	Liabilities	Equity	Revenues	Expenses	Net Income	Cash

6.   Foutz Co. provided $4,000 worth of services to its customers who had previously given it
      cash (see transaction 4).

_____   _____   _____

_____   _____   _____

Assets	Liabilities	Equity	Revenues	Expenses	Net Income	Cash

7.   Grant Co. purchased equipment for $12,000 cash. The equipment has an expected life of
      five years and estimated salvage value of $2,000.

_____   _____   _____

_____   _____   _____

Assets	Liabilities	Equity	Revenues	Expenses	Net Income	Cash

8.   Montana Co. made a $5,000 cash distribution to its owners.

_____   _____ _____
_____   _____ _____

Assets	Liabilities	Equity	Revenues	Expenses	Net Income	Cash

9.   Sperry Co. purchased $20,000 of land using a note payable.

_____   _____ _____
_____   _____ _____

Assets	Liabilities	Equity	Revenues	Expenses	Net Income	Cash

10.   Inman Co. purchased $1,000 of office supplies for cash.

_____   _____ _____
_____   _____ _____

Assets	Liabilities	Equity	Revenues	Expenses	Net Income	Cash

11.   Sperry Co. paid off the $20,000 note payable it had used to purchase land (see transaction 9). There was no interest on this note.

_____   _____ _____
_____   _____ _____

Assets	Liabilities	Equity	Revenues	Expenses	Net Income	Cash

12.   Jackson Co. paid cash in advance of $6,000 for a three-year lease of office space.

_____   _____ _____
_____   _____ _____

Assets	Liabilities	Equity	Revenues	Expenses	Net Income	Cash

13. Sperry Co. sold land for $8,000. The land had originally been purchased for $6,000. Show the net effects in the articulation chart.

Assets	Liabilities	Equity	Revenues	Expenses	Net Income	Cash

14. Grant Co. made a year-end adjustment to record depreciation on the equipment it purchased in transaction 7.

Assets	Liabilities	Equity	Revenues	Expenses	Net Income	Cash

15. Jackson Co. made a year-end adjustment related to the prepaid lease of office space that occurred in transaction 12. Jackson has used the office space for six months by year-end.

Assets	Liabilities	Equity	Revenues	Expenses	Net Income	Cash

16. Inman Co. made a year-end adjustment after it determined that only $300 of the office supplies purchased in transaction 10 were still on hand.

Assets	Liabilities	Equity	Revenues	Expenses	Net Income	Cash

Multiple-Choice Problems

1. Kramer Co. purchased land by issuing a note payable. The journal entry to record this transaction would require a:
    a. Debit to land and a credit to notes payable.
    b. Debit to notes payable and a credit to land.
    c. Debit to land and a debit to notes payable.
    d. Credit to land and a credit to notes payable.

2. How would the following journal entry affect the accounting equation?

Prepaid Rent	500	
Cash		500

    a. Assets would increase and equity would decrease.
    b. Liabilities would increase and assets would decrease.
    c. Liabilities would decrease and assets would decrease.
    d. There would be no effect on total assets, liabilities, or equity.

3. Debit entries act to:
    a. Decrease assets.
    b. Increase retained earnings.
    c. Increase expenses.
    d. Increase liabilities.

4. What type event does the following journal entry describe?

Accounts Payable	1,000	
Cash		1,000

    a. Provided services on account.
    b. Paid cash owed to suppliers.
    c. Incurred expenses on account.
    d. Collected cash from customers.

5.   The following account balances are available for the Lincoln Co.

Cash	$ 5,000	Common Stock	$12,000
Accounts Payable	6,000	Land	20,000
Supplies	1,000	Accumulated Depreciation	4,000
Equipment	15,000	Retained Earnings	19,000

If the account balances above were placed in a trial balance, the total of the debits column would be equal to:
a. $27,000
b. $37,000
c. $41,000
d. $60,000

6.   Which of the following accounts would <u>not</u> be closed to retained earnings at the end of the accounting period?
a.   Accumulated Depreciation.
b.   Rent Expense.
c.   Dividends.
d.   Interest Revenue.

7.   James Co. had the following trial balance before its closing entries were made.

Account	Debit	Credit
Cash	$10,000	$
Equipment	8,000	
Accumulated Depreciation		4,000
Common Stock		2,000
Retained Earnings		4,000
Revenues		20,000
Expenses	12,000	
Totals	$30,000	$30,000

After closing entries have been made and posted to the accounts, the balance in Retained Earnings will be:
a. $ 4,000
b. $ 8,000
c. $12,000
d. $24,000

8. Which of the following statements is true?
    a. A journal entry may have one account debited and two accounts credited.
    b. Accumulated depreciation is an asset account that has a debit balance.
    c. Liability accounts have debit balances.
    d. The amount of a company's total assets will equal the amount of its total debits.

9. Which of the following statements is true?
    a. Adjusting journal entries often involve cash.
    b. Adjusting journal entries are made after closing entries.
    c. Adjusting journal entries involve accruals but not deferrals.
    d. Adjusting journal entries are needed to correctly determine a company's net income.

10. An adjusting journal entry to record accrued interest on a note payable would involve:
    a. A debit to an asset account.
    b. A debit to a contra asset account.
    c. A credit to a liability account.
    d. A credit to a revenue account.

11. Which of the following journal entries would affect *cash flows from operating activities* on the Statement of Cash Flows?

a.	Land	10,000	
	Cash		10,000
b.	Prepaid Rent	10,000	
	Cash		10,000
c.	Cash	10,000	
	Common Stock		10,000
d.	Accounts Receivable	10,000	
	Revenue		10,000

12. Kenya Co. made the following journal entry:

Accounts Receivable	5,000	
Revenue		5,000

Which of the following choices reflects how this journal entry would affect the company's financial statements?

	Assets	=	Liab.	+	Equity	Rev.	–	Exp.	=	Net Inc.	Cash Flow
a.	I		N		I	I		N		I	N
b.	I		N		N	I		N		N	N
c.	D		N		D	D		N		D	N
d.	D		N		N	D		N		N	N

Multiple True-False Problems

1. Consider the following journal entry that was made by the Erie Co.:

Rent Expense	1,200	
Prepaid Rent		1,200

Base on this journal entry, indicate if each of the following statements are true or false.
a.   Erie's total assets increased.
b.   This was a claim exchange event.
c.   Erie's net income decreased.
d.   The Prepaid Rent account was credited.
e.   This journal entry is a transaction entry, not an adjusting entry.

2. Indicate if each of the following events related to the record keeping process is true or false.
a.   Expense accounts are closed with credit entries.
b.   Liability accounts are closed with debit entries.
c.   July 31, would be a good time to end the fiscal year and close the books at a company that does most of its business during the summer months.
d.   Adjusting journal entries are made before closing journal entries.
e.   The Accumulated Depreciation account is not closed at year-end.

3.   The following pre-closing trial balance was prepared for Montana Co.

Account Titles	Debits	Credits
Cash	$ 8,000	$
Accounts Receivable	21,000	
Equipment	80,000	
Accumulated Depreciation		9,000
Accountants Payable		16,000
Common Stock		11,000
Retained Earnings		50,000
Revenues		94,000
Expenses	71,000	
Totals	$180,000	$180,000

Based on the preceding trial balance, indicate if each of the following statements is true or false.

a.   Montana's total assets are $180,000.

b.   After Montana's books have been closed, the Common Stock account will have a balance of $11,000.

c.   Montana's net income is $23,000.

d.   After Montana's books have been closed, the Retained Earnings account will have a balance of $50,000.

e.   Montana's equipment has a book value of $80,000.

Exercise-Type Problem

P-1   Perez Co. began operations on January 1, 2005. On January 1, 2006, the company
records showed the following account balances:

Cash	$10,000	Accounts Payable	$ 3,500
Accounts Receivable	5,000	Wages Payable	500
Supplies	1,000	Common Stock	8,000
		Retained Earnings	4,000

The following events occurred during 2006:

a.   Paid the Wages Payable of $500.
b.   Purchased supplies of $3,000 with cash.
c.   Provided services of $12,000 on account.
d.   Purchased office equipment for $5,000 with cash. The equipment has an expected life of
four years and expected salvage value of $1,000.
e.   A customer gave Perez $6,000 for services that Perez agreed to perform in the future.
f.   Incurred expenses of $7,000 on account.
g.   Collected $11,000 from Accounts Receivable.
h.   Paid cash of $8,500 on Accounts Payable.
i.   Made a $2,000 distribution to the owners.
j.   A count of the supplies revealed that $1,500 remained on hand. (Adjustment required.)
k.   A review of the contract with the customer that gave Perez the cash advance (transaction
e) revealed that Perez had completed one-third of the promised work.   (Adjustment
required.)
l.   Perez determined that a full year of depreciation should be recognized on the equipment
purchased in transaction (d). (Adjustment required.)

Required:
1.   Prepare the proper journal entry for each of the above events. Use the space provided on
the following page.
2.   Post the journal entries to the T-accounts provided on a following page.
3.   Prepare a trial balance. A partially completed worksheet is provided on a following page.
4.   Prepare closing journal entries. Use the space provided on the following page.

Space for requirement 1

a. _____   _____   _____
   _____   _____   _____

b. _____   _____   _____
   _____   _____   _____

c. _____   _____   _____
   _____   _____   _____

d. _____   _____   _____
   _____   _____   _____

e. _____   _____   _____
   _____   _____   _____

f. _____   _____   _____
   _____   _____   _____

g. _____   _____   _____
   _____   _____   _____

h. _____   _____   _____
   _____   _____   _____

i. _____   _____   _____
   _____   _____   _____

j. _____   _____   _____
   _____   _____   _____

k. _____   _____   _____
   _____   _____   _____

l. _____   _____   _____
   _____   _____   _____

T-accounts for requirement 2

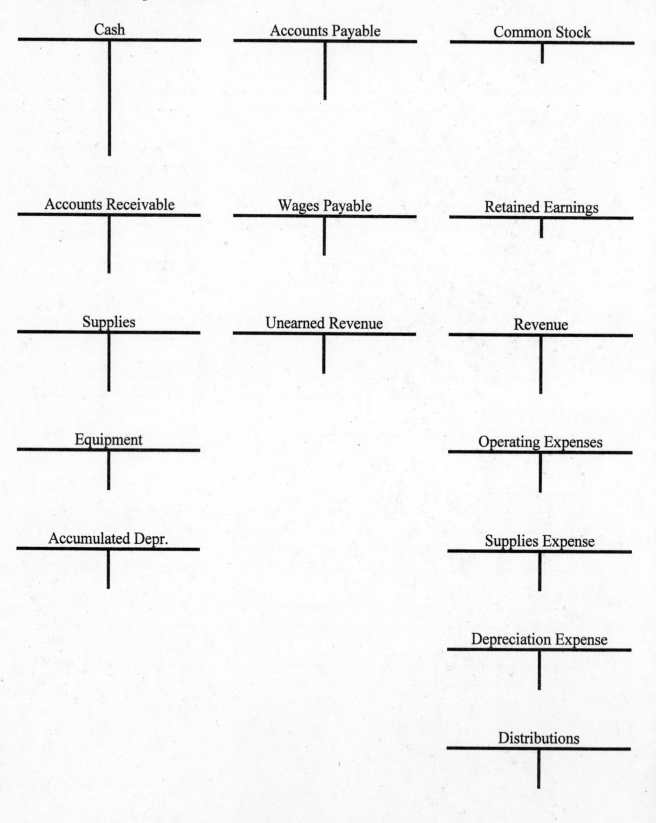

Cash

Accounts Payable

Common Stock

Accounts Receivable

Wages Payable

Retained Earnings

Supplies

Unearned Revenue

Revenue

Equipment

Operating Expenses

Accumulated Depr.

Supplies Expense

Depreciation Expense

Distributions

Form for requirement 3

Account	Balances	
	Debit	Credit
Cash	$	$
Accounts Receivable		
Supplies		
Equipment		
Accumulated Depreciation		
Accounts Payable		
Wages Payable		
Unearned Revenue		
Common Stock		
Retained Earnings		
Revenue		
Operating Expenses		
Supplies Expense		
Depreciation Expense		
Dividends		
Totals	$	$

Space for requirement 4

Rev.
Accts.

Exp.
Accts.

Distri-
bution

Solutions to Self-Study Problems

Articulation Problems

1.   The owners of Dover Co. began their business by investing $10,000 cash.

    Cash   10,000
          Common Stock   10,000

Assets	Liabilities	Equity	Revenues	Expenses	Net Income	Cash
I	N	I	N	N	N	I

2.   Epstein Co. provided services to customers for $15,000 cash.

    Cash   15,000
          Revenue   15,000

Assets	Liabilities	Equity	Revenues	Expenses	Net Income	Cash
I	N	I	I	N	I	I

3.   Epstein Co. provided services to its customers for $20,000 on account.

    Accounts Receivable   20,000
          Revenue   20,000

Assets	Liabilities	Equity	Revenues	Expenses	Net Income	Cash
I	N	I	I	N	I	N

4.   Foutz Co. collected $8,000 cash from customers for services that Foutz agreed to perform in the future.

    Cash   8,000
          Unearned Revenue   8,000

Assets	Liabilities	Equity	Revenues	Expenses	Net Income	Cash
I	I	N	N	N	N	I

5.   Epstein Co. collected $13,000 cash from accounts receivable.

    Cash   13,000
          Accounts Receivable   13,000

Assets	Liabilities	Equity	Revenues	Expenses	Net Income	Cash
N	N	N	N	N	N	I

6.   Foutz Co. provided $4,000 worth of services to its customers who had previously given it cash (see transaction 4).

    Unearned Revenue   4,000
          Revenue   4,000

Assets	Liabilities	Equity	Revenues	Expenses	Net Income	Cash
N	D	I	I	N	I	N

7.   Grant Co. purchased equipment for $12,000 cash. The equipment has an expected life of five years and estimated salvage value of $2,000.

       Equipment   12,000
           Cash   12,000

Assets	Liabilities	Equity	Revenues	Expenses	Net Income	Cash
N	N	N	N	N	N	D

8.   Montana Co. made a $5,000 cash distribution to its owners.

       Dividends   5,000
           Cash   5,000

Assets	Liabilities	Equity	Revenues	Expenses	Net Income	Cash
D	N	D	N	N	N	D

9.   Sperry Co. purchased $20,000 of land using a note payable.

       Land   20,000
           Notes Payable   20,000

Assets	Liabilities	Equity	Revenues	Expenses	Net Income	Cash
I	I	N	N	N	N	N

10.   Inman Co. purchased $1,000 of office supplies for cash.

       Supplies   1,000
           Cash   1,000

Assets	Liabilities	Equity	Revenues	Expenses	Net Income	Cash
N	N	N	N	N	N	D

11.   Sperry Co. paid off the $20,000 note payable it had used to purchase land (see transaction 9). There was no interest on this note.

       Notes Payable   20,000
           Cash   20,000

Assets	Liabilities	Equity	Revenues	Expenses	Net Income	Cash
D	D	N	N	N	N	D

12.   Jackson Co. paid cash in advance of $6,000 for a three-year lease of office space.

       Prepaid Rent   6,000
           Cash   6,000

Assets	Liabilities	Equity	Revenues	Expenses	Net Income	Cash
N	N	N	N	N	N	D

13.   Sperry Co. sold land for $8,000. The land had originally been purchased for $6,000. Show the net effects in the articulation chart.

Cash	8,000
Land	6,000
Gain on Sale of Land	2,000

Assets	Liabilities	Equity	Revenues	Expenses	Net Income	Cash
I	N	I	I	N	I	I

The gain on the sale of the land is not exactly the same thing as revenue, but because it has the same effect on net income, it is shown here as if it were revenue.

14.   Grant Co. made a year-end adjustment to record depreciation on the equipment it purchased in transaction 7.

Depreciation Expense	2,000
Accumulated Depreciation	2,000
[($12,000 - $2,000) ÷ 5 years = $2,000]	

Assets	Liabilities	Equity	Revenues	Expenses	Net Income	Cash
D	N	D	N	I	D	N

15.   Jackson Co. made a year-end adjustment related to the prepaid lease of office space that occurred in transaction 12. Jackson had used the office space for six months by year-end.

Rent Expense	1,000
Prepaid Rent	1,000
[($6,000 ÷ 3 years) X 6/12 = $1,000]	

Assets	Liabilities	Equity	Revenues	Expenses	Net Income	Cash
D	N	D	N	I	D	N

16.   Inman Co. made a year-end adjustment after it determined that only $300 of the office supplies purchased in transaction 10 were still on hand.

Supplies Expense	700
Supplies [$1,000 - $300]	700

Assets	Liabilities	Equity	Revenues	Expenses	Net Income	Cash
D	N	D	N	I	D	N

Multiple-Choice Questions

1.   a.

2.   d.

3.   c.

4.   b.

5.   c.   Cash + Supplies + Equipment + Land

6.   a.   Accumulated Depreciation is a contra asset that appears on the balance sheet.

7.   c.   Beginning balance [$4,000] + Revenues [$20,000] − Expenses [$12,000]

8.   a.

9.   d.

10.   c.   Interest Payable, a liability, would be credited.

11.   b.

12.   a.   The debit entry increases accounts receivable, which causes assets to increase. The credit entry increases revenues, which caused net income to increase. An increase in net income causes retained earnings, a part of owners' equity, to increase.

Multiple True-False Problems

1.   a.   **False**, total assets decreased because the asset, prepaid rent, decreased.
      b.   **False**, this was an asset use event.
      c.   **True**, rent expense increased, which caused net income to decrease.
      d.   **True**.
      e.   **False**, this was an adjusting entry. Prepaid rent decreases with the passage of time, but, generally, the account is updated only when the company wishes to prepare financial statements.

2.   a.   **True**, the closing process requires that expense accounts be credited and Retained Earnings is debited for the same amount.
      b.   **False**, liability accounts, like other accounts that appear on the balance sheet, are not closed.
      c.   **False**, a company that is very busy during the summer would want to close its books at a time of year when business is slower.
      d.   **True**, adjusting entries must be made before the income statement is prepared. The income statement should be prepared before closing entries are made.
      e.   **True**, it is an account that is reported on the balance sheet. Therefore, it is not closed at year-end.

3.   a.   **False**, total assets are $100,000 ($8,000 + $21,000 + $80,000 − $9,000).
      b.   **True**, the Common Stock account is not affected by closing entries.
      c.   **True**. ($94,000 − $71,000 = $23,000)
      d.   **False**, after the books are closed the Retained Earnings account will have a balance of $73,000. (Beginning Retained Earnings of $50,000 plus Net Income of $23,000 equals ending Retained Earnings of $73,000.)
      e.   **False**, Montana's equipment has a book value of $71,000 ($80,000 − $9,000).

Exercise-Type Problem

Solution for requirement 1

a.	Wages Payable	500	
	Cash		500
b.	Supplies	3,000	
	Cash		3,000
c.	Accounts Receivable	12,000	
	Revenue		12,000
d.	Equipment	5,000	
	Cash		5,000
e.	Cash	6,000	
	Unearned Revenue		6,000
f.	Operating Expenses	7,000	
	Accounts Payable		7,000
g.	Cash	11,000	
	Accounts Receivable		11,000
h.	Accounts Payable	8,500	
	Cash		8,500
i.	Dividends	2,000	
	Cash		2,000
j.	Supplies Expense	2,500	
	Supplies		2,500

[Beg. bal. [$1,000] + Supplies purchased [$3,000] - Supplies remaining [$1,500] = $2,500]

k.	Unearned Revenue	2,000	
	Revenue		2,000
l.	Depreciation Expense	1,000	
	Accumulated Depreciation		1,000

[($5,000 - $1,000) ÷ 4 years = $1,000]

Solution for requirement 2

Cash		
Bal. 10,000	500	
6,000	3,000	
11,000	5,000	
	8,500	
	2,000	
Bal. 8,000		

Accounts Payable	
8,500	3,500 Bal.
	7,000
	2,000 Bal.

Common Stock	
	8,000 Bal.

Accounts Receivable	
Bal. 5,000	11,000
12,000	
Bal. 6,000	

Wages Payable	
500	500 Bal.
	0 Bal.

Retained Earnings	
	4,000 Bal.

Supplies	
Bal. 1,000	2,500
3,000	
Bal. 1,500	

Unearned Revenue	
2,000	6,000
	4,000 Bal.

Revenue	
	12,000
	2,000
	14,000 Bal.

Equipment	
5,000	
Bal. 5,000	

Operating Expense	
7,000	
Bal. 7,000	

Accumulated Depr.	
	1,000
	1,000 Bal.

Supplies Expense	
2,500	
Bal. 2,500	

Depreciation Expense	
1,000	
Bal. 1,000	

Distributions	
2,000	
Bal. 2,000	

Solution for requirement 3

Account	Debit	Credit
		Balances
Cash	$ 8.000	$
Accounts Receivable	6,000	
Supplies	1,500	
Equipment	5,000	
Accumulated Depreciation		1,000
Accounts Payable		2,000
Wages Payable		0
Unearned Revenue		4,000
Common Stock		8,000
Retained Earnings		4,000
Revenue		14,000
Operating Expenses	7,000	
Supplies Expense	2,500	
Depreciation Expense	1,000	
Dividends	2,000	
Totals	$33,000	$33,000

Solution for requirement 4

Revenues	14,000	
Retained Earnings		14,000
Retained Earnings	10,500	
Operating Expenses		7,000
Supplies Expense		2,500
Depreciation Expenses		1,000
Retained Earnings	2,000	
Dividends		2,000

Chapter Five
Accounting for Merchandising Businesses

Learning Objectives for the Chapter

After completing this chapter you should be able to:

1.   Distinguish between service and merchandising businesses.
2.   Identify and explain the primary features of the perpetual inventory system.
3.   Explain the meaning of terms used to describe transportation costs, cash discounts, returns or allowances, and financing costs.
4.   Compare and contrast single and multistep income statements.
5.   Show the effects of lost, damaged, or stolen inventory on financial statements.
6.   Use common-size financial statements to evaluate managerial performance.
7.   Use ratio analysis to evaluate managerial performance.
8.   Identify the primary features of the periodic inventory system. (Appendix)

Brief Explanation of the Learning Objectives

1.   Distinguish between service and merchandising businesses.

A business that sells goods must purchase the goods before they can be resold. This causes the *merchandising* business to have inventory and incur the cost of financing inventory. A service business usually does not have significant amounts of inventory. The implications of needing to maintain significant amounts of inventory are enormous.

2.   Identify and explain the primary features of the perpetual inventory system.

When inventory is purchased, the inventory account, an asset, is increased. When goods are sold, the inventory account is reduced and an expense account, cost of goods sold, is increased. The sale is recorded at the same time by increasing revenues and increasing assets, either cash or accounts receivable.

3.   Explain the meaning of terms used to describe transportation costs, cash discounts, returns or allowances, and financing costs.

FOB means *free on board*. For the purposes of this course it indicates whether the buyer or seller will be responsible for paying shipping costs. FOB destination means the seller will pay; FOB shipping point means the buyer will pay. The term FOB actually tells when legal title to goods is passed from the seller to the buyer, which has implications beyond shipping costs.

Cash discount terms, such as 1/10, n/30 tell when the buyer is supposed to pay for the goods, and indicates if there is a discount for paying early. Terms of 1/10, n/30 mean there is a 1% discount granted if payment is made by the 10th day following the date of sale. If payment is not made in the first ten days, the buyer has an **additional** 20 days, for a total of 30, to pay for the goods at the full price.

A purchase or sales ***return*** means that purchased goods were returned to the seller for a full refund. An ***allowance*** implies that the purchaser kept goods that did meet his or her original expectations, but that the seller reduced the price that the buyer had originally agreed to pay.

The money a company uses to purchase inventory cannot be used elsewhere. For example, if the money were not tied up in inventory it could be in a bank earning interest. For the purpose of this course, consider the cost of financing inventory to be the interest lost on money that was invested in inventory from the time the inventory was paid for until it was sold.

4.   Compare and contrast single and multistep income statements.

Single-step income statements list revenues from operating activities and nonoperating activities together, and they list operating and nonoperating expenses together. Single-step income statements **do not** subtract *cost of goods sold* from *sales* to display *gross margin*. Multistep income statements do subtract *cost of goods sold* from *sales* to display *gross margin*, and then they lists all other *operating* expenses. Nonoperating revenues and expenses are shown separately, after operating items, on a multistep income statement. Both forms of income statements must list *discontinued operations, extraordinary items*, and *cumulative effects of changes in accounting principles* in separate sections at the bottom of the statement.

5.   Show the effects of lost, damaged, or stolen inventory on financial statements.

The cost of goods that are purchased is assigned either to goods that remain on-hand, in which case they are assets (inventory), or the cost is assigned to an expense or loss. If inventory is *lost or stolen*, it cannot be considered an asset, so inventory is decreased and expenses (cost of goods sold) or losses are increased, which in-turn, decreases net income. The carrying value of goods that are ***damaged*** must be written down and an expense or loss of the same amount must be recognized.

6.   Use common-size financial statements to evaluate managerial performance.

Common-size income statements convert all of the revenues and expenses on the income statement into percentages, where sales equal 100% and all other items are expressed as a percentage of sales. Common-size balance sheets can also be prepared, where total assets equal 100% and all other items are stated as a percentage of total assets. Common-size financial statements make it much easier to compare a company's financial results for the current accounting period to those of earlier periods. They also make it easier to compare one company's results to those of another.

7.   Use ratio analysis to evaluate managerial performance.

Two ratios are discussed in this chapter; the gross margin percentage and the return-on-sales. These are computed as follows:

Gross margin percentage   =   Gross margin ÷ Sales

Return on sales   =   Net income ÷ Sales

The gross margin percentage helps explain a company's pricing strategy. The higher percentage, the more a company marks up its goods. Specialty shops tend to have higher gross profit percentages while discount stores tend to have lower percentages.

The return-on-sales ratio, expressed as a percentage, indicates how much of each dollar of sales remains as profit after all expenses have been deducted. Discount stores do not necessarily have lower return-on-sales percentages than specialty shops. The higher the return-on-sales ratio is the better.

8.   Identify the primary features of the periodic inventory system. (Appendix)

The periodic method records inventory purchases in the purchases account. When goods are sold, only the revenue transaction is recorded. At the end of the accounting period, *cost of goods sold* is determined by adding inventory from the beginning of the period to the balance in the *purchases* account (this total is called *goods available for sale*) and subtracting the inventory that exists at the end of the accounting period. Ending inventory is determined by a physical count.

Be sure you understand the differences between the perpetual inventory system (learning objective 2) and periodic inventory system (learning objective 8). The perpetual system requires that the inventory account be increased each time inventory is purchased and decreased each time inventory is sold. The periodic system does not update the inventory account each time goods are purchased or sold. Purchased goods are recorded in the Purchases account, and the amount of *cost of goods sold* and the proper balance in the *inventory* account is determined only at the end of the accounting period. The perpetual system is more accurate, while the periodic system requires less record keeping. Both methods require a physical count of inventory at year-end.

Self-Study Problems

Articulation Problems

For each situation below, indicate its effects on the accounting elements shown on the accompanying chart. Use the following letters to indicate your answer (you do not need to enter amounts):

Increase = **I**   Decrease = **D**   No effect = **N**

1.   Owners of Quinn Co. invested inventory in the business.

Assets	Liabilities	Equity	Revenues	Expenses	Net Income	Cash

2.   Richard Co. purchased merchandise inventory for cash.

Assets	Liabilities	Equity	Revenues	Expenses	Net Income	Cash

3.   Sarah Co. sold merchandise to customers. The inventory originally cost Sarah $500 and was sold for $700, on account. Sarah uses the perpetual method. Show the net effects of this exchange.

Assets	Liabilities	Equity	Revenues	Expenses	Net Income	Cash

4.   Redbud Co. paid the transportation costs required for having goods delivered to its place of business **from a supplier**. Redbud had purchased the goods FOB shipping point.

Assets	Liabilities	Equity	Revenues	Expenses	Net Income	Cash

5.   Redbud Co. paid the transportation costs required for having goods delivered **to one of its customers**. Redbud had sold the goods FOB destination.

Assets	Liabilities	Equity	Revenues	Expenses	Net Income	Cash

6.   A customer who had purchased goods from Salsa Co. returned some of the goods to Salsa. These goods had originally cost Salsa $1,000 and had been sold to the customer for $1,200, on account. The customer had not paid for the goods. Show the net effects of the return. Salsa uses the perpetual inventory method.

Assets	Liabilities	Equity	Revenues	Expenses	Net Income	Cash

7.   A customer who had purchased goods from Salsa Co. complained that some of the goods were slightly damaged. Salsa agreed to give the customer a $100 allowance on the goods. These goods had been sold to the customer for $1,200, on account. The customer had not paid for the goods. Show the effects of the allowance event.

Assets	Liabilities	Equity	Revenues	Expenses	Net Income	Cash

8.   Salsa Co. returned some goods it had purchased from one of its suppliers. Salsa had purchased the goods for $600 on account. Salsa had not paid for the goods at the time they were returned. Salsa uses the perpetual inventory method. Show the effects of the return.

Assets	Liabilities	Equity	Revenues	Expenses	Net Income	Cash

Multiple-Choice Problems

1.   Rayes Co. purchased $10,000 of merchandise inventory on account. Assuming Rayes uses the perpetual inventory method, which of the following correctly describes the journal entry needed to record this transaction?
      a.   **Debit** cost of goods sold, and **credit** accounts payable.
      b.   **Debit** inventory, and **credit** accounts payable.
      c.   **Debit** purchases, and **credit** accounts receivable.
      d.   **Debit** inventory, and **credit** cost of goods sold.

2.   Which of the following is <u>not</u> a period cost?
      a.   Interest cost.
      b.   Advertising cost.
      c.   Cost of salaries paid to sales staff.
      d.   Cost of transportation-in.

3.   Tulsa Co. purchased $6,000 of inventory for cash. Later in the same year one-half of the inventory was sold for $4,000 on account. Based on these facts alone, the amount of *net income* and *net cash flow from operating activities* for Tulsa Co. would be:

	Net Income	Cash Flow
a.	$ 1,000	$ 3,000 outflow
b.	$ 1,000	$ 6,000 outflow
c.	$ 2,000	$ 3,000 outflow
d.	$ 2,000	$ 6,000 outflow

The following information applies to questions 4 through 6.

Vega Co. had the following account balances at the beginning of 2008:

Cash	$10,000	Accounts Payable	$ 8,000
Accounts Receivable	20,000	Common Stock	12,000
Inventory	15,000	Retained Earnings	25,000

The following events occurred during 2008:
      a.   Vega purchased $40,000 of inventory.
      b.   Vega sold goods that cost $30,000 for $45,000.
      c.   Operating expenses amounted to $10,000.

4.   The gross margin that should be shown on the 2008, income statement is:
    a. $ 0
    b. $ 5,000
    c. $15,000
    d. $30,000

5.   The balance in retained earnings at December 31, 2008, would be:
    a. $40,000
    b. $30,000
    c. $15,000
    d. $ 5,000

6.   The balance in inventory on December 31, 2008, would be:
    a. $ 5,000
    b. $10,000
    c. $15,000
    d. $25,000

The following information applies to questions 7 and 8.

Walton Co. had the following account balances in 2007, prior to the closing entries.

Purchases	$30,000	Sales	$45,000
Transportation-out	2,500	Transportation-in	2,000
Beginning Inventory	10,000	Ending Inventory	9,000
Purchase Returns	3,000	Sales Discounts	1,000
Sales Returns	2,000	Unearned Revenue	10,000

7.   What amount of *net sales* would appear on Walton's income statement?
    a. $32,000
    b $39,500
    c. $42,000
    d. $52,000

8.   Assuming Walton Co. uses the **periodic** inventory method, what was Walton's *cost of goods sold* for 2007?
    a. $39,000
    b. $32,500
    c. $30,000
    d. $29,000

9.   Which of the following is true?
   a.   If the perpetual inventory method is used, a physical inventory count is <u>not</u> required.
   b.   Other things being equal, a company's *net income* and *net cash flow from operating activities* will be the same whether it uses the perpetual or periodic inventory method.
   c.   The payments of transportation-in and transportation-out costs both tend to decrease the total assets of a company.
   d.   A company's gross margin will decrease if it makes a purchase of merchandise inventory at the end of the year.

10.   The records at Xenon Co. indicate that $125,000 of inventory should be on hand on December 31, 2008.   A physical count of the inventory reveals that $122,000 of inventory exists. The entry to reconcile these differences will cause:
   a.   cost of goods sold to decrease by $3,000.
   b.   net earnings to decrease by $3,000.
   c.   net cash flows from operating activities to decrease by $3,000.
   d.   total assets to remain the same.

11.   Arch Co. purchased $10,000 of inventory on June 1, 2005, on account, with terms n/30. Arch paid for these goods on July 1.   These same goods were sold to Bass Co. on November 1, 2005, for $15,000 cash. When Arch Co. has excess cash, it invests it in certificates of deposit that pay 9% interest.   What was Arch's cost to finance this inventory?
   a. $ 300.00
   b. $ 375.00
   c. $ 450.00
   d. $ 562.50

12.   Which of the following is an expense?
   a.   Accumulated depreciation.
   b.   Sales discount.
   c.   Cost of goods sold.
   d.   Transportation-in cost.

13. Benson Co. **purchased** merchandise inventory for cash. Benson uses the perpetual inventory method. Which of the following choices reflects how this event would affect the company's financial statements?

	Assets	=	Liab.	+	Equity		Rev	–	Exp.	=	Net Inc.		Cash
a.	N		N		D		N		I		D		D
b.	N		N		N		N		N		N		N
c.	D		N		D		N		I		D		D
d.	N		N		N		N		N		N		D

14. Benson Co. **sold** merchandise inventory for cash. Benson uses the perpetual inventory method. Which of the following choices reflects how this event would affect the company's financial statements?

	Assets	=	Liab.	+	Equity		Rev	–	Exp.	=	Net Inc.		Cash
a.	I		N		N		I		I		N		I
b.	I		N		I		I		I		I		I
c.	D		N		D		N		I		D		N
d.	N		N		N		N		N		N		N

The following information applies to questions 15 through 17.

The following account balances are available for Carlsbad Co.:

Assets	$100,000	Sales	$70,000
Liabilities	60,000	Cost of Goods Sold	45,500
Common Stock	10,000	Operating Expenses	6,500
Retained Earnings	30,000	Net Earnings	18,000

15. What is Carlsbad's gross margin percentage?
    a. 24%
    b. 35%
    c. 54%
    d. 65%

16. What is Carlsbad's return-on-sales ratio?
    a. 18%
    b. 26%
    c. 45%
    d. 54%

17. Assume Carlsbad sells goods for $4,000 that were originally purchased for $3,000. What will Carlsbad's gross margin percentage be <u>after</u> this sale?
    a. 25%
    b. 34%
    c. 36%
    d. 39%

Multiple True-False Problems

1. Douglas Co. purchased inventory for $500, cash, on June 1, 2007. These goods were sold on August 1 for $750, cash. When Douglas has excess cash, it invests the cash in an account that pays 4% interest. Based only on the information provided above, indicate if each of the following statements is true or false.
    a. On June 1, Douglas' total assets were not affected by its purchase of inventory.
    b. On August 1, Douglas' total assets increased by $750 as a result of its sale of goods.
    c. Douglas had a gross margin percentage of 50% on the sale of these goods.
    d. The opportunity cost of financing the inventory was $3.33.
    e. Assuming that Douglas' gross margin percentage averages 30% and that its competitors gross margin percentages average 25%, it may be assumed that Douglas is a discount retailer.

2. On March 1, 2007, Benson Co. purchased merchandise inventory for $10,000, on account, with the following terms: FOB destination, 2/10, n/30. Indicate if each of the following statements is true or false.
    a. If Benson pays for these goods on March 15, the amount to be paid will be $10,000.
    b. Regardless of when the bill is paid, Benson must pay the freight company for the shipping cost.
    c. Benson Co. has a total of 40 days to pay for the goods if it is willing to not take the discount.
    d. If Benson pays for these goods on March 8, the amount to be paid will be $ $9,800.
    e. If Benson has **not** paid for the goods by March 10, it should wait until March 30, to pay for them rather than paying earlier.

3.   Indicate if each of the following statements about the **periodic** inventory method is true or false.

    a.   A company that uses the periodic method will have the same balance in its Cost of Goods Sold account and its Inventory account as if the company had used the perpetual method.

    b.   The Purchases account is an expense account.

    c.   If a company's fiscal year ends on December 31, 2005, the balance in its Inventory account on May 3, 2006, will be the same as it was on December 31, 2005.

    d.   The balance in the Purchase Returns and Allowances account causes the amount of Cost of Goods Available for Sale to be lower.

    e.   The main advantage the periodic inventory method has over the perpetual method is that it is more accurate since it relies on a physical count of inventory.

Exercise-Type Problems

P-1.   The following selected events occurred at Earth Co. during the first half of 2008.

Date	Event	Amount
Jan. 1	Beginning inventory	$11,000
Jan. 25	Purchased goods, FOB shipping point	20,000
Feb. 10	Returned goods to supplier	3,000
Feb. 15	Paid freight on goods purchased	1,000
Mar. 20	Sold goods	19,000
Apr. 5	Purchased goods, FOB destination	34,000
May 1	Sold goods	14,000
June 1	Sold goods	23,000
June 18	Customer returned goods to Earth	2,000
June 30	Physical count of ending inventory	18,000

Required: Prepare a *Schedule of Cost of Goods Sold* for Earths Co. assuming the periodic inventory method is used. Use the form provided below.

Beginning inventory $

Purchases $

Purchase returns

Transportation-in   _____   _____

Cost of goods available for sale

Ending inventory   _____

Cost of goods sold $_____

P-2.

Mars Co. had the following account balances on January 1, 2008:

Cash	$ 3,000	Accounts Payable	$ 8,000
Accounts Receivable	9,000	Common Stock	10,000
Inventory	15,000	Retained Earnings	23,000
Equipment	17,000	Accumulated Depreciation	3,000

The following events occurred during 2008:

a. Purchased inventory for $55,000, on account.
b. Some of the goods purchased were slightly defective. The supplier granted Mars a $500 allowance.
c. On March 1, 2008, borrowed $20,000 from the Local Bank. This was a one-year loan at 9%.
d. Sold merchandise inventory for $40,000 cash. The cost of these goods to Mars was $28,000.
e. Made a $50,000 payment on accounts payable.
f. Incurred cash operating expenses of $10,500.
g. Owners invested merchandise inventory in the business. The inventory had a value of $5,000.
h. Sold merchandise inventory for $47,000 on account. The cost of these goods to Mars was $32,400.
i. Merchandise that had been sold for $2,000 was returned to Mars. These goods had been sold on account and had not been paid for when they were returned. The returned goods had cost Mars $1,400.
j. Collected $42,000 from accounts receivable.
k. Mars made the end of the year adjustment related to the note payable (event c).
l. Mars made the end-of-the-year adjustment to depreciate the equipment. This equipment had been purchased in 2007. It had an expected useful life of five years and an estimated salvage value of $2,000.

Required:
1. Post these events to the T-accounts provided on the following page. The beginning balances have been entered for you.
2. Prepare an income statement, a statement of changes in stockholders' equity, a balance sheet, and a statement of cash flows. Use the forms provided on the following pages.

T-accounts for requirement 1

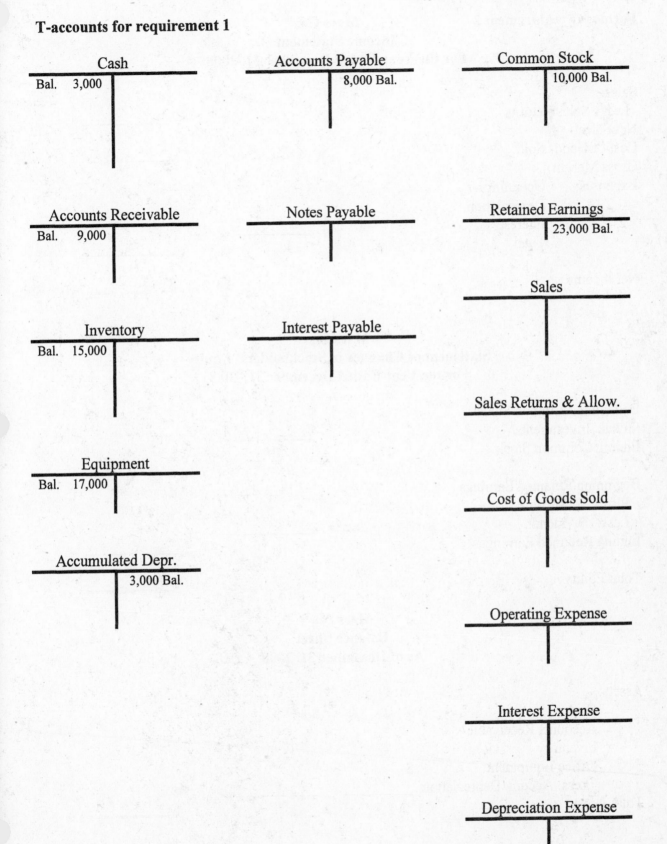

Cash

Bal.   3,000

Accounts Payable

8,000 Bal.

Common Stock

10,000 Bal.

Accounts Receivable

Bal.   9,000

Notes Payable

Retained Earnings

23,000 Bal.

Inventory

Bal.   15,000

Interest Payable

Sales

Sales Returns & Allow.

Equipment

Bal.   17,000

Cost of Goods Sold

Accumulated Depr.

3,000 Bal.

Operating Expense

Interest Expense

Depreciation Expense

Forms for requirement 2

Mars Co.
Income Statement
For the Year Ended December 31, 2008

Sales $ _____
  Less: Sales Returns
Net Sales   _____
Cost of Goods Sold
Gross Margin   _____
Expenses: Operating $ _____
            Depreciation
            Interest
            Total   _____

Net Income $ _____

Mars Co.
Statement of Changes in Stockholders' Equity
For the Year Ended December 31, 2008

Beginning Common Stock $ _____
  Plus: Investments   _____
Ending Common Stock $ _____

Beginning Retained Earnings
  Plus: Net Income
  Less: Dividends   _____
Ending Retained Earnings   _____

Total Equity $ _____

Mars Co.
Balance Sheet
As of December 31, 2008

Assets:
    Cash $ _____
    Accounts Receivable
    Inventory
    Office Equipment $ _____
      Less: Accum. Depreciation   _____   _____
Total Assets $ _____

P-2   Balance Sheet (continued)

Liabilities:
    Accounts Payable $
    Interest Payable
    Notes Payable
Total Liabilities $

Equity:
    Common Stock
    Retained Earnings
Total Equity

Total Liabilities and Equity $

Mars Co.
Statement of Cash Flows
For the Year Ended December 31, 2008

Cash Flows from Operating Activities:
    Inflows from Customers $
    Outflows for Operating Expenses
    Outflows for Inventory
Net Cash Flow from Operating Activities $

Cash Flow from Investing Activities:

Cash Flows from Financing Activities:
    Inflows from Bank Loan
Net Cash Flow from Financing Activities

Net Increase in Cash
Add: Beginning Cash Balance
Cash Balance at December 31, 2006 $

Solutions to Self-Study Problems

Articulation Problems

1.   Owners of Quinn Co. invested inventory in the business.

Assets	Liabilities	Equity	Revenues	Expenses	Net Income	Cash
I	N	I	N	N	N	N

Assets increased because of the inventory received. Equity increased because the owners' investment increased common stock.

2.   Richard Co. purchased merchandise inventory for cash.

Assets	Liabilities	Equity	Revenues	Expenses	Net Income	Cash
N	N	N	N	N	N	D

Merchandise inventory, an asset, increased while another asset, cash, decreased by the same amount.

3.   Sarah Co. sold merchandise to customers. The inventory originally cost Sarah $500 and was sold for $700, on account. Sarah uses the perpetual method. Show the net effects of this exchange.

Assets	Liabilities	Equity	Revenues	Expenses	Net Income	Cash
I	N	I	I	I	I	N

One asset, accounts receivable, increased by $700 while another asset, inventory, decreased by $500. Thus, the net effect on assets was a $200 increase. Revenues increased by the amount of the sale, $700, while expenses increased by $500, the amount of cost of goods sold, the expense. Thus, net income increased by the net difference of $200. The increase in net income caused retained earnings to increase.

4.   Redbud Co. paid the transportation costs required for having goods delivered to its place of business **from a supplier**. Redbud had purchased the goods FOB shipping point.

Assets	Liabilities	Equity	Revenues	Expenses	Net Income	Cash
N	N	N	N	N	N	D

Cash decreased, but inventory, another asset, increased by the same amount. Transportation-in costs are a part of inventory. The transportation-in costs do not become expenses until the inventory is sold.

5.   Redbud Co. paid the transportation costs required for having goods delivered **to one of its customers**. Redbud had sold the goods FOB destination.

Assets	Liabilities	Equity	Revenues	Expenses	Net Income	Cash
D	N	D	N	I	D	D

The costs of shipping goods **to** a customer, transportation-out, are expenses. The increase in expenses caused net income and retained earnings to decrease. Assets decreased because of the decrease in cash.

6.   A customer who had purchased goods from Salsa Co. returned some of the goods to Salsa. These goods had originally cost Salsa $1,000 and had been sold to the customer for $1,200, on account. The customer had not paid for the goods. Show the net effects of the return. Salsa uses the perpetual inventory method.

Assets	Liabilities	Equity	Revenues	Expenses	Net Income	Cash
D	N	D	D	D	D	N

Two asset accounts were affected. Inventory increased by $1,000 because the returned goods were replaced in inventory. Accounts receivable decreased by $1,200 because the customer does not have to pay for the returned goods. Therefore, there was a net reduction of $200 for assets. Revenues decreased because the sale that Salsa Co. thought it had made was not completed (revenues would be decreased through the use of the contra account, Sales Returns and Allowances). Expenses were reduced by $1,000 because the Cost of Goods Sold that was recorded when the goods were sold is now removed. Thus, there was a $200 reduction of net income because of the reduction in revenue and expenses. This, in turn, reduced equity.

7.   A customer who had purchased goods from Salsa Co. complained that some of the goods were slightly damaged. Salsa agreed to give the customer a $100 allowance on the goods. These goods had been sold to the customer for $1,200, on account. The customer had not paid for the goods. Show the effects of the allowance event.

Assets	Liabilities	Equity	Revenues	Expenses	Net Income	Cash
D	N	D	D		D	N

Accounts receivable was reduced and revenues were red_____ he use of the Sales Returns and Allowances account). The reduction in revenues reduced_____ equity.

8.   Salsa Co. returned some goods it had purchased from _____ rs. Salsa had purchased the goods for $600 on account. Salsa had not paid for the go_____ they were returned. Salsa uses the perpetual inventory method. Show the effects of the r_____

Assets	Liabilities	Equity	Revenues	Expenses	Net Income	Cash
D	D	N	N	N	N	N

Assets were reduced because the returned goods were in inventory. Liabilities were reduced because Salsa will not have to pay the accounts payable associated with the returned goods.

Multiple-Choice Problems

1.   b.

2.   d.

3.   b.

Net Income		Cash Flows	
Sales	$ 4,000	Inflows	$ 0
Cost of Goods Sold	3,000	Outflows for Purchases	(6,000)
Net Income	**$ 1,000**	Net Cash Flow	**$(6,000)**

4.   c.   Sales $45,000
                   Cost of Goods Sold   30,000
                   Gross Margin   **$15,000**

5.   b.   Net Income   Retained Earnings
                   Gross Margin (see No. 4) $15,000   Balance Jan. 1, 2008 $25,000
                   Operating Expenses   10,000   Net Income   5,000
                   Net Income $ 5,000   Balance Dec. 31, 2008   **$30,000**

6.   d.   Balance Jan. 1, 2008 $15,000
                   + Purchases   40,000
                   Goods Available   55,000
                   – Cost of Goods Sold   30,000
                   Balance Dec. 31, 2008   **$25,000**

7.   c.   **Sales** – **Sales Discounts** – **Sales Returns** = **Net Sales**
                   $45,000 – $1,000   – $2,000   =   **$42,000**

8.   c.   Beginning Inventory $10,000
                   + Purchases   30,000
                   – Purchase Returns   3,000
                   + Transportation-In   2,000
                   Goods Available   39,000
                   – Ending Inventory   9,000
                   Cost of Goods Sold   **$30,000**

9.   b.   Note: Choice (c) is false because transportation-in increases inventory, an asset.
                   Choice (d) is false because the gross margin is affected by Sales and Cost of Goods Sold.
                   Purchasing inventory at year-end affects inventory, not Sales or Cost of Goods Sold.

10.   b.   The decrease in inventory causes assets to decrease, which causes expenses to increase,
                   which causes net earnings to decrease. Cash flows are not affected.

11.   a.   Arch is financing the inventory from the date the supplier is paid, July 1, to the date the
                   inventory is sold, November 1. Therefore, the financing cost is computed as follows:
                   $10,000 x .09 x 4/12 = **$300.00**

12.   c.

13.   d.   See articulation problem 2 for an explanation of the correct answer.

14.   b.   See articulation problem 3 for an explanation of the correct answer.

15.   b.   First, compute gross margin: Sales $70,000
                                               Cost of goods sold   45,500
                                               Gross margin $24,500

            Then the gross margin percentage can be computed:

            Gross Margin   ÷   **Sales**   =   **%**
               $24,500   ÷ $70,000   =   **35%**

16.   b. | **Net Earnings** | ÷ | **Sales** | = | **%** |
|---|---|---|---|---|
| $18,000 | ÷ | $70,000 | = | **25.7%** |

17.   b.

Ratio	Before Sale		Effect of Sale		After Borrowing		
Gross Margin	$24,500	+	$1,000 [(1)]	=	$25,500		
Sales	$70,000	+	$4,000	=	$74,000	=	**34.5%**

(1) | Sale | $4,000 |
|---|---|
| Cost of goods sold | 3,000 |
| Gross margin | $1,000 |

Multiple True-False Problems

1.   a.   **True**, cash decreased, but inventory increased by the same amount.
b.   **False**, cash did increase by $750, but inventory decreased by $500. Thus, total assets increased by $250, not $750.
c.   **False**, Douglas' gross margin percentage was 33.33% [($750 − $500) ÷ $750]
d.   **True**, had it not purchased the inventory, Douglas could have invested the $500 for two months at 4%   ($500 x .04 x 2/12 = $3.33).
e.   **False**, if Douglas has a higher gross margin percentage than its competitors, this indicates Douglas is charging more fore the same items, not less.

2.   a.   **True**, Benson will not get a discount if it pays 15 days after they were purchased.
b.   **False**, when goods are sold FOB destination the shipping cost is the responsibility of the seller, not the buyer.
c.   **False**, 2/10, n/30 indicates that the buyer has a total of 30 days to pay.
d.   **True**.
e.   **True**, when a company does not pay in time to get a purchase discount, it should wait as long as possible to pay without incurring a penalty. The longer it waits to pay, the longer its cash can be invested elsewhere.

3.   a.   **True**, although when more advanced inventory accounting topics are presented in Chapter 8, there will be some exceptions to this statement. However, for the purposes of Chapter 5, it is a true statement.
b.   **False**, the Purchases account is neither an expense nor an asset account. It is merely a "bookkeeping account." It is eliminated before either the income statement or the balance sheet is prepared.
c.   **True**, if a company used the periodic method, the inventory that was bought and sold between December 31, 2005, and May 3, 2006, was **not** recorded in the Inventory account, so the balance in the Inventory account would not change.
d.   **True**, the more goods that are returned to suppliers, the lower will be the goods available for sale.
e.   **False**, both the perpetual and the periodic methods require a physical count of inventory. The main advantage of the periodic inventory method is that it requires less record keeping than the perpetual method.

Exercise-Type Problems

P-1   Solution

Earth Co.
Schedule of Cost of Goods Sold
for the Period January 1, 2008 to June 30, 2008

Beginning inventory		$11,000
Purchases	$54,000	
Purchase returns	(3,000)	
Transportation-in	1,000	52,000
Cost of goods available for sale		
Ending inventory		(18,000)
Cost of goods sold		$45,000

P-2   Solution to requirement 1

Cash		
Bal.	3,000	50,000 e.
c.	20,000	10,500 f.
d.	40,000	
j.	42,000	
Bal.	44,500	

Accounts Payable		
b.	500	8,000 Bal.
e.	50,000	55,000 a.
		12,500 Bal.

Common Stock	
	10,000 Bal.
	5,000 g.
	15,000 Bal.

Accounts Receivable		
Bal.	9,000	2,000 i.
h.	47,000	42,000 j.
Bal.	12,000	

Notes Payable	
	20,000 c.
	20,000 Bal.

Retained Earnings	
	23,000 Bal.

Inventory		
Bal.	15,000	500 b.
a.	55,000	28,000 d.
g.	5,000	32,400 h.
Bal.	15,500	

Interest Payable	
	1,500 k.
	1,500 Bal.

Sales	
	40,000 d.
	47,000 h.
	87,000 Bal.

Equipment	
Bal.	17,000

Sales Returns & Allow.	
i.	2,000
Bal.	2,000

Accumulated Depr.	
	3,000 Bal.
	3,000 l.
	6,000 Bal.

Cost of Goods Sold		
d.	28,000	1,400 i.
h.	32,400	
Bal.	59,000	

Operating Expense	
f.	10,500
Bal.	10,500

Interest Expense	
k.	1,500
Bal.	1,500

Depreciation Expense	
l.	3,000
Bal.	3,000

P-2.   Solution for requirement 2

Mars Co.
Income Statement
For the Year Ended December 31, 2008

Sales		$87,000
Less: Sales Returns		2,000
Net Sales		85,000
Cost of Goods Sold		59,000
Gross Margin		26,000
Expenses: Operating	$10,500	
Depreciation	3,000	
Interest	1,500	
Total		15,000
Net Income		$11,000

Mars Co.
Statement of Changes in Stockholders' Equity
For the Year Ended December 31, 2008

Beginning Common Stock	$10,000	
Plus: Investments	5,000	
Ending Common Stock		$15,000
Beginning Retained Earnings	23,000	
Plus: Net Income	11,000	
Less: Dividends	0	
Ending Retained Earnings		34,000
Total Equity		$49,000

Mars Co.
Balance Sheet
As of December 31, 2008

Assets:

Cash		$44,500
Accounts Receivable		12,000
Inventory		15,500
Office Equipment	$17,000	
Less: Accum. Depreciation	6,000	11,000
Total Assets		$83,000

Liabilities:

Accounts Payable	$12,500	
Interest Payable	1,500	
Notes Payable	20,000	
Total Liabilities		34,000

Equity:

Common Stock	15,000	
Retained Earnings	34,000	
Total Equity		49,000
Total Liabilities and Equity		$83,000

Mars Co.
Statement of Cash Flows
For the Year Ended December 31, 2008

Cash Flows from Operating Activities:

Inflows from Customers	$82,000	
Outflows for Operating Expenses	(10,500)	
Outflows for Inventory	(50,000)	
Net Cash Inflow from Operating Activities		$21,500

Cash Flow from Investing Activities: 0

Cash Flows from Financing Activities

Inflows from Bank Loan	20,000	
Net Cash Inflow from Financing Activities		20,000

Net Increase in Cash	41,500
Add: Beginning Cash Balance	3,000
Cash Balance at December 31, 2006	$44,500

Chapter Six
Accounting for Merchandising Businesses –
Advanced Topics

Learning Objectives for the Chapter

After completing this chapter you should be able to:

1. Explain how different inventory cost flow methods (specific identification, FIFO, LIFO, and weighted average) affect financial statements.
2. Demonstrate the computational procedures for FIFO, LIFO, and weighted average.
3. Apply the lower-of-cost-or-market rule to inventory valuation.
4. Explain how fraud can be avoided through inventory control.
5. Use the gross margin method to estimate ending inventory.
6. Explain the importance of inventory turnover to a company's profitability.
7. Explain how accounting for investment securities differs when the securities are classified as held-to-maturity, trading, or available-for-sale. (Appendix)

Brief Explanation of the Learning Objectives

1. **Explain how different inventory cost flow methods (specific identification, FIFO, LIFO, and weighted average) affect financial statements.**

The effect that an inventory cost flow assumption has on inventory and related items depends on whether the prices of inventory are rising or falling. If prices do not change, then all inventory cost flow methods will give the exact same results. *For purposes of this discussion, assume prices are **rising**.* The following chart shows the effects of different cost flow assumptions.

	Effects on		
Cost Flow Assumption	**Ending Inventory**	**Cost of Goods Sold**	**Cash Flows**
FIFO	Highest	Lowest	Lowest
LIFO	Lowest	Highest	Highest
Weighted Avg.	In between	In between	In between

The *only* reason the inventory cost flow assumption affects cash flows is because of taxes. The lower a company's cost of goods sold, the higher its gross margin and taxable income. The higher its taxable income, the more cash it must pay for tax expense. All other cash flows associated with inventory are the same regardless of whether the company uses FIFO, LIFO, or weighted average. Remember, *if prices were **falling***, the effects of using FIFO versus LIFO would be reversed.

2.   Demonstrate the computational procedures for FIFO, LIFO, and weighted average.

These procedures are demonstrated at length in the textbook. They are also examined with the self-study problems.

3.   Apply the lower-of-cost-or-market rule to inventory valuation.

The lower-of-cost-or-market rule (LCM) requires that inventory should be written down to its market value (replacement cost) if that value is less than its original (historical) cost. This write-down causes assets and net earnings (and in-turn, retained earnings) to decrease. The decrease in net earnings is shown as a *loss* if the decline in market value is material; it is added to *cost of goods sold* if it is not material. Inventory should **not** be written up to a market value that is higher than the inventory's original cost.

4.   Explain how fraud can be avoided through inventory control.

The cost of goods that are purchased is assigned either to goods that remain on hand, in which case they are assets (inventory), or the cost is assigned to an expense or loss. If an error occurs when accounting for inventory that causes inventory to be *understated*, then cost of goods sold (expenses) must be *overstated* to keep the balance sheet in balance. Remember, cost of goods sold is an expense, so if it is *overstated*, then net earnings and retained earnings will be *understated*.

If an error occurs that causes inventory to be *overstated*, then cost of goods must be *understated* (which causes net earnings and retained earnings to be *overstated*). A company wishing to deliberately overstate its earnings might try to do so by overstating its inventory. Because cost of goods sold is usually a company's single largest expense item, understating this account (by overstating inventory) is a tempting way to fraudulently inflate earnings. One of the main reasons a physical inventory must be conducted, and observed by the independent auditor, is to prevent this type of fraud.

5.   Use the gross margin method to estimate ending inventory.

When a company uses the periodic method of inventory and is not able to establish the amount of ending inventory with a physical count, the amount of inventory that should be reported on the balance sheet can be estimated with the gross margin method. The computational details of this method are addressed with the self-study problems.

6.   Explain the importance of inventory turnover to a company's profitability.

When a company purchases inventory, it is making a financial investment somewhat like depositing money in a bank account that pays interest. However, instead of earning interest, inventory earns gross margin when sold, and there is more risk with the inventory investment than the bank account. For example, two banks that promise to pay $100 interest on a bank account with a $1,000 balance appear to be equal. But, if the first bank agrees to pay the $100 of interest every six months, while the second pays only every twelve months, the first bank is obviously offering a much better deal. Inventory turnover works the same way. A company that can sell inventory and receive its gross margin in one month is better off than a company earning the same gross margin after waiting two months to sell its inventory. This is another example of the cliché, "time is money."

7.   Explain how accounting for investment securities differs when the securities are classified as held-to-maturity, trading, or available-for-sale. (Appendix)

Marketable securities (stocks and bonds) that a company owns that are classified as *trading* or *available-for-sale* should be shown on the company's balance sheet at market value. This is true whether the market value is lower or higher than the securities' original (historical) cost. Merchandise inventory is shown on the balance sheet at the lower of its historical cost or market value. Thus, in some cases (but not most) inventory may be reported at its market value.

Marketable securities that a company owns that are classified as *trading* or *available-for-sale* should be shown on the company's balance sheet at market value. Debt securities that a company purchases and plans to keep until they mature should be classified as *held-to-maturity*, and should be reported at amortized cost. When they are written-up or written-down from historical cost to market value, total equity must also be adjusted in order to keep the balance sheet in balance.

This is accomplished in two different ways. For *trading securities*, the change in the asset value is balanced by recording a gain or loss on the income statement, which in turn, increases or decreases retained earnings on the balance sheet. For securities classified as *available-for-sale*, the change in the asset value is balanced by increasing or decreasing a special account in the stockholders' equity section of the balance sheet. In other words, net earnings are not affected by changes in the market value of *available-for-sale* securities.

Self-Study Problems

Articulation Problems

Note: *The articulation problems presented here are intended primarily to review some issues first covered in Chapter 5. You will have difficulty understanding the topics in Chapter 8 if you did not understand the concepts presented in Chapter 5. Review Chapter 5 if necessary.*

For each situation below, indicate its effects on the accounting elements shown on the accompanying chart. Use the following letters to indicate your answer (you do not need to enter amounts):

Increase = **I**   Decrease = **D**   No effect = **N**

1. Window Co. purchased merchandise inventory for cash.

Assets	Liabilities	Equity	Revenues	Expenses	Net Income	Cash

2. Window Co. purchased merchandise inventory on account.

Assets	Liabilities	Equity	Revenues	Expenses	Net Income	Cash

3. Door Co. sold merchandise to customers. The inventory originally cost Door $500 and was sold for $700 cash. Door uses the perpetual method. Show the net effects of this exchange.

Assets	Liabilities	Equity	Revenues	Expenses	Net Income	Cash

4.   Door Co. sold merchandise to customers. The inventory originally cost Door $500 and was sold for $700, on account. Door uses the perpetual method. Show the net effects of this exchange.

Assets	Liabilities	Equity	Revenues	Expenses	Net Income	Cash

Multiple-Choice Problems

1.   If prices are rising:
  a.   Cost of goods sold will be higher if LIFO is used instead of FIFO.
  b.   Inventory will be higher if LIFO is used instead of FIFO.
  c.   A company's gross margin will be higher if LIFO is used instead of FIFO.
  d.   Cash flows, including the effect of taxes, will be the same whether a company uses LIFO or FIFO.

2.   Other things being equal, if prices are rising, a company will have a higher current ratio if it uses:
  a.   FIFO.
  b.   LIFO.
  c.   Weighted average.
  d.   The inventory cost flow method used has no effect on the current ratio.

3.   If prices are rising, a company wishing to minimize tax cost would use:
  a.   FIFO.
  b.   LIFO.
  c.   Weighted average.
  d.   The inventory cost flow method used has no effect on tax cost.

The following information applies to questions 4 through 6.

The following events occurred at Denver Co.:

January 2:	Purchased 20 units @ $10.
January 4:	Purchased 30 units @ $11.
January 7:	Purchased 15 units @ $12.
January 10:	Sold 25 units @ $18.

4.   What will be the cost of goods sold be if Denver Co. uses the FIFO cost flow method?
    a. $195
    b. $250
    c. $255
    d. $290

5.   What will be the cost of goods sold be if Denver Co. uses the LIFO cost flow method?
    a. $255
    b. $290
    c. $300
    d. $450

6.   What will be the cost of goods sold be if Denver Co. uses the weighted average cost flow method?
    a. $273
    b. $275
    c. $319
    d. $710

The following information applies to questions 7 through 9.

The following information is available for Phoenix Co.:

March 1:	Beginning inventory was 10 units @ $20.
March 6:	Purchased 12 units @ $19.
March 8:	Purchased 8 units @ $24.
March 12:	Sold 17 units @ $35.

7.   What will Phoenix's ending inventory be if it uses the FIFO cost flow method?
    a. $257
    b. $287
    c. $333
    d. $363

8.   What will Phoenix's ending inventory be if it uses the LIFO cost flow method?
    a. $363
    b. $333
    c. $287
    d. $257

9.   What will Phoenix's ending inventory be if it uses the weighted average cost flow method (rounded to the nearest $1)?
    a. $269
    b. $273
    c. $351
    d. $357

10.   Which of the following statements is <u>false</u>?
    a.   The cost of financing inventory is the same regardless of which inventory cost flow method is used.
    b.   The price that a company charges for the goods it sells will depend on the cost flow method it uses.
    c.   The *lower-of-cost-or-market* rule must be applied regardless of which inventory cost flow method is used.
    d.   The inventory cost flow method a company uses will probably depend on whether management expects the prices of goods to be rising or falling.

The following information applies to questions 12 and 13.

The following events occurred at Austin Co.:
September 5: Purchased 10 units @ $20.
September 9: Purchased 10 units @ $22.
September 10: Sold 14 units @ $30.

11.   What will Austin's gross margin be if it uses the FIFO cost flow method?
    a. $300
    b. $288
    c. $132
    d. $120

12.   What will Austin's gross margin be if it uses the LIFO cost flow method?
    a. $120
    b. $132
    c. $288
    d. $300

13.   On April 1, 2007, a fire destroyed a store belonging to Aquinas Co. All of the store's inventory was destroyed in the fire, and the company is trying to determine what its insurance claim for lost inventory should be. The following information is available for the first three months of 2007:

Inventory at January 1	$ 3,000
Purchases from January 1 to March 31	$ 9,000
Purchase returns from January 1 to March 31	$ 1,000
Sales from January 1 to March 31	$10,000
Aquinas's gross margin has traditionally been	40%

What was the amount of inventory lost in the fire?
a. $5,000
b. $6,000
c. $7,000
d. $8,000

14.   The following selected events occurred at Quail Co. during 2006 and 2007:

November 5, 2006:	Purchased $1,000 of goods on account.
November 30, 2006:	Paid for the goods purchased on November 5.
January 7, 2007:	Sold the goods purchased on November 5, 2006, for $1,500.
February 3, 2007:	Received payment for the goods sold on January 7.

Based only on the facts above, which of the following statements is true, regarding *net cash flows from operating activities* (Net CFO) for 2006 and 2007?

	Net CFO 2006	Net CFO 2007
a.	$1,000 outflow	$ 500 inflow
b.	$1,000 outflow	$1,500 inflow
c.	$ 0	$ 500 inflow
d.	$ 0	$1,500 inflow

15.   Saturn Co. purchased $10,000 of inventory on March 1, 2006, with terms of n/30. The account payable was paid on April 1, 2006. The same goods were sold on October 1, 2006, for $15,000 cash. If Saturn could invest idle cash for 6%, what was its cost of financing this inventory?
a. $525
b. $450
c. $350
d. $300

The following information applies to questions 16 and 17.

The following account balances are available for Topaz Co.:

Accounts Receivable	$ 12,000	Stockholders' Equity	$ 70,000
Inventory	15,000	Sales	430,000
Current Assets	40,000	Cost of Goods Sold	260,000
Total Assets	200,000	Operating Expenses	135,000
Accounts Payable	18,000	Net Earnings	35,000
Current Liabilities	25,000		
Total Liabilities	130,000		

16.   What is Topaz's inventory turnover ratio?
   a.   11 times
   b.   13 times
   c.   17 times
   d.   29 times

17.   On average, how many days does it take Topaz to sell its inventory?
   a.   10 days
   b.   13 days
   c.   21 days
   d.   24 days

18.   (Appendix) Consider the following facts related to Risky Capital Company's investment in Digital-Stuff Co.

Date	Event
June 17	Purchased 100 shares of Digital-Stuff at $40 per share.
Nov. 1	Digital-Stuff paid a dividend of $.25 per share.
Dec. 31	The market value of Digital-Stuff's stock is $38 per share.

If Risky Capital accounts for its investment in Digital-Stuff as trading securities, which of the following accurately describes how its investment would be reported on its balance sheet and income statement?

	Investment balance on Dec. 31, Balance Sheet	Effect on Net Income
a.	$3,800	$ 25
b.	$3,800	($175)
c.	$4,000	$ 25
d.	$4,000	($175)

19.   (Appendix) Consider the following facts related to Risky Capital Company's investment in Home-Lending Corp.

Date	Event
May 1	Purchased bonds of Home-Lending for $100,000.
Nov. 1	Home-Lending paid $4,000 of interest to Risky Capital.
Dec. 31	The market value of the Home-Lending's bonds held by Risky Capital is $102,000.

If Risky Capital accounts for its investment in Home-Lending as held-to-maturity securities, which of the following accurately describes how its investment would be reported on its balance sheet and income statement?

	Investment balance on Dec. 31, Balance Sheet	Effect on Net Income
a.	$100,000	$4,000
b.	$100,000	$6,000
c.	$102,000	$4,000
d.	$102,000	$6,000

Multiple True-False Problems

1.   Ellington, Inc. reports its inventory using the lower-of-cost-or-market (LCM) rule. Data related to its inventory are as follows:

Item	Quantity	Cost per Unit	Replacement Value per Unit
Q	100	$12	$11
R	80	20	23
S	120	15	16
T	250	10	8

Indicate if each of the following statements related to Ellington is true or false.

a.   If Ellington reports on an individual item basis, its balance sheet will report ending inventory at $6,500.

b.   If Ellington reports on an aggregate (total inventory) basis, its balance sheet will report ending inventory at $7,100.

c.   **ASSUMING** Ellington inventory had a cost of $8,000 and a replacement market-value of $7,600, writing down its inventory to the lower-of-cost-or-market will cause the company's net income to increase by $400.

d.   **Rather** than use the lower-of-cost-or-market rule, Ellington could have chosen to use the FIFO or LIFO method.

e.   Inventory should only be "written down" from cost to a lower market value when the value of inventory has declined due to unusual circumstances.

2.   (Appendix) Indicate if each of the following statements related to marketable securities is true or false.
      a.   Investments in the common stock of another company cannot be accounted for as held-to maturity securities.
      b.   Marshall Co. has excess cash on hand that it does not need today, but that it does expect to need in two months. If Marshall invests this money in the stock of Fast-Mart, this investment should be accounted for as available-for-sale securities.
      c.   Changes in the market value of securities classified as available-for-sale securities affects the net income of the investor company even if the securities have not been sold as of the end of the fiscal-year.
      d.   Changes in the market value of securities classified as trading securities affects the net income of the investor company even if the securities have not been sold as of the end of the fiscal-year.
      e.   Berkeley co. owns 55% of the outstanding stock of Fantasy Co. Berkeley should account for its investment in Fantasy using the equity method.

3.   (Appendix) Consider the following facts related to Music Company's investment in Anthony Corp.:

Date	Event
Feb. 9	Purchased 500 shares of Anthony at $100 per share.
Oct. 1	Anthony paid a dividend of $1.00 per share.
Dec. 31	The market value of Anthony's stock is $106 per share.

      Indicate if each of the following statements related to Edward's investment in Anthony is true or false.
      a.   If Music properly classifies its investment as trading securities, the total affect of the investment on its net income would be $500.
      b.   If Music properly classifies its investment as available-for-sale securities, the total affect of the investment on its stockholders' equity would be $3,500.
      c.   If Music properly classifies its investment as available-for-sale securities, the total affect of the investment on its net income would be $500.
      d.   If Music properly classifies its investment as trading securities, the investment would be reported on its balance sheet at $53,000.
      e.   If Music properly classifies its investment as trading securities, the affect of the above events on its *net cash flow from investing activities* would be ($50,000).

Exercise-Type Problem

P-1. The following events occurred at Maplewood Co. during the month of January 2005:

January 1:	Beginning inventory was 50 units @ $20.
January 10:	Purchased 60 units @ $22.
January 16:	Sold 70 units @ $35.
January 21:	Purchased 40 units @ $24.
January 27:	Sold 60 units @ $36.
For the month:	Operating expenses totaled $500.

Maplewood Co.'s tax rate was 30%. All purchases and sales of inventory were for cash, as were operating expenses. Maplewood uses the perpetual inventory method.

Required:
1. Assuming that Maplewood Co. uses the **FIFO** inventory cost flow method, determine January's: (Use the forms provided on the following pages.)
    - a. Cost of goods sold
    - b. Ending inventory
    - c. Sales
    - d. Gross margin
    - e. Tax expense
    - f. Net cash flow from operating activities

2. Assuming that Maplewood Co. uses the **LIFO** inventory cost flow method, determine January's: (Use the forms provided on the following pages.)
    - a. Cost of goods sold
    - b. Ending inventory
    - c. Sales
    - d. Gross margin
    - e. Tax expense
    - f. Net cash flow from operating activities

3. Assuming that Maplewood Co. uses the **moving average** inventory cost flow method, determine January's: (Use the forms provided on the following pages.)
    - a. Cost of goods sold
    - b. Ending inventory
    - c. Sales
    - d. Gross margin
    - e. Tax expense
    - f. Net cash flow from operating activities

P-1.   Forms for requirement 1   (FIFO)

Table for parts (a), and (b).

Date	Purchases Units	Purchases Cost/Unit	Purchases Total Cost	Cost of Goods Sold Units	Cost of Goods Sold Cost/Unit	Cost of Goods Sold Total Cost	Inventory Units	Inventory Cost/Unit	Inventory Total Cost
Jan. 1							50	$20	$1,000
Jan. 10									
Jan. 16									
Jan. 21									
Jan. 27									
Bals.									

Form for parts (c), (d), and (e)

Sales [(70 @ $35) + (60 @ $36)]	$ _____
Cost of goods sold (from table)	_____
Gross margin	
Operating expenses	(500)
Taxable income	
Tax rate	.30
Tax expense	$ _____

Form for part (f)

Cash Flows from Operating Activities

Inflows from sales	$
Outflows for purchases (from table)	
Outflows for operating expenses	
Outflows for taxes	(500)
Net cash flow from oper. activity	$ _____

P-1. Forms for requirement 2 (LIFO)

Table for parts (a), and (b).

Date	Purchases			Cost of Goods Sold			Inventory		
	Units	Cost/Unit	Total Cost	Units	Cost/Unit	Total Cost	Units	Cost/Unit	Total Cost
Jan. 1							50	$20	$1,000
Jan. 10									
Jan. 16									
Jan. 21									
Jan. 27									
Bals.									

Form for parts (c), (d), and (e)

Sales [(70 @ $35) + (60 @ $36)]	$ _____
Cost of goods sold (from table)	_____
Gross margin	_____
Operating expenses	(500)
Taxable income	_____
Tax rate	.30
Tax expense	$ _____

Form for part (f)

Cash Flows from Operating Activities

Inflows from sales	$ _____
Outflows for purchases (from table)	_____
Outflows for operating expenses	(500)
Outflows for taxes	_____
Net cash flow from oper. activity	$ _____

P-1.   Forms for requirement 3   (Moving Average)

Table for parts (a), and (b).

Date	Purchases			Cost of Goods Sold			Inventory		
	Units	Cost/Unit	Total Cost	Units	Cost/Unit	Total Cost	Units	Cost/Unit	Total Cost
Jan. 1							50	$20	$1,000
Jan. 10									
Jan. 16									
Jan. 21									
Jan 27									
Bals.									

Form for parts (c), (d), and (e)

Sales [(70 @ $35) + (60 @ $36)]	$ _____
Cost of goods sold (from table)	_____
Gross margin	_____
Operating expenses	(500)
Taxable income	_____
Tax rate	.30
Tax expense	$ _____

Form for part (f)

Cash Flows from Operating Activities

Inflows from sales	$ _____
Outflows for purchases (from table)	_____
Outflows for operating expenses	_____
Outflows for taxes	(500)
Net cash flow from oper. activity	$ _____

Solutions to Self-Study Problems

Articulation Problems

1. Window Co. purchased merchandise inventory for cash.

Assets	Liabilities	Equity	Revenues	Expenses	Net Income	Cash
N	N	N	N	N	N	D

Merchandise inventory, an asset, increased while another asset, cash, decreased by the same amount.

2. Window Co. purchased merchandise inventory on account.

Assets	Liabilities	Equity	Revenues	Expenses	Net Income	Cash
I	I	N	N	N	N	N

Merchandise inventory, an asset, increased. Because the goods acquired were not paid for, accounts payable, a liability, also increased.

3. Door Co. sold merchandise to customers. The inventory originally cost Door $500 and was sold for $700 cash. Door uses the perpetual method. Show the net effects of this exchange.

Assets	Liabilities	Equity	Revenues	Expenses	Net Income	Cash
I	N	I	I	I	I	I

One asset, cash, increased by $700 while another asset, inventory, decreased by $500. Thus, the net effect on assets was a $200 increase. Revenues increased by the amount of the sale, $700, while expenses increased by $500, the amount of cost of goods sold. Thus, net income increased by the net difference of $200. The increase in net income caused retained earnings to increase.

4. Door Co. sold merchandise to customers. The inventory originally cost Door $500 and was sold for $700, on account. Door uses the perpetual method. Show the net effects of this exchange.

Assets	Liabilities	Equity	Revenues	Expenses	Net Income	Cash
I	N	I	I	I	I	N

One asset, accounts receivable, increased by $700 while another asset, inventory, decreased by $500. Thus, the net effect on assets was a $200 increase. Revenues increased by the amount of the sale, $700, while expenses increased by $500, the amount of cost of goods sold. Thus, net income increased by the net difference of $200. The increase in net income caused retained earnings to increase.

Multiple-Choice Problems

1.   a.

2.   a.   Using FIFO causes ending inventory to be higher. The higher ending inventory causes current assets to be higher. Other things being equal, higher current assets will result in a higher current ratio (which is current assets ÷ current liabilities).

3.   b.   Using LIFO causes a company's cost of goods sold to be higher, which, in turn, causes gross margin to be lower. If a company's gross margin is lower, its taxable income, the amount on which it pays taxes, will also be lower. The lower taxable income results in lower taxes.

4.   c.
20 units @ $10	=	$200
5 units @ $11	=	55
Cost of goods sold		**$255**

5.   b.
15 units @ $12	=	$180
10 units @ $11	=	110
Cost of goods sold		**$290**

6.   a.

Step 1

Units	Cost/Unit	Total Costs
20	$10	$200
30	11	330
15	12	180
65		$710

Step 2
Weighted av. cost per unit = $710 ÷ 65 units = **$10.92**

Step 3
25 units @ $10.92 = **$273**

7.   b.

Step 1
Units available (10 + 12 + 8)	30
– Units sold	17
Units of ending inventory	13

Step 2
8 units @ $24	=	$192
5 units @ $19	=	95
		$287

8.   d.   It was determined in Problem (7) that there are 13 units of ending inventory.
10 units @ $20	=	$200
3 units @ $19	=	57
		$257

9.   a.

Step 1
Units	Cost/Unit	Total Costs
10	$20	$200
12	19	228
8	24	192
30		$620

Step 2
Weighted av. cost per unit = $620 ÷ 30 units = **$20.67**

Step 3
13 units @ $20.67 = **$268.71**

10.   b.   Economic theory suggests that a company will price its goods based on "what the market will bear."

11.   c.
Sales (14 units @ $30)			$420
– Cost of Goods Sold	10 units @ $20	$200	
	4 units @ $22	88	288
Gross Margin			**$132**

12. a.

Sales (14 units @ $30)				$420
− Cost of goods Sold	10 units @ $22	$220		
	4 units @ $20	80		300
Gross Margin				**$120**

13. a.

Step 1 **Compute Cost of Goods Sold** **Based on Gross Margin Percentage**		**Step 2** **Compute the Estimated Cost** **of Ending Inventory**	
Sales	$10,000	Beginning Inventory	$ 3,000
− Gross margin ($10,000 x 40%)	4,000	+ Purchases (net of returns)	8,000
Cost of Goods Sold	$ 6,000	Goods Available for Sale	11,000
		− Cost of Goods Sold	6,000
		Estimated Ending Inventory	**$ 5,000**

14. b.   The only cash flow in 2006 was the **outflow** resulting from the payment of the accounts payable. The only cash flow in 2007 was the **inflow** resulting from the collection of the accounts receivable.

15. d.

Cost of the inventory	$10,000
Company's interest rate	.06
Part of the year during which the inventory was financed	6/12
Cost of financing inventory	**$ 300**

16. c.

Cost of Goods Sold	÷	**Inventory**	=	**Turnover**
$260,000	÷	$15,000	=	**17.3 times**

17. c.

Days in Year	÷	**Inventory Turnover**	=	**Average Days to Sell**
365	÷	17.3 times	=	**21 days**

18. b.

On the balance sheet:	100 shares at $38 per share = $3,800	
On the income statement:	Unrealized loss due to decline in mkt. value ($4,000 - $3,800)	= $200)
	Income from dividends (100 shares x $.25)	= 25
	Net effects on net income	($175)

19. a.

On the balance sheet:	The bonds are reported at cost = $100,000
On the income statement:	Only the interest income is reported = $4,000

Multiple True-False Problems

1.   a.   **True**:   Items reported at cost:

R (80 units x $20)	$1,600
S (120 units x $15)	1,800

                                  Items reported at market:

Q (100 units x $11)	1,100
T (250 units x $8)	2,000
Total of LCM item by item	$6,500

   b.   **False,** Total "cost" of all items   = $7,100
                     Total "market" of all items =   6,860   Thus, inventory should be reported at $6,860.

   c.   **False**, when inventory is written down from cost to market, net income **decreases** rather than increases.

   d.   **False**, LCM is not an alternative to FIFO, LIFO, or weighted average methods. Rather, it is an additional step that must be followed after inventory's "cost" has been determined using the FIFO, LIFO, or weighted average methods.

   e.   **False**, inventory should be written down anytime its replacement value declines below its historical cost, even if the reason for the decline is not due to unusual events.

2.   a.   **True**, only debt securities may be accounted for as held-to-maturity.

   b.   **False**, because these securities will be sold in two months, they should be accounted for as trading securities.

   c.   **False**, even though available-for-sale securities are reported on the investor's balance sheet at their fair market value, changes in the fair market value are reported directly as changes in stockholders' equity; they are not reported on the income statement. Changes in the market value of "trading securities" are reported on the income statement.

   d.   **True**, see the explanation for "c" above.

   e.   **False**, the equity method is used to account for investments when the investor owns from approximately 20% to 50% of the outstanding stock of the investee company. If more than 50% of the investee's stock is owned, consolidated financial statements must be presented.

3.   a.   **False**, when investments are accounted for as trading securities, changes in their market value must also be reported on the income statement. Thus, Music would report $3,500 [(500 x $1) + (500 x $6] on its income statement related its investment in Anthony.

   b.   **True**, if the investment is classified as available-for-sale, both the $500 of income from dividends, which affects net income and **retained earnings**, and the $3,000 change in market value, which is shown as an **unrealized gain in a separate equity account**, would affect Edward's stockholders' equity.

   c.   **True**, if the investment is classified as available-for-sale, only the dividends ($500) would be reported on Edward's income statement.

   d.   **True**, both trading securities and available-for-sale securities are reported as assets at their market value as of the balance sheet date. At December 31, Edward's 500 shares of Anthony's stock are worth $53,000 (500 x $106).

   e.   **False**, the cash paid to purchase securities classified as trading securities is reported in the *operating activities* section of the statement of cash flows. However, this statement would be true if the investment was accounted for as available-for-sale securities.

P-1.   Solution for requirement 1   (FIFO)

Table for parts (a), and (b).

Date	Purchases Units	Purchases Cost/Unit	Purchases Total Cost	Cost of Goods Sold Units	Cost of Goods Sold Cost/Unit	Cost of Goods Sold Total Cost	Inventory Units	Inventory Cost/Unit	Inventory Total Cost
Jan. 1							50	$20	$1,000
Jan. 10	60	$22	$1,320				50	$20	$1,000
							60	$22	$1,320
Jan. 16				50	$20	$1,000			
				20	$22	$ 440	40	$22	$ 880
Jan. 21	40	$24	$ 960				40	$22	$ 880
							40	$24	$ 960
Jan. 27				40	$22	$ 880			
				20	$24	$ 480	20	$24	$ 480
Bals.	100		$2,280	130		$2,800	20	$24	$ 480

Form for parts (c), (d), and (e)

Sales [(70 @ $35) + (60 @ $36)]	$4,610
Cost of goods sold (from table)	(2,800)
Gross margin	1,810
Operating expenses	(500)
Taxable income	1,310
Tax rate	.30
Tax expense	$ 393

Form for part (f)

Cash Flows from Operating Activities

Inflows from sales	$4,610
Outflows for purchases (from table)	(2,280)
Outflows for operating expenses	(500)
Outflows for taxes	(393)
Net cash flow from oper. activity	$1,437

P-1.   Solution for requirement 2   (LIFO)

Table for parts (a), and (b).

Date	Purchases			Cost of Goods Sold			Inventory		
	Units	Cost/Unit	Total Cost	Units	Cost/Unit	Total Cost	Units	Cost/Unit	Total Cost
Jan. 1							50	$20	$1,000
Jan. 10	60	$22	$1,320				50	$20	$1,000
							60	$22	$1,320
Jan. 16				60	$22	$1,320			
				10	$20	$ 200	40	$20	$ 800
Jan. 21	40	$24	$ 960				40	$20	$ 800
							40	$24	$ 960
Jan. 27				40	$24	$ 960			
				20	$20	$ 400	20	$20	$ 400
Bals.	100		$2,280	130		$2,880	20	$20	$ 400

Form for parts (c), (d), and (e)

Sales [(70 @ $35) + (60 @ $36)]	$4,610
Cost of goods sold (from table)	(2,880)
Gross margin	1,730
Operating expenses	(500)
Taxable income	1,230
Tax rate	.30
Tax expense	$ 369

Form for part (f)

Cash Flows from Operating Activities

Inflows from sales	$4,610
Outflows for purchases (from table)	(2,280)
Outflows for operating expenses	(500)
Outflows for taxes	(369)
Net cash flow from oper. activity	$ 1,461

P-1.   Solution for requirement 3   (Moving Average)

Table for parts (a), and (b).

Date	Purchases Units	Cost/Unit	Total Cost	Cost of Goods Sold Units	Cost/Unit	Total Cost	Inventory Units	Cost/Unit	Total Cost
Jan. 1							50	$20.00	$1,000
Jan. 10	60	$22	$1,320				110	$21.09 (1)	$2,320
Jan. 16				70	$21.09	$1,476	40	$21.09	$ 844
Jan. 21	40	$24	$ 960				80	$22.55 (2)	$1,804
Jan. 27				60	$22.55	$1,353	20	$22.55	$ 451
Bals.	100		$2,280	130		$2,829	20	$22.55	$ 451

(1) [$1,000 + $1,320] ÷ [110 units] = $21.09.

(2) [$844 + $960] ÷ [80 units] = $22.55.

Form for parts (c), (d), and (e)

Sales [(70 @ $35) + (60 @ $36)]	$4,610
Cost of goods sold (from table)	(2,829)
Gross margin	1,781
Operating expenses	(500)
Taxable income	1,281
Tax rate	.30
Tax expense	$ 384

Form for part (f)

Cash Flows from Operating Activities

Inflows from sales	$4,610
Outflows for purchases (from table)	(2,280)
Outflows for operating expenses	(500)
Outflows for taxes	(384)
Net cash flow from oper. activity	$ 1,446

Chapter Seven
Internal Control and Accounting for Cash

Learning Objectives for the Chapter

After completing this chapter you should be able to:

1.   Identify the key elements of a strong system of internal control.
2.   Identify special internal controls for cash.
3.   Prepare a bank reconciliation.
4.   Explain the use of a petty cash fund.
5.   Prepare a classified balance sheet.
6.   Use the current ratio to assess the level of liquidity.

Brief Explanation of the Learning Objectives

1.   Identify the key elements of a strong system of internal control.

There are two basic types of internal controls: *accounting controls* and *administrative controls*. Accounting controls are intended to help safeguard a company's resources and assure that its accounting records contain reliable information. Administrative controls help assure that management's plans and policies are followed by the company's employees.

Consult the textbook for a more complete list of elements of internal control, and for an explanation of the elements listed here. Some key elements of internal control are:

- Separation of duties.
- Proper physical control over assets and accounting records.
- Documentation of procedures to be followed.
- Clear lines of authority and responsibility.
- Adequate insurance and bonding of key employees.
- Careful hiring and training of employees.
- Formal performance evaluations of employees.
- Required periods of absence.

In addition to the normal internal control procedures, computerized accounting systems should have:

- Additional tests of reasonableness. Computers do not automatically recognize data that looks unreasonable unless programmed to do so.
- Careful management to insure that technically and ethically competent employees are hired to operate the computer system.

- Additional controls in place to insure the integrity of data input into the system, because paper documentation is eliminated in a computerized system.
- Additional documentation for the computer system itself, including software documentation.
- Controls to prevent "hackers" from accessing the system.
- Back up copies of all important electronic data and programs. These should be kept off-site.

2.   **Identify special internal controls for cash.**

In addition to the normal internal control procedures, controls over cash should include:

- More physical safeguards, since cash can be stolen more easily than many other assets; also it is more tempting to steal.
- Systematic reconciliation of bank statements.
- Prenumbering of all documents related to the checking account.

3.   **Prepare a bank reconciliation.**

This learning objective is examined further through the use of the self-study problems. Exercise-type Problem P-2 is especially intended to help you achieve this objective.

4.   **Explain the use of the petty cash fund.**

The petty cash fund allows a business to make relatively small payments of cash without going through the more formal process of issuing a purchase order, preparing a voucher, and writing a check. The use of a petty cash fund allows small purchases to be made quickly and without the added expense the normal purchasing system imposes, with an acceptable loss of internal control.

5.   **Prepare a classified balance sheet.**

The assets and liabilities on the balance sheet may be separated into current items and non-current items. To understand the definition of **current**, one must know the meaning of an *operating cycle* (explained below).

A *current asset* is an asset that will be converted into cash, or consumed within one year or within an operating cycle, whichever is longer. Generally, a *current liability* is one that must be repaid within one year or an operating cycle, whichever is longer. A more precise explanation of current liabilities is given in the textbook.

The *current ratio* is used to make relative comparisons of current assets and current liabilities. The current ratio is: Current assets ÷ Current liabilities.

A classified balance sheet is one that separates assets and liabilities into current and non-current sections. Within each section, items are usually listed in order of descending *liquidity*.

6.   Use the current ratio to assess the level of liquidity.

Liquidity refers to how quickly noncash assets can be converted into cash. The more quickly assets can be converted into cash, the more liquid they are, and the more useful they are for paying liabilities that must be paid in the near future. The current ratio provides a measure of how a company's more liquid assets (current assets) compare to its current liabilities. Other things being equal, the higher a company's current ratio, the easier it can pay its currently maturing debts.

The current ratio is defined as:

$$\frac{\text{Current assets}}{\text{Current liabilities}}$$

Self-Study Problems

Matching Problem

The terms in the left column on the following page describe elements of internal control. The right column contains examples of internal control procedures that might exist at a branch bank for a large bank. Match each of the terms from the left column with the correct example of that term from the right column.

Term	Example of Term
_____ **Prenumbered documents**	**a.** Limiting access to the bank vault to a few designated employees.
_____ **Physical control**	**b.** An insurance policy to protect the bank against a loss if a cashier steals money from his or her cash register.
_____ **Authority and responsibility**	**c.** The bank has a policy that prohibits the person who orders supplies from verifying that the goods were actually received.
_____ **Fidelity bond**	**d.** When bank employees give receipts to customers, these receipts come from a "booklet" and must be used in the order they are in the booklet to prevent employees from giving receipts that are not recorded.
_____ **Separation of duties**	**e.** The purchase of office equipment that cost less than $1,500 may be approved by the bank's branch manager. Purchases that cost more than $1,500 must be approved by the regional manager of branch banks.

Multiple-Choice Problems

1. Which of the following is true?
    a. Internal controls would not be needed if all employees were honest.
    b. Use of a Petty Cash Fund does not improve internal controls.
    c. Separation of duties is not needed if employees are covered by fidelity bonds.
    d. Documentation of procedures is not needed in a computerized system.

2. The use of prenumbered documents:
    a. is an example of physical controls.
    b. is a way of reducing printing costs.
    c. helps prevent employees from failing to record transactions.
    d. is helpful only where the receipt of cash is involved.

3. Which of the following is true?
    a. Good hiring and training procedures are intended to help eliminate the need for performance evaluations.
    b. The person who writes the checks should be responsible for insuring that they are reconciled to the bank statement.
    c. Physical control of assets is an element of *administrative* controls.
    d. Proper separation of duties will eliminate many opportunities for fraud by employees.

4. The Cash Short and Over account is always:
    a. an asset account.
    b. an expense account.
    c. a revenue account.
    d. an account closed to retained earnings at year-end.

Use the following designations for problems 5 and 6. A bank reconciliation consists of two parts. One part begins with the Balance on the Bank Statement; this is designated the "bank side." The other part begins with the Unadjusted Balance in the Cash Account; this is designated as the "book side."

5. Which of the following is true?
    a. A deposit in transit requires an adjustment on the bank side.
    b. An NSF check requires an adjustment on the bank side.
    c. A note receivable collected for the company by the bank requires an adjustment on the bank side.
    d. Adjusting journal entries relate to bank reconciliation items that required adjustments on the bank side.

6.   Which of the following is <u>false</u>?
   a.   A bank service charge requires an adjustment on the book side.
   b.   Interest earned on a checking account requires an adjustment on the book side.
   c.   Outstanding checks require an adjustment on the book side.
   d.   An error made by the company's bookkeeper in recording a check that the company wrote requires an adjustment on the book side.

7.   Which of the following statements about the use of a Petty Cash Fund is <u>false</u>?
   a.   Journal entries are not made when individual payments are made from petty cash.
   b.   Payments from petty cash are so small that receipts do not need to be kept.
   c.   The Petty Cash Fund is an example of an imprest fund.
   d.   The custodian of the Petty Cash Fund is an example of an employee who should be covered by a fidelity bond.

8.   Which of the following correctly describes the effects on the accounting equation caused by a company replenishing its Petty Cash Fund.

	Assets	Liabilities	Equity
a.	Decrease	None	Decrease
b.	Decrease	Decrease	None
c.	None	Increase	Decrease
d.	Increase	None	Increase

9.   The following information is available for Kelly Co.:
   1.   On August 31, 2006, the unadjusted balance in the Cash account was $2,914.
   2.   There was a deposit in transit of $376.
   3.   There was a bank service charge of $30.
   4.   There were outstanding checks that totaled $262.
   5.   A customer's NSF check of $41 was reported on the bank statement.

   The true cash balance for Kelly Co. on August 31, 2006 is:
   a. $2,308
   b. $2,843
   c. $2,957
   d. $3,039

10.   The bank reconciliation for Shark Co. included an adjustment for a customer's NSF check. The correct journal entry to record this adjustment is:
   a.   debit Expenses and credit Cash.
   b.   debit Accounts Payable and credit Cash.
   c.   debit Accounts Receivable and credit Cash.
   d.   debit Cash and credit Accounts Receivable.

The following information applies to questions 11 through 14.

The following account balances are available for Arkin Co.:

Current Assets	$ 50,000	Sales	$250,000
Long-term Assets	100,000	Cost of Goods Sold	175,000
Current Liabilities	30,000	Operating Expenses	155,000
Long-term Liabilities	50,000	Net Earnings	20,000
Owners' Equity	70,000		

11. What is Arkin's debt-to-assets ratio?
    a. 33%
    b. 50%
    c. 53%
    d. 80%

12. What is Arkin's current ratio?
    a. .6
    b. 1.7
    c. 2.0
    d. 2.5

13. Assume Arkin purchases land for $10,000 cash. What effect will this have on Arkin's current ratio and debt-to-assets ratio?

	Current Ratio	Debt-to-Assets Ratio
a.	Decrease	Increase
b.	Decrease	No effect
c.	No effect	Increase
d.	No effect	No effect

14. Assume Arkin purchases land using a $10,000 note payable that matures in five years. What effect will this have on Arkin's current ratio and debt-to-assets ratio?

	Current Ratio	Debt-to-Assets Ratio
a.	Decrease	Increase
b.	Decrease	No effect
c.	No effect	Increase
d.	No effect	No effect

Multiple True-False Problems

1.   Indicate if each of the following statements related to bank reconciliations is true or false.
     a.   A *deposit in transit* will cause the unadjusted **bank** balance to be lower than the unadjusted **book** balance.
     b.   The journal entry to record a *bank service charge* will include a credit entry to the Cash account.
     c.   An *outstanding check* will cause the unadjusted **bank** balance to be higher than the unadjusted **book** balance.
     d.   The bank reconciliation should be prepared by the person who writes the checks.
     e.   The journal entry to record that a *customer's NSF check* that is returned by the bank will include a crebit entry to the Accounts Receivable account.

2.   Indicate if each of the following statements related to classified balance sheets and liquidity are true or false.
     a.   A company that has a current ratio of less than 1.0 will not be able to pay its debts during the next year.
     b.   Office Equipment is a current asset account.
     c.   Office Supplies is a current asset account.
     d.   Assume the Argon Co. and the Zenon Co. are in the same industry. If Argon sells goods on account but Zenon sell goods only for cash, Zenon's operating cycle will be shorter than Argon's.
     e.   Assume Berry Co. and Antique Co. both sell goods only on a cash basis. If Berry Co. sells fresh strawberries and Antique Co. sells furniture, Antique's operating cycle will be shorter than Berry's.

Exercise-Type Problems

P-1.   The Sleepy Valley Transit Authority (SVTA) operates a toll road that goes through the beautiful countryside of Sleepy Valley. Persons driving on the road must stop at a tollbooth and pay a 50¢ toll either in an exact change lane or at a booth operated by a cashier.

       Because the toll road was established more to collect money from tourists who visit the valley than to collect money from local residents who use the road on a frequent basis, an alternate method of payment is available. Frequent users may purchase a book of 100 coupons for $20, thus reducing the cost of a toll to 20¢. To use the coupon, drivers must go through a booth operated by a cashier.

       Fred K. Rook was hired by SVTA as a cashier. Fred recently devised a way to make some extra cash while working as a cashier. He purchased several books of toll coupons that he takes to work. When a driver comes through his booth and pays the toll with cash, Fred puts the 50¢ cash in his pocket and deposits one of **his** coupons in the toll box as payment for the driver, thus making 30¢ on the "deal." (The drivers are not aware of what Fred is doing.) On a good day Fred can make an extra $20 to $30.

Required: Suggest ways the SVTA can prevent Fred's scheme from working and ways to identify cashiers when they do attempt it.

P-1.   **Suggestions:**

P-2   The following information is available for the Prince Co. for the month of April 2007:

a.   The unadjusted balance in the cash account on Prince's books was $ 8,715.71.

b.   The April 30 balance shown on Prince's bank statement was $ 8,472.36.

c.   A customer who owed Prince $700 on a note payable paid the $700 and $35 for interest, directly to Prince's bank. Prince did not know about this payment prior to receiving its bank statement.

d.   Prince had made a deposit of $1,635.25 near the end of April that had not cleared the bank when it prepared Prince's bank statement.

e.   Prince discovered that a check it had written for $153.15 had been erroneously recorded in its books as $135.15. This check had been written to pay an account payable.

f.   Three checks that Prince had written during April had not cleared the bank by April 30. The amounts of these checks were $147.90, $372.15, and $209.45.

g.   Prince has a checking account that earns interest on the minimum monthly balance. The bank statement showed that $35.12 of interest was earned during April.

h.   The bank statement showed that a check written by one of Prince's customers was returned for NSF. The check was for $79.72. Prince did not know about the NSF check before receiving its bank statement.

i.   The bank charged Prince a $10.00 service charge for the month of April.

Required:

1.   Prepare Prince's bank reconciliation for the month of April. Use the form provided on the following page.

2.   Record the adjusting journal entries necessary to correct the unadjusted book balance. Use the space provided on the following page.

P-2.   Forms for requirement 1

Prince Company
Bank Reconciliation Schedule
April 30, 2007

Balance per bank statement, April 30, 2007 $
Add:

Less: $

                                                    _____ (_____)
True cash balance, April 30, 2007 $

Unadjusted balance per the books, April 30, 2007 $
Add: $
                                                    _____

Less:

                                                    _____ (_____)
True cash balance, April 30, 2007 $

Space for requirement 2   **Debits**   **Credits**

Solutions to Self-Study Problems

Solution to Matching Problem

	Term			Term
d	Prenumbered documents		b	Fidelity bond
a	Physical control		c	Separation of duties
e	Authority and responsibility			

Multiple-Choice Problems

1. b.

2. c.

3. d.

4. d.   A *debit* balance indicates an expense; a *credit* balance indicates revenue. Both are closed to retained earnings.

5. a.

6. c.

7. b.

8. a.

9. b.

Unadjusted balance in the cash account	$ 2,914
Less: Service charge	(30)
Customer's NSF check	(41)
True cash balance August 31, 2006	$ 2,843

10. c.

11. c.

Total Debt	÷	Total Assets	=	%
$30,000 + 50,000	÷	$50,000 + 100,000	=	53.3%

12. b.

Current Assets	÷	Current Liab.	=	Ratio
$50,000	÷	$30,000	=	1.67 to 1

13.   b.   Current Ratio:

Ratio	Before Purchase		Effect of Purchase		After Borrowing			
Current Assets	$50,000	−	$10,000	=	$40,000			
Current Liab.	$30,000	+	$ 0	=	$30,000	=	1.3	= <u>Decrease</u>

Debt-to-Assets Ratio:

Ratio	Before Purchase		Effect of Purchase		After Purchase			
Total Debt	$80,000	+	$ 0	=	$80,000			
Total Assets	$150,000	+	$ 0	=	$150,000	=	53.3%	= <u>No effect</u>

14.   c.   Current Ratio:

Ratio	Before Purchase		Effect of Purchase		After Borrowing			
Current Assets	$50,000	+	$ 0	=	$50,000			
Current Liab.	$30,000	+	$ 0	=	$30,000	=	1.67	= <u>No effect</u>

Debt-to-Assets Ratio:

Ratio	Before Purchase		Effect of Purchase		After Purchase			
Total Debt	$80,000	+	$10,000	=	$90,000			
Total Assets	$150,000	+	$10,000	=	$160,000	=	56.2%	= <u>Increase</u>

Multiple True-False Problems

1.   a.   **True**, the deposit will have been recorded in the company's books but not in the bank's.

   b.   **True**, a service charge decreases cash.

   c.   **True**, the check that was written by the company will have been recorded in the company's books but not in the bank's.

   d.   **False**, separation of duties is an important element of internal control. Allowing the person who writes checks to prepare the bank reconciliation violates the separation of duties rule.

   e.   **False**, if a customer's check is returned by the bank, the customer still owes the company money. Thus, the accounts receivable for this customer should be increased with a debit, not decreased with a credit.

2.   a.   **False**, while most companies have current ratios greater than 1.0, a ratio of less than 1.0 does not mean a company cannot pay its debts during the next year. For example, the company may have cash sales during the next year sufficient to pay its bills as they come due.

   b.   **False**, office equipment has a life greater than one year, so it is a long-term asset.

   c.   **True**.

   d.   **True**, the length operating cycle is the average time it takes a company to sell inventory and collect the cash from that sale. Because Zenon only sells goods for cash, it does not have to wait for accounts receivable to be collected as does Argon.

   e.   **False**, a company that sells perishable goods, such as fresh fruit, must sell its inventory more quickly than a company that sells furniture. Therefore, its operating cycle will be shorter, assuming both companies only make cash sales.

Exercise-Type Problems

P-1   Suggestions for Sleepy Valley Transit Authority:

1.   The coupons should have serial numbers on them so that coupons coming from the same book can be detected because it is unlikely that a real coupon-using customer would go through the same toll booth several times on the same day. If tickets from Fred's toll box are compared and it is found that an unusually high number came from the same coupon book, this would be cause for further investigation.

2.   Compare the ratio of cash tolls to coupon tolls for different cashiers. If Fred always has a larger percentage of coupon tolls than other cashiers, this would be cause for further investigation. Having Fred operate different booths on different days would further assist this method because Fred could not argue, "the coupon-paying drivers always use the same booth."

3.   An "undercover" internal auditor could go through Fred's tollbooth and try to detect his "switch."

4.   Cameras could be placed in the tollbooths to discourage cashiers from using Fred's scheme. This would be especially helpful when used along with suggestion 3.

5.   The SVTA could initiate random searches of tollbooths to search for coupon books brought in by cashiers. The tollbooths are not private property.

P-2   Solution for requirement 1

Prince Company
Bank Reconciliation Schedule
April 30, 2007

Balance per bank Statement, April 30, 2007		$ 8,472.36
Add: Deposit in transit		1,635.25
Less: Outstanding checks	$ 147.90	
	372.15	
	209.45	(729.50)
True cash balance, April 30, 2007		$ 9,378.11
Unadjusted balance per the books, April 30, 2007		$ 8,715.71
Add: Note receivable (plus interest) collected by bank	$ 735.00	
Interest on checking account	35.12	770.12
Less: NSF check	79.72	
Bookkeeping error ($153.15 – $135.15)	18.00	
Bank service charge	10.00	(107.72)
True cash balance, April 30, 2007		$ 9,378.11

P-2   Solution for requirement 2

Cash	735.00	
Notes Receivable		700.00
Interest Revenue		35.00
Cash	35.12	
Interest Revenue		35.12
Accounts Receivable	79.72	
Cash		79.72
Accounts Payable	18.00	
Cash		18.00
Bank Service Charge Expense	10.00	
Cash		10.00

Chapter Eight
Accounting for Accruals -- Advanced Topics:
Receivables and Payables

Learning Objectives for the Chapter

After completing this chapter you should be able to:

1. Explain the importance of offering credit terms to customers.
2. Explain how the allowance method of accounting for bad debts affects financial statements.
3. Show how the direct write-off method of accounting for bad debts affects financial statements.
4. Explain how accounting for credit card sales affects financial statements.
5. Explain how accounting for warranty obligations affects financial statements.
6. Explain the effects of the cost of financing credit sales.
7. Show how discount notes and related interest charges affect financial statements. (Appendix)

Brief Explanation of the Learning Objectives

1.   Explain the importance of offering credit terms to customers.

By offering customers the opportunity to purchase goods on account, companies often can increase their sales. With proper management of such credit sales, the additional profit earned on credit sales will exceed the additional cost they generate (such as bad debts expense). A company may also have to offer credit terms to keep-up with competition if competitors are offering such terms.

2.   Explain how the allowance method of accounting for bad debts affects financial statements.

There are two ways to account for bad debt: the direct write-off method and the allowance method. The allowance method is preferred because it gives the best estimate of cash that will ultimately be collected from accounts receivable (i.e., the *net realizable value* of accounts receivable). When a company estimates the amount of bad debt that will result from the credit sales of a given period the company increases its **bad debt expense** account and **allowance for doubtful accounts**. The allowance for doubtful accounts is a *contra-asset account*, contra to accounts receivable. When the allowance account increases, the net realizable value of accounts receivable is reduced. This reduces total assets. When a specific customer's account is deemed uncollectible and written off, the write-off has **no** effect on expenses or assets. This objective is further investigated with the articulation problems.

3.   **Show how the direct write-off method of accounting for bad debts affects financial statements.**

Under the direct write-off method, no allowance account is used. When a customer's account receivable is deemed uncollectible, the balance in accounts receivable is decreased and bad debts expense is increased by the same amount. This method is only acceptable for companies that have very small amounts of bad debts.

4.   **Explain how accounting for credit card sales affects financial statements.**

When a customer pays with a credit card, the company will not receive the full amount of the sale from the credit card company, because the credit card company deducts a fee for handling the collections. The fee charged by the credit card company is an expense to the business that is recognized at the time of the sale, not when the cash is received.

5.   **Explain how accounting for warranty obligations affects financial statements.**

Liabilities, such as those caused by guaranteeing the quality of products sold are known as estimated liabilities because at the time of the sale the company cannot be sure how much the actual warranty costs will be. Thus, these costs must be estimated if the matching principle is to be followed. Specifically, the estimated cost of repairing products under warranty should be recorded as an expense during the same year the revenue is recognized. Because this expense has not been paid, a liability for future payment is also created. When a warranty repair is made, this liability is reduced, along with the assets that were used to make the repair.

6.   **Explain the effects of the cost of financing credit sales.**

There are two primary costs related to credit sales. The most obvious is the cost caused by bad debts. The other is the opportunity cost incurred by not getting cash at the time the sale is made. If the cash were collected at the time of sale, rather than later, it could be invested and be earning more income for the company. If a company is going to allow credit sales, it must satisfy itself that the additional profits these credit sales generate are greater than the additional costs caused by such sales.

7.   **Show how discount notes and related interest charges affect financial statements.**

A note that requires the borrower to repay **only** the face value to the lender is known as a *discount note*. (They are also known as *non-interest bearing notes*, but this term is misleading because there is an interest cost associated with discount notes.) Because the borrower will pay only the face value to the creditor, the lender will give the borrower less than face value in cash. The difference between the cash the borrower receives and the amount that must be repaid (the face value) is the interest that the lender will earn on the loan. This amount is also known as the *discount*. From the borrower's perspective the discount is a contra liability account, contra to the note payable.

The balance in the discount account is amortized over the life of the note. The liabilities on the balance sheet are increased as the discount is amortized (reduced). As the company reduces the discount account, it also records an equal amount in interest expense.

Self-Study Problems

Articulation Problems

For each situation below, indicate its effects on the accounting elements shown on the accompanying chart. Use the following letters to indicate your answer (you do not need to enter amounts):

Increase = **I**   Decrease = **D**   No effect = **N**

1.   Neptune Co. provided services of $100,000 to customers on account.

Assets	Liabilities	Equity	Revenues	Expenses	Net Income	Cash

2.   Neptune Co. estimated it will have $1,000 of bad debt costs related to credit sales. Neptune uses the allowance method to account for bad debt.

Assets	Liabilities	Equity	Revenues	Expenses	Net Income	Cash

3.   Neptune Co. wrote off a $200 account receivable from Wiggins Co. Wiggins had recently declared bankruptcy.

Assets	Liabilities	Equity	Revenues	Expenses	Net Income	Cash

4.   Wiggins Co., whose account was written off in event 3, decided to pay its debt to Neptune Co. despite their declaration of bankruptcy. Wiggins's account was reestablished and the $200 was collected. Record the net effects.

Assets	Liabilities	Equity	Revenues	Expenses	Net Income	Cash

5.   Pluto Co. made a $1,000 sale to a customer who paid with a credit card. Pluto has submitted the invoice for payment to the credit card company. The company charges a 3% fee for its services. Pluto has not been paid.

Assets	Liabilities	Equity	Revenues	Expenses	Net Income	Cash

6.   Pluto collected the $970 from the credit card company (see event 5).

Assets	Liabilities	Equity	Revenues	Expenses	Net Income	Cash

7.   Pet-Proof Co. sells and installs carpet with a two-year warranty. The company estimated that its warranty cost related to this year's sales will total $5,000.

Assets	Liabilities	Equity	Revenues	Expenses	Net Income	Cash

8.   Pet-Proof Co. had to repair a customer's carpet that was under warranty. The company paid cash to another company that actually did the repair for Pet-Proof Co.

Assets	Liabilities	Equity	Revenues	Expenses	Net Income	Cash

9.   On September 1, 2007, Augusta Co. needed to borrow cash for its business. To do so it issued a one-year discount note to the Corner Bank. The note had a face value of $10,000. The bank's discount rate on the note was 9%.

Assets	Liabilities	Equity	Revenues	Expenses	Net Income	Cash

10.   On December 31, 2007, Augusta Co. made the appropriate year-end adjustment related to the discount note it had issued in September to the Corner Bank (see event 9).

Assets	Liabilities	Equity	Revenues	Expenses	Net Income	Cash

Multiple-Choice Problems

The following information applies to questions 1 and 2.

The following information is available for Columbia Co. for 2005:

- Sales (all on account) $ 50,000
- Beginning accounts receivable   0
- Cash collected from accounts receivable   43,000
- Uncollectible accounts are estimated to be 1% of the ending balance of accounts receivable.
- No accounts receivable had been written off during the year.

1.   What was Columbia's bad debt expense for 2005?
      a. $500
      b. $430
      c. $ 70
      d. $ 0

2.   What was the net realizable value of Columbia's accounts receivable at the end of 2005?
      a. $ 6,500
      b. $ 7,000
      c. $ 7,500
      d. $49,500

The following information applies to questions 3 and 4.

The following information is available for Miami Co. for 2006:

- Sales (all on account) $100,000
- Beginning accounts receivable   7,000
- Cash collected from accounts receivable   89,700
- Beginning balance in allowance for doubtful accounts   350
- Accounts receivable written off during the year   300
- Uncollectible accounts are estimated to be 2% of credit sales.

3.   What was Miami's bad debt expense for 2006?
    a. $ 300
    b. $ 340
    c. $1,794
    d. $2,000

4.   What was the net realizable value of Miami's accounts receivable at the end of 2006?
    a. $17,000
    b. $15,000
    c. $14,950
    d. $10,000

5.   Which of the following is the correct way to record bad debt expense?
    a.   Debit bad debt expense and credit accounts receivable.
    b.   Debit allowance for doubtful accounts and credit accounts receivable.
    c.   Debit allowance for doubtful accounts and credit bad debt expense.
    d.   Debit bad debit expense and credit allowance for doubtful accounts.

6.   Boise Co. wrote off a customer's account receivable that had a balance of $500. What effect did this have on Boise's current ratio?
    a.   The current ratio did not change.
    b.   The current ratio increased.
    c.   The current ratio decreased.
    d.   The answer depends on what the current ratio was prior to the write-off.

The following information applies to questions 7 and 8.

On September 1, 2008, Madison Co. issued a discount note to the Town & Country Bank. The note had a one-year term and was discounted by the bank at 9%. The face value of the note was $5,000.

7.   What was the carrying value of the note on December 31, 2008?
      a. $4,550
      b. $4,700
      c. $4,850
      d. $5,150

8.   How much interest expense was recognized by Madison in 2008 and 2009, respectively?

	2008	2009
a.	$ 0.00	$150.00
b.	$112.50	$337.50
c.	$150.00	$300.00
d.	$225.00	$225.00

The following information applies to questions 9 and 10.

Maine Co. gives customers a three-year warranty for the products it sells. Maine's sales in 2005 were $500,000. The company estimates warranty costs will total 2% of sales over the life of the warranty. During 2005 customers' goods were repaired at a cost of $4,000. There was no balance in the warranty payable account on January 1, 2005.

9.   How much warranty expense should Maine recognize for 2005?
      a. $10,000
      b. $14,000
      c. $ 4,000
      d. $ 6,000

10.   What amount of warranty liability should Maine Co. report on its December 31, 2005, balance sheet?
      a. $10,000
      b. $14,000
      c. $ 4,000
      d. $ 6,000

11.   On December 31, 2005, Dakota Co. recorded the estimated bad debt expense it expects to incur as the result of sales made on account during the current year. Which of the following choices reflects how this event would affect the company's financial statements?

	Assets	=	Liab.	+	Equity		Rev	–	Exp.	=	Net Inc.		Cash
a.	N		N		N		N		N		N		N
b.	D		N		D		N		I		D		N
c.	D		N		D		D		N		D		N
d.	N		N		N		N		N		N		N

12.   During 2006, Dakota wrote off customers' accounts receivables deemed to be uncollectible. Dakota uses the allowance method to account for bad debt expense. Which of the following choices reflects how writing-off the uncollectible accounts would affect the company's financial statements?

	Assets	=	Liab.	+	Equity		Rev	–	Exp.	=	Net Inc.		Cash
a.	N		N		D		D		N		D		N
b.	N		N		N		D		N		D		N
c.	D		N		D		N		I		D		N
d.	N		N		N		N		N		N		N

13.   York Co. sells merchandise for which it provides a two-year warranty. At the end of 2006, York properly recorded the estimated warranty cost that will result from this year's sales. Which of the following choices reflects how this event would affect the company's financial statements?

	Assets	=	Liab.	+	Equity		Rev	–	Exp.	=	Net Inc.		Cash
a.	D		N		D		N		I		D		D
b.	D		I		N		N		N		N		D
c.	N		I		D		N		I		D		N
d.	N		N		N		N		N		N		N

The following account balances are available for Michigan Co.:

Accounts Receivable	$ 10,000	Common Stock	$15,000
Current Assets	40,000	Retained Earnings	20,000
Total Assets	100,000	Sales	80,000
Accounts Payable	18,000	Cost of Goods Sold	55,000
Current Liabilities	30,000	Operating Expenses	41,000
Total Liabilities	65,000	Net Earnings	14,000

14. What are Michigan's *accounts receivable turnover* ratio and *average days to collect accounts receivable*?

	A/R Turnover	Av. Days to Collect A/R
a.	4.4 times	5 days
b.	4.4 times	83 days
c.	8.0 times	36 days
d.	8.0 times	46 days

15. Which of the following statements is true?
   a. A company would prefer its *accounts receivable turnover ratio* to be higher rather than lower.
   b. The higher a company's *accounts receivable turnover ratio*, the longer it takes it to collect its accounts receivables.
   c. Other things equal, the faster a company collects its accounts receivable, the higher its costs of making credit sales will be.
   d. The only significant cost of making credit sales is bad debt expense.

The following information applies to questions 16 through 18.

The following account balances are available for Nebraska Co.:

Accounts Receivable	$ 12,000	Stockholders' Equity	$ 70,000
Inventory	15,000	Sales	430,000
Current Assets	40,000	Cost of Goods Sold	260,000
Total Assets	200,000	Operating Expenses	135,000
Accounts Payable	18,000	Net Earnings	35,000
Current Liabilities	25,000		
Total Liabilities	130,000		

16. What is Nebraska's inventory turnover ratio?
   a. 11 times
   b. 13 times
   c. 17 times
   d. 29 times

17.   On average, how many days does it take Nebraska to sell its inventory?
    a.   10 days
    b.   13 days
    c.   21 days
    d.   24 days

18.   What is Nebraska's *accounts receivable turnover* ratio?
    a.   17 times
    b.   22 times
    c.   29 times
    d.   36 times

19.   Assume that Nebraska has an *inventory turnover* of 14 times and an *accounts receivable turnover* of 9 times. What is the length of Nebraska's *operating cycle*?
    a.   16 days
    b.   23 days
    c.   67 days
    d.   126 days

20.   The following information was available for Duluth Co. on December 31, 2007:

Accounts Receivable	$10,000	Accounts Payable	$ 12,000
Inventory	15,000	Current Liabilities	25,000
Current Assets	50,000	Sales	120,000
Cost of Goods Sold	90,000	Net Income	8,000

    What was the length of Duluth's operating cycle (rounded to the nearest day)?
    a.   182 days
    b.   91 days
    c.   86 days
    d.   18 days

Multiple True-False Problems

1.   The following information is available for the first year of operations at the Medford Co.

Credit sales	$1,000,000
Collections of accounts receivable	850,000
Bad debt expense recorded	15,000
Accounts receivable written off	5,000

Based on the information above, indicate if each of the following statement is true or false.

a.   The balance in Medford's Accounts Receivable account is $150,000.

b.   The balance in the Allowance for Doubtful Accounts account is 10,000.

c.   **Assuming** the balance in Medford's Accounts Receivable account is $125,000, its accountants receivable turnover ratio is 8 times.

d.   **Assuming** Medford has an accounts receivable turnover ratio of 9 times. If it sells goods with collection terms of "net 30" it should be satisfied with its current rate of collections. (Hint: calculations are required.)

e.   **Assuming** the balance in Medford's Allowance for Doubtful Accounts account is $15,000, and the balance in its Accounts Receivable account is $145,000, the amount of receivables that would be included in its total assets would be $130,000.

2.   Indicate if each of the following statements is true of false.

a.   The only reason a company would not make sales on account is because of the fear of not being paid by customers.

b.   If Eckert Co. provides $500 of services to a customer who pays with a credit card, Eckert's revenues will increase by $500 as a result of the transaction.

c.   If Eckert Co. provides $500 of services to a customer who pays with a credit card, Eckert's net income will increase by $500 as a result of the transaction.

d.   Companies that cannot make precise estimates about uncollectible accounts receivable should use the direct write-off method of accounting for bad debts.

e.   If a company provides a one-year warranty with the goods it sells, it should expect its net earnings to be less than if it did not provide a warranty.

3.   On April 1, 2007, St. Louis Co. borrowed funds by issuing a 1-year note with a face value of $20,000 and an interest rate of 8%.

On the same day, April 1, 2007, Parker Co. borrowed funds by issuing a discount note with a face value of $20,000 and a discount rate of 8%.

Indicate if each of the following statement, related to the transactions described above, is true or false.
a.   On April 1, 2007, total liabilities of St. Louis increased by $20,000.
b.   On April 1, 2007, total liabilities of Parker increased by $20,000.
c.   The effective interest rate of the note issued by St. Louis is 8%.
d.   The effective interest rate of the note issued by Parker is 8%.
e.   The total liabilities of St. Louis Co. will increase by $1,200 on December 31, 2007, as a result of the adjusting entry that must be made related to the note payable that was issued on April 1.
f.   The total liabilities of Parker Co. will increase by $1,200 on December 31, 2007, as a result of the adjusting entry that must be made related to the note payable that was issued on April 1.

Exercise-Type Problems

P-1.   The following events occurred at the Platte Co. during 2009. (Ignore any beginning balances on Platte' books as well as any other events that may have occurred during the year.)
a.   Provided services to customers for $30,000, on account.
b.   Collected $23,000 from accounts receivable.
c.   Estimated that 1% of the uncollected accounts receivable would never be collected. Platte uses the allowance method to account for bad debts.
d.   Wrote-off as uncollectible the $100 account of Regal Co.

Required:
1.   Record the events above in journal entry form. Use the space provided below.
2.   Show the effects of these events on Platte's accounting equation. Use the table provided on the next page. Note that the table includes only the affected accounts. Use ( ) to show subtractions from accounts.
3.   Answer the following questions related to Platte Co. Use the space provided on the next page.
   ▪ What was the net realizable value of Platte's accounts receivable after event (b)?
   ▪ What was the net realizable value of Platte's accounts receivable after event (c)?
   ▪ What was the net realizable value of Platte's accounts receivable after event (d)?
   ▪ What was the effect of event (d) on Platte's current ratio?

P-1.   Forms for requirement 1

a.

b.

c.

d.

Table for requirement 2

Event	Asset Accounts Affected			Liabilities	Equity Accounts Affected	
	Cash	Acct. Rec.	Allow D/A	*NONE*	Revenue	Bad Debt
a.						
b.						
c.						
d.						

Space for answering requirement 3

	Accounts Rec.	-	Allowance	=	Net Realizable Value
Net realizable value after event (b)?	$		$		$
Net realizable value after event (c)?	$		$		$
Net realizable value after event (d)?	$		$		$

Effect of event (d) on
        Platte's current ratio?   **Increase**   **Decrease**   **No Effect**

P-2   The following events occurred at the Oklahoma Co. during 2009.

a.   During 2009 Oklahoma sold $50,000 of sports equipment for cash. These goods had originally cost Oklahoma $35,000. Oklahoma gives its customers a two-year warranty on the goods it sells.

b.   Based on past experience, Oklahoma estimated that warranty cost on the products sold would be 2 percent of sales. Oklahoma established a warranty liability for this amount.

c.   During 2009 customers returned for repair some of the products they had purchased. Oklahoma had the goods repaired by an outside repair shop to which Oklahoma paid cash. The repair costs totaled $200.

Required:

1.   Show the effects of these events on Oklahoma's accounting equation. Use the table provided on the next page. Note that the table includes only the affected accounts. Use ( ) to show subtractions from accounts.

2.   Answer the following questions, using the space provided on the next page:

- What were the total expenses related to these events?
- What would be the amount of warranty liability on Oklahoma's 2009 balance sheet?
- What were the cash flows related to Oklahoma's warranty policy for 2009?

Table for requirement 1

Event	Asset Accounts Affected		Liabilities	Equity Accounts Affected		
	Cash	Inventory	Warranty Payable	Sales	Cost of Goods Sold	Warranty Expense
a.						
b.						
c.						

Space for answering requirement 2

Expenses for 2009: $_____ + $_____ = $_____

Liability on the 2009 balance sheet: $_____

Cash flows for warranty costs in 2009: $_____

P-3   The following events occurred at the Idaho Co. during 2006 and 2007:

a.   On July 1, 2006, Idaho Co. issued a discount note to the Big Bank. This note had a face value of $10,000 and matured in one year. The bank used an 8% discount rate to determine how much cash to give (loan) Idaho.

b.   On December 31, 2006, Idaho recorded the appropriate adjustment related to the discount note.

c.   On December 31, 2006, Idaho made the closing entry for interest expense.

d.   On June 30, 2007, Idaho repaid the discount note.

Required:
1.   Post these events to Idaho's T-accounts, using the T-accounts provided on the next page.
2.   Answer the following questions, using the space provided:
   ▪ How would the discount note be presented on Idaho's December 31, 2006, balance sheet?
   ▪ What information would be disclosed on Idaho's 2006 and 2007 statements of cash flows? Describe both the amounts and the section(s) of the statement in which they would appear.

T-accounts for requirement 1

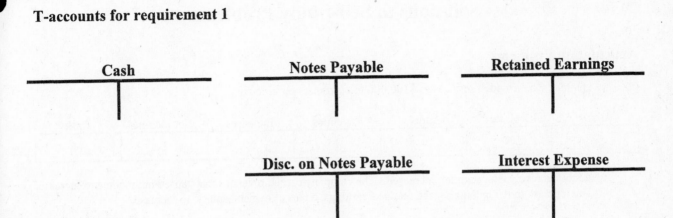

| Cash | Notes Payable | Retained Earnings |

| Disc. on Notes Payable | Interest Expense |

P-3   Space for answering requirement 2

2006 balance sheet disclosure:

Liabilities:
Notes Payable $
Less: Disc. on Notes Pay.   _____
                                                  $ _____

Information on statements of cash flows:

	Amount	Inflow or Outflow	Section of the Statement
2006:	_____	_____	_____
2007:	_____	_____	_____
	_____	_____	_____

Solutions to Self-Study Problems

Articulation Problems

1. Neptune Co. provided services of $100,000 to customers on account.

Assets	Liabilities	Equity	Revenues	Expenses	Net Income	Cash
I	N	I	I	N	I	N

Accounts receivable, an asset, increased. The company earned revenues that caused net income to increase. The increase in net income caused retained earnings, a part of owners' equity, to increase.

2. Neptune Co. estimated it will have $1,000 of bad debt costs related to credit sales. Neptune uses the allowance method to account for bad debt.

Assets	Liabilities	Equity	Revenues	Expenses	Net Income	Cash
D	N	D	N	I	D	N

Allowance for doubtful accounts, a contra asset account, **increased**; this caused total assets to **decrease**. Bad debt expense increased, which caused net income to decrease. The decrease in net income caused retained earnings, a part of owners' equity, to decrease.

3. Neptune Co. wrote off a $200 account receivable from Wiggins Co. Wiggins had recently declared bankruptcy.

Assets	Liabilities	Equity	Revenues	Expenses	Net Income	Cash
N	N	N	N	N	N	N

Accounts receivable was decreased, which caused total assets to decrease. Allowance for doubtful accounts was also decreased, but the decrease in a contra asset account causes total assets to increase. These two actions offset each other.

4. Wiggins Co., whose account was written off in event 3, decided to pay its debt to Neptune Co. despite their declaration of bankruptcy. Wiggins's account was reestablished and the $200 was collected. Record the net effects.

Assets	Liabilities	Equity	Revenues	Expenses	Net Income	Cash
N	N	N	N	N	N	I

This is best understood if you think of it as two separate events. First, the customer's account was reestablished; this is accomplished by reversing the things done in event (3) above. This did not affect any of the accounting elements listed. Second, consider the collection of the cash for payment of an account receivable. This decreased accounts receivable and increased cash. Because these two effects offset each other, total assets were not affected, but cash flows increased.

5.   Pluto Co. made a $1,000 sale to a customer who paid with a credit card. Pluto has submitted the invoice for payment to the credit card company. The company charges a 3% fee for its services. Pluto has not been paid.

Assets	Liabilities	Equity	Revenues	Expenses	Net Income	Cash
I	N	I	I	I	I	N

Accounts receivable increased by the amount Pluto expected to receive from the credit card company, $970 [$1,000 X 97%]. Revenues increased by the selling price of the goods, $1,000, which in turn increased net income and retained earnings. Expenses increased by the amount the credit card company will withhold from its payment to Pluto, $30 [$1,000 x 3%]. The $30 increase in expenses decreased net income and retained earnings.

6.   Pluto collected the $970 from the credit card company (see event 5).

Assets	Liabilities	Equity	Revenues	Expenses	Net Income	Cash
N	N	N	N	N	N	I

Cash increased by $970; accounts receivable decreased by the same amount. Thus, total assets were not affected.

7.   Pet-Proof Co. sells and installs carpet with a two-year warranty. The company estimated its warranty cost related to this year's sales will total $5,000.

Assets	Liabilities	Equity	Revenues	Expenses	Net Income	Cash
N	I	D	N	I	D	N

Because the company obligated itself to make a future payment, its liabilities increased, specifically, the warranty payable account. Because this liability resulted from a cost incurred in the hopes of producing more revenue, it was also an expense. The increase in expenses caused net income and retained earnings to decrease.

8.   Pet-Proof Co. had to repair a customer's carpet that was under warranty. The company paid cash to another company that actually did the repair for Pet-Proof Co.

Assets	Liabilities	Equity	Revenues	Expenses	Net Income	Cash
D	D	N	N	N	N	D

Cash was obviously decreased. This decrease occurred because the company repaid one of its obligations. This reduced liabilities. There was no effect on expenses because the expense had been estimated and recorded earlier (event 7).

9.   On September 1, 2007, Augusta Co. needed to borrow cash for its business. To do so it issued a one-year discount note to the Corner Bank. The note had a face value of $10,000. The bank's discount rate on the note was 9%.

Assets	Liabilities	Equity	Revenues	Expenses	Net Income	Cash
I	I	N	N	N	N	I

Cash increased by the amount received from the bank, $9,100 [$10,000 x 91%]. Liabilities also increased by $9,100, but two liability accounts were affected. First, notes payable increased by $10,000. Second, *discount on notes payable*, a contra liability account, increased by $900 [$10,000 x 9%]. The net effect was to increase liabilities by $9,100.

10.   On December 31, 2007, Augusta Co. made the appropriate year-end adjustment related to the discount note it had issued in September to the Corner Bank (see event 9).

Assets	Liabilities	Equity	Revenues	Expenses	Net Income	Cash
N	I	D	N	I	D	N

Because Augusta had used the bank's money for four months, it incurred an expense, specifically, interest expense. Because of the special way discount notes are recorded, the interest expense did **not** result in *interest payable* being recorded. Rather, one-third of the *discount on notes payable* account was removed from the books. When a contra liability account decreased, total liabilities increased.

Multiple-Choice Problems

1.   a.
Credit sales	$50,000
x % uncollectible	1%
Bad debt expense	$ 500

2.   a.
Sales on account	$50,000
– Cash collections	43,000
Ending accounts receivable	7,000
– Allowance for doubtful accounts	500*
Net realizable value	$ 6,500

* Since there was no beginning balance in the Allowance for Doubtful Accounts account, and no accounts receivable were written off during the year, the ending balance is the same as bad bets expense. (See problem 1 above)

3.   d.
Credit sales	$100,000
x % uncollectible	2%
Bad debt expense	$ 2,000

4. c.

Step 1	
Beg. accounts rec.	$ 7,000
+ Sales on acct.	100,000
	107,000
− Cash collections	89,700
	17,300
− Acct. rec. written off	300
End. accounts rec.	$ 17,000

Step 3	
End. accounts rec.	$17,000
− Allowance for doubtful accounts	2,050
Net realizable value of A/R	**$14,950**

Step 2	
Beg. allowance for doubt. accts.	$ 350
− Accts written-off	300
+ Bad debt expense for 2006	2,000
End. allowance for doubt. accts.	$2,050

5. d.

6. a. The write-off had no effect on the net realizable value of accounts receivable. Therefore, it had no effect on current assets or the current ratio.

7. b.

Step 1	
Face value	$5,000
x Disc. rate	.09
Discount	$ 450

Step 3	
Disc. per month	$ 37.50
x 9/1 - 12/31	4 months
Disc. amtz. 2008	$150.00

Step 2	
Discount	$ 450.00
÷ Term of note	12 months
Disc. per month	$ 37.50

Step 4	
Face value	$5,000
− Disc. bal.	300
Carrying value	**$4,700**

8. c. 2008: $37.50 x 4 months = **$150**
2009: $37.50 x 8 months = **$300**

9. a.

Sales	$500,000
x	.02
Warranty expense	**$ 10,000**

10. d.

Warranty expense	$10,000
− Repairs made	4,000
Warranty payable Dec. 31, 2005	**$ 6,000**

11. b. See articulation problem 2 for an explanation of the correct answer.

12. d. See articulation problem 3 for an explanation of the correct answer.

13. c. See articulation problem 7 for an explanation of the correct answer.

14. d.   First, compute the accounts receivable turnover ratio:

Sales	÷	**Accounts Receivable**	=	**Turnover**
$80,000	÷	$10,000	=	**8 times**

Then, compute average days to collect receivables:

Days in Year	÷	**Accounts Receivable Turnover**	=	**Average Days to Collect**
365	÷	8 times	=	**45.6 days**

15. a.   The higher the accounts receivable turnover, the more quickly accounts receivable are being collected. The more quickly receivables are collected, the lower the cost of financing inventory.

16. c.

Cost of Goods Sold	÷	**Inventory**	=	**Turnover**
$260,000	÷	$15,000	=	**17.3 times**

17. c.

Days in Year	÷	**Inventory Turnover**	=	**Average Days to Sell**
365	÷	17.3 times	=	**21 days**

18. d.

Sales	÷	**Accounts Receivable**	=	**Turnover**
$430,000	÷	$12,000	=	**35.8 times**

19. c.

Average days to sell inventory (365 ÷ 9)	=	40.55 days
Average days to collect receivables (365 ÷ 14)	=	26.07 days
Length of operating cycle	=	**66.62 days**

20. b.   1.

Cost of Goods Sold	÷	**Inventory**	=	**Inv. Turnover**
$90,000	÷	$15,000	=	6 times

2.

365 days	÷	**Inv. Turnover**	=	**Av. Days to Sell Inv.**
365	÷	6 times	=	60.8 days

3.

Sales	÷	**Acct. Receivable**	=	**A/R Turnover**
$120,000	÷	$10,000	=	12 times

4.

365 days	÷	**A/R Turnover**	=	**Av. Days to Collect Rec.**
365	÷	12 times	=	30.4 days

The **operating cycle** is the sum of the answers to steps 2 and 4:

60.8 days	+	30.4 days	=	**91.2 days**

Multiple True-False Problems

1.   NOTE: This problem is for the first year of operations at Medford Co., so there are no beginning account balances in Accounts Receivable or Allowance for Doubtful Accounts.

   a.   **False**, the Accounts Receivable account has a balance of $145,000, computed as follows:

Sales on account	$1,000,0000
less collections	850,000
Acc. rec. balance before write-offs	150,000
less acct. rec. written off	5,000
Ending balance in acc. rec.	$ 145,0000

   b.   **True**, allowance for doubtful accounts would have increased by the $15,000 of bad debt expense, and decreased by the $5,000 of accounts receivable written off, leaving a balance of $10,000.

   c.   **True**. ($1,000,000 ÷ $125,000 = 8)

   d.   **False**, if Medford's accounts receivable turnover ratio is 9 times, then it is taking approximately 41 days to collect its receivables (365 ÷ 9 = 40.55). If its customers are supposed to pay in 30 days, but they are taking 41 days, Medford needs to take corrective action.

   e.   **True**, it is the net realizable value (NRV) of accounts receivable that is included in total assets, and given these assumptions, Medford's NRV would be $130,000 ($145,000 – $15,000).

2.   a.   **False**, even if all customers pay their debts, a company granting credit still has to consider the opportunity cost related to financing its accounts receivable.

   b.   **True**.

   c.   **False**, although revenue increases $500, there is an expense associated with allowing customers to pay with credit cards. This is because the credit card company will not pay the company the full face value of the amount charged. Thus, increase in net income on a $500 credit card sale will be less than $500.

   d.   **False**, the direct write-off method is permitted by GAAP only when the amount of a company's uncollectible accounts receivable is immaterial.

   e.   **False**, the main reason for extending warranties on sales is to increase profits. By granting warranties, a company hopes it will generate additional sales, and that the profit from these additional sales will more than offset the cost of repairing any defective products that are sold.

3.   a.   **True**.

   b.   **False**, although the Notes Payable account increased by $20,000, the Discount on Notes Payable account, a contra liability, increased by $1,600 ($20,000 x .08). Since contra liabilities cause total liabilities to decrease, the total liabilities at Parker increased only $18,400 ($20,000 – $1,600).

   c.   **True**.

   d.   **False**, the effective interest rate on Parker's discount note is 8.7% ($1,600 ÷ $18,400 [see b. above]).

   e.   **True**, total liabilities at St. Louis increased $1,200 due to the increase in the Interest Payable account. ($20,000 x .08 x 9/12 = $1,200)

   f.   **True**, total liabilities at Parker increased because $1,200 of the Discount on Notes Payable account was amortized ($1,600 x 9/12 = $1,200). If a contra liability account decreases, total liabilities increase.

Exercise-Type Problems

P-1   Solution to requirement 1

a.	Accounts Receivable	30,000	
	Revenue		30,000
b.	Cash	23,000	
	Accounts Receivable		23,000
c.	Bad Debt Expense	300	
	Allowance for Doubtful Accounts		300
	[$30,000 x .01]		
d.	Allowance for Doubtful Accounts	100	
	Accounts Receivable		100

Solution for requirement 2

Event	Asset Accounts Affected			Liabilities	Equity Accounts Affected	
	Cash	Acct. Rec.	Allow D/A	*NONE*	Revenue	Bad Debt
a.		30,000			30,000	
b.	23,000	(23,000)				
c.			300			300
d.		(100)	(100)			

Solution for requirement 3

	Accounts Rec. –	Allowance =	Net Realizable Value
Net realizable value after event (b)?	$7,000	$ 0	$7,000
Net realizable value after event (c)?	$7,000	$ 300	$6,700
Net realizable value after event (d)?	$6,900	$ 200	$6,700
Effect of event (d) on Platte's current ratio? Decrease		Decrease	**No effect**

There would be no effect on the current ratio because neither the amount of current assets nor current liabilities were changed as a result of event (d).

P-2   Solution for requirement 1

Event	Asset Accounts Affected		Liabilities	Equity Accounts Affected		
	Cash	Inventory	Warranty Payable	Sales	Cost of Goods Sold	Warranty Expense
a.	50,000	(35,000)		50,000	35,000	
b.			1,000			1,000
c.	(200)		(200)			

Solution for requirement 2

Expenses for 2009:	$ 35,000	+	$ 1,000	=	$ 36,000

Liability on the 2009 balance sheet: $ 800

Cash flow for warranty cost in 2009: $ 200

P-3   Solution for requirement 1

Cash				Notes Payable				Retained Earnings	
a.	9,200	10,000	d.	d.	10,000	10,000	a.	c.	400

Disc. on Notes Payable				Interest Expense			
a.	800	400	b.	b.	400	400	c.
		400	d.	d.	400		

P-3   Solution for requirement 2

2006 balance sheet disclosure:

Liabilities:
Notes Payable $ 10,000
Less: Disc. on Notes Payable   400
                                                   $ 9,600

Information on statements of cash flows:

	Amount	Inflow or Outflow	Section of the Statement
2006:	$ 9,200	Inflow	Financing
2007:	$ 9,200	Outflow	Financing (repayment of principal)
	$ 800	Outflow	Operating (payment of interest)

Chapter Nine
Accounting for Long-Term Operational Assets

Learning Objectives for the Chapter

After completing this chapter you should be able to:

1. Identify different types of long-term operational assets.
2. Determine the cost of long-term operational assets.
3. Explain how different depreciation methods affect financial statements.
4. Determine how gains and losses on disposals of long-term operational assets affect financial statements.
5. Identify some of the tax issues that affect financial statements.
6. Show how revising estimates affects financial statements.
7. Explain how continuing expenditures for operational assets affects financial statements.
8. Explain how expense recognition for natural resources (depletion) affects financial statements.
9. Explain how expense recognition for intangible assets (amortization) affects financial statements.
10. Understand how expense recognition choices and industry characteristics affect financial performance measures.

Brief Explanation of the Learning Objectives

1.   Identify different types of long-term operational assets.

Most assets are considered to be *tangible* because they have physical existence, i.e., they can be touched. *Intangible* assets do not have physical existence, but they do represent an economic resource to the business. Most intangible assets exist primarily due to legal protection or contractual agreements. *Goodwill* is a unique type of intangible asset that exists due to the perceived excess earnings power of a particular business rather than a specific legal right.

Property, Plant and Equipment: This includes such tangible assets as land, buildings, equipment and furnishings. Except for land, these assets are **depreciated**.

Natural Resources: This includes such tangible assets as coal deposits, gas and oil reserves, gravel pits, and timber. These assets are **depleted**.

Intangible Assets: Included in intangible assets are copyrights, patents, trademarks, franchise agreements, and goodwill. Intangible assets are **amortized**.

2.   Determine the cost of long-term operational assets.

The recorded cost of a long-term asset is *the sum of the costs necessary to get that asset ready for its intended use*. All **necessary** costs are included, such as sales taxes on the asset, cost of having the asset delivered, and installation costs. Any unnecessary cost related to the long-term asset should not be included in the cost of the asset, but should be expensed. To illustrate, assume equipment was purchased for which a 2% discount was allowed for prompt payment. If the company did not make prompt payment, the 2% discount not taken should be recorded as an expense, not as part of the cost of the asset.

3. Explain how different depreciation methods affect financial statements.

When a long-term asset is acquired, its cost is not expensed immediately because the asset will be used to produce revenue over more than one accounting period, not just in the year of purchase. Instead, a portion of the cost is expensed in each period that the asset is used to produce revenue. This is accomplished through the use of depreciation. Recording depreciation causes the *carrying value* of the asset to decrease (which reduces total assets) and causes expenses to increase (which reduces net income and retained earnings).

Different methods of depreciation cause different amounts of depreciation expense to be recorded in each year for the same asset. This, in turn, affects the company's net earnings and total assets for each year the asset is used. It should be remembered that *over the total life* of a given asset *the total amount of depreciation expense will be the same* regardless of which method is used. Because depreciation is a noncash expense, the statement of cash flows is not directly affected by the method of depreciation that a company uses

The text explains three depreciation methods that are allowed under GAAP: *straight-line*, *double-declining balance*, and *units of production*. There is a separate method, *MACRS*, which is allowed for tax purposes. Each of these methods is explained in detail in the text, and is examined further in the self-study problems.

4. Determine how gains and losses on disposal of long-term operational assets affect financial statements.

When a long-term asset is disposed of at an amount different than its book value, the difference is recognized as a gain or loss. Assets sold for more than their book value produce *gains*, which increase net earnings and retained earnings. Because the asset was sold for more than its book value, total assets will also increase. Assets sold for less than their book value produce *losses,* which reduce net earnings, retained earnings, and total assets.

5. Identify some of the tax issues which affect long-term operational assets.

Long-term assets affect income taxes because depreciation expense is a tax-deductible expense. Thus, depreciation reduces the amount of income taxes that must be paid. The same is true for the cost of inventory that is sold, but there is a significant accounting difference. Most companies use the same inventory method for financial reporting purposes (GAAP) and for tax reporting purposes. For depreciation, however, the tax method used by most companies, MACRS, is **not** allowed for financial reporting purposes. Under GAAP, companies may choose from among several depreciation methods for their financial reporting, but these methods generally are not acceptable for tax reporting. Because the only cash flow effect of depreciation is its tax effect, and because all companies must use the same method for tax purposes, **the effect of depreciation on cash flows for a given situation will be the same regardless of which**

GAAP method of depreciation a company uses. [At this point you are probably thinking that taxes make the businessperson's job much more complicated. You are RIGHT! Now you know why some accountants get graduate degrees in tax accounting.]

6.   **Show how revising estimates affects financial statements.**

Accounting measurements are based on many estimates. When a company changes an estimate, the change affects *current and future* accounting periods, but *not past* periods. Accountants refer to this as "prospective" treatment. When the estimates are revised related to a depreciable asset, the *book value* at the time of the change is depreciated over the future life of the asset based on the *new estimates* for remaining useful life and/or book value. This will cause depreciation expense, and all related accounts, for future years to be different than it would have been if the estimates had not been changed.

7.   **Explain how continuing expenditures for operational assets affect financial statements.**

Costs that are related to a long-term asset that are incurred after the asset has been placed into service are referred to as continuing expenditures. Most of these costs are *expensed* as repair and maintenance expenses.

In two situations the costs of continuing expenditures are *capitalized*. If the cost *improves the quality* of the asset to which it relates (that is, increases its productive capacity) the cost is recorded in an asset account, *equipment*, for example. If the continuing expenditure does not increase the productive capacity of the asset, but does *extend its useful life*, the cost is capitalized by **reducing** the contra-asset, accumulated depreciation. Reducing the accumulated depreciation causes the book value of the asset to increase. A continuing expenditure that is capitalized will increase depreciation expense in future accounting periods.

8.   **Explain how expense recognition for natural resources (depletion) affects financial statements.**

Depletion of natural resources affects financial statements similarly to the way depreciation of equipment affects financial statements. (See objective 5.) Two differences between depreciation and depletion should be noted. Depletion is almost always calculated using a *units-of-production* approach, whereas depreciation is calculated in several different ways. Also, as with depreciation of equipment, some companies use a *contra-asset account*, *accumulated depletion*, to reduce assets for the depletion charge, but others simply reduce the asset account itself.

9.   **Explain how expense recognition for intangible assets (amortization) affects financial statements.**

Amortization of intangible assets affects financial statements similarly to the way depreciation of equipment affects financial statements. (See objective 5.) Two differences between depreciation and amortization should be noted. Amortization is almost always calculated using a *straight-line* approach, whereas depreciation is calculated in several different ways. Also, with depreciation of equipment, companies use a *contra-asset account*, accumulated depreciation, to reduce assets for the depreciation charge, but to amortize an intangible asset most companies simply reduce the asset account itself.

10.   Understand how expense recognition choices and industry characteristics affect financial performance measures.

As Chapter 9 demonstrated, companies can use different methods for computing depreciation, and they can use many different estimates for the useful life and salvage value of the same type of asset. Each of these differences can affect the amount a company reports for *total assets, depreciation expense, net earnings* and *retained earnings*. Therefore, any financial ratio that includes any of these accounting elements will be affected by the method used to account for long-term assets.

Self-Study Problems

Articulation Problems

For each situation below, indicate its effects on the accounting elements shown on the accompanying chart. Use the following letters to indicate your answer (you do not need to enter amounts):

Increase = **I**   Decrease = **D**   No effect = **N**

1.   In 2005 Ohio Co. purchased a packaging machine for $20,000 cash.

Assets	Liabilities	Equity	Revenues	Expenses	Net Income	Cash

2.   In 2005 Ohio Co. paid $1,000 to have the packaging machine delivered to its factory.

Assets	Liabilities	Equity	Revenues	Expenses	Net Income	Cash

3.   At the end of 2005 Ohio Co. recorded the first year's depreciation on the packaging machine.

Assets	Liabilities	Equity	Revenues	Expenses	Net Income	Cash

4.   During 2006 Ohio Co. paid $500 for the annual maintenance cost on the packaging machine.

Assets	Liabilities	Equity	Revenues	Expenses	Net Income	Cash

5.   During 2007 Ohio Co. paid $2,000 to have the packaging machine fitted with a computer controller. Previously the machine had been manually controlled. This new device is considered to have improved the quality of the packaging machine.

Assets	Liabilities	Equity	Revenues	Expenses	Net Income	Cash

6.   During 2008 Ohio Co. spent $4,000 to replace several major parts on the packaging machine. Although these repaired parts did not increase the productive capacity of the machine, they did extend its useful life by three years.

Assets	Liabilities	Equity	Revenues	Expenses	Net Income	Cash

7.   At the end of 2008 Ohio Co. sold the packaging machine for $7,000. At the time of the sale, the cost of the machine in Ohio' books was $24,000 and accumulated depreciation totaled $15,000. Thus, the book value of the machine was $9,000. Record the net effects of this sale.

Assets	Liabilities	Equity	Revenues	Expenses	Net Income	Cash

Multiple-Choice Problems

1. Toronto Co. made a basket purchase for $180,000 that included land, a building, and equipment. The estimated market values of the three assets were: land, $80,000; building, $90,000; and equipment, $30,000. How much cost should be allocated to the land?
    a. $88,889
    b. $80,000
    c. $72,000
    d. $60,000

2. Which of the following correctly matches the type of long-term asset with the term used to identify how that asset's cost is expensed?

	Building	Oil Reserve	Copyright
a.	Amortization	Depreciation	Depletion
b.	Depletion	Amortization	Depletion
c.	Amortization	Depletion	Depreciation
d.	Depreciation	Depletion	Amortization

3. On January 1, 2005, the Windsor Co. purchased a machine for $25,000. The machine had an expected useful life of five years and estimated salvage value of $5,000. Windsor uses the double-declining balance method of depreciation. What amount of depreciation should Windsor recognize in **2006?**
    a. $8,000
    b. $6,000
    c. $5,000
    d. $4,000

4. Which of the following statements regarding depreciation methods is true?
    a.   Use of double-declining balance versus straight-line causes cash flows to be **lower**.
    b.   Use of double-declining balance versus straight-line causes cash flows to be **higher**.
    c.   Use of double-declining balance versus straight-line has **no effect** on cash flows.
    d.   Use of double-declining balance versus straight-line causes cash flows to be lower in the early years of an asset's life and higher in the later years of an asset's life.

5.   On January 1, 2005, the Alberta Co. purchased a new furnace for $26,000. The furnace had an expected useful life of 10 years and estimated salvage value of $2,000. If Alberta uses the straight-line method of depreciation, what would be the depreciation expense on the furnace for **2006**, and the book value of the furnace as of December 31, **2006**?

	2006 Depr. Exp.	Dec. 2006 Book Value
a.	$2,400	$21,200
b.	$2,400	$19,200
c.	$2,600	$20,800
d.	$2,600	$18,800

6.   Regina Co. owns and operates a copper mine. The company paid $1,000,000 for the mine, which is expected to produce 50,000 tons of copper ore over its 10-year life. During 2007, 4,000 tons of ore were extracted. What amount of depletion should Regina record for 2007?
   a. $100,000
   b. $125,000
   c. $ 80,000
   d. $ 20,000

7.   Which of the following is <u>false</u>?
   a.   MACRS is the depreciation method <u>most</u> companies use for income tax purposes.
   b.   A company that uses MACRS for tax purposes <u>must</u> use another depreciation method for financial reporting (GAAP) purposes.
   c.   Under MACRS, the <u>shorter</u> the period over which an asset is depreciated, (e.g., 5-year property versus 7-year property), the <u>lower</u> the amount of taxes the company will have to pay.
   d.   Companies using MACRS are <u>prohibited</u> from using the "half-year convention."

8.   In 2007, Calgary Co. paid $15,000 cash to purchase a truck. The company recorded depreciation of $3,000 on the asset for that year. What was the effect of these events on Calgary' cash flows for 2007?
   a. $ 3,000 decrease
   b. $15,000 decrease
   c. $18,000 decrease
   d.   There was no effect on cash flows.

9. Spokane Co. purchased a machine in 2005 for $12,000. The machine had an estimated useful life of 10 years and an expected salvage value of $2,000. Spokane uses the straight-line method of depreciation. At the beginning of 2009 Spokane spent $3,000 to improve the quality of the machine. If accumulated depreciation at December 31, 2008 was $4,000, what would be the depreciation expense for 2009?
    a. $1,833
    b. $1,500
    c. $1,300
    d. $1,000

10. Which of the following is true?
    a.   The book value of an asset is its estimated market value.
    b.   The primary purpose of recording depreciation expense on the income statement is to reduce income tax expense.
    c.   Recording depreciation expense decreases the book value of the asset in the year it was used to produce revenue.
    d.   The accumulated depreciation for an asset provides the cash needed to replace the asset at the end of its useful life.

11. Chime Co. purchased an asset in **2005** and estimated it would have a useful life of five years. At the beginning of **2007** Chime revised its estimate of the asset's life to a total of seven years (versus five years). This change had **no** effect on Chime's income taxes. Regarding this revision, which of the following is true?
    a.   The change in the estimate will require that the financial statements for 2005 and 2006 be restated.
    b.   Because of the change in the estimate, **net income** for 2007 will be **higher** than if the change in the estimate had not been made.
    c.   Because of the change in the estimate, **cash flows** for 2007 will be **higher** than if the change in the estimate had not been made.
    d.   Because of the change in the estimate, **cash flows** for 2007 will be **lower** than if the change in the estimate had not been made.

12. Drink Co. purchased Bottle Co. for $1,000,000 and agreed to assume its liabilities. Prior to the purchase the balance sheet for Bottle Co. showed the following:

Cash	$100,000	Liabilities	$200,000
Inventory	400,000	Common Stock	300,000
Equipment (net)	700,000	Retained Earnings	700,000

An independent appraiser estimated the market value of the inventory to be $350,000 and the market value of the equipment to be $500,000. How much goodwill, if any, should Drink record for this purchase?
  a. $ 0
  b. $ 50,000
  c. $200,000
  d. $250,000

13. Apple Co. recorded amortization on a patent it holds. Which of the following choices reflects how this event would affect the company's financial statements?

	Assets	=	Liab.	+	Equity	Rev	–	Exp.	=	Net Inc.	Cash
a.	D		N		D	N		I		D	D
b.	N		N		N	N		I		D	N
c.	D		N		D	N		I		D	N
d.	D		N		D	N		N		N	D

14. Kalispell Co. paid $5,000 to install a new controller mechanism on a piece of its equipment. This expenditure will improve the quality of the equipment, but will not extend its useful life. Which of the following choices reflects how this event would affect the company's financial statements?

	Assets	=	Liab.	+	Equity	Rev	–	Exp.	=	Net Inc.	Cash
a.	N		N		N	N		N		N	D
b.	N		N		N	N		+		D	D
c.	D		N		D	N		+		D	D
d.	D		N		D	N		N		N	D

The following information applies to questions 15 through 17.

The following account balances are available for Portland Co. <u>before</u> it purchased a new truck:

Current Assets	$100,000	Common Stock	$20,000
Total Assets	300,000	Retained Earnings	80,000
Current Liabilities	70,000	Net Earnings	40,000
Total Liabilities	200,000		

Assume that Portland purchases a new truck for $30,000 cash.

15.   What immediate effect does this purchase have on Portland's debt-to-assets ratio?
    a.   Increase
    b.   Decrease
    c.   No effect

16.   What immediate effect does this purchase have on Portland's current ratio?
    a.   Increase
    b.   Decrease
    c.   No effect

17.   What immediate effect does this purchase have on Portland's return-on-assets ratio?
    a.   Increase
    b.   Decrease
    c.   No effect

Multiple True-False Problems

1.   The Overland Co., which hauls freight for other businesses, owns several large trucks. The following events occurred at Overland during 2007. Indicate if the statement related to each of the events is true or false.

   a.   Overland paid $10,000 to replace the engine in truck #2179, which was purchased in 2005. The new engine will extend the life of the truck by 3 years, and the truck will get significantly better gas mileage due to the new engine. Overland should record the $10,000 as a decrease in cash and an increase in the Equipment account.

   b.   Overland paid $10,000 to replace the engine in truck #2235, which was purchased in 2005. The new engine will extend the life of the truck by 4 years, but the overall quality of the truck will not be better than it was before the original engine failed. Overland should record the $10,000 as a decrease in cash and an increase in the Repair and Maintenance Expense account.

   c.   A third truck, #2461, was taken to the shop to have several things done at the same time. The rear bumper, which was severely dented, was replaced. The windshield, which had a crack, was replaced. The tires were changed, and the truck received its scheduled 25,000 miles service. The $4,000 cost of these items was recorded as a decrease in cash and an increase in the Repair and Maintenance Expense account.

   d.   Truck #2088 was purchased in 2003 for $80,000. At the time, Overland expected the truck would have a useful life of 8 years and a salvage value of $12,000. This year, 2007, the expected life of the truck was extended by 3 years, but the estimated salvage value was not changed. As a result of this change, the depreciation expense in **2008** will be higher than if the original expected life had not been changed.

   e.   Truck #2353 was purchased in 2005 for $60,000. At the time, Overland expected the truck would have a useful life of 8 years and a salvage value of $10,000. This year, 2007, the estimated salvage value was reduced to $5,000, but the expected useful life was not changed. As a result of this change, the depreciation expense in **2008** will be higher than if the original expected life had not been changed.

2.   On July 1, 2005, the Hampton Co. purchased a stamping machine for $100,000 cash. Hampton uses the units of production method of depreciation. The machine had an expected useful life of 10,000 machine hours of operation, and an estimated salvage value of $20,000. The machine was used as follows:

Year	Hours Used
2005	600
2006	3,000
2007	4,000
2008	2,000
2009	1,000
Total	10,600

The machine was sold on September 15, 2009, for $17,000. Indicate if each of the following statements related to this machine is true or false.

a.   During 2005 Hampton should report a negative cash flow from investing activities of $100,000.

b.   Depreciation expense for 2005 would be $6,000.

c.   Depreciation expense for 2006 would be $24,000.

d.   **Assuming** the correct depreciation expense was $9 per unit for this machine, depreciation expense for 2009 would be $9,000.

e.   When the machine was sold in 2009, Hampton would report a Loss on Disposal of Assets of $3,000.

3.   Indicate if each of the following statements about long-term operational assets is true or false.

a.   Assume Giant Co. buys Little Co. for $1,000,000. At the date of this transaction Little's books show assets of $950,000 and liabilities of $100,000. Because Giant paid more for Little's net assets than their book value, Giant will have to record goodwill on its books.

b.   For tax purposes, a company may choose to use MACRS or the double-declining-balance method of depreciation for its assets.

c.   Even though a copyright has a legal life of at least 50 years, it cannot be amortized over a life of 50 years.

d.   Other things being equal, when a company records depreciation, its debt-to-assets ratio increases.

e.   If a company purchases a machine for $40,000 and pays $5,000 to have it delivered, the delivery cost will cause the depreciation expense on the machine to be higher than it otherwise would have been.

Exercise-Type Problem

P-1   On January 1, 2005, Suffolk Co. purchased an automobile for use in its business. The following facts relate to this asset:

Cost		$14,000
Estimated salvage value		2,000
Estimated life:	in years:	4
	in miles:	100,000
Miles driven:	2005	26,000
	2006	29,000
	2007	23,000
	2008	20,000

Required:
1.   Compute the **depreciation expense** for 2005, 2006, 2007, and 2008 using:
   a.   Straight-line method.
   b.   Double-declining balance method.
   c.   Units of production method.

Record your answers on the chart provided on the following page.

2.   Using the forms provided, compute the **book value** of the automobile at the end of 2005, 2006, 2007, and 2008 using:
   a.   Straight line method.
   b.   Double-declining balance method.
   c.   Units of production method.

3.   Using information developed in completing requirements (1) and (2), answer the following questions:
   a.   Which method of depreciation produced the highest net income in **2005?**
   b.   Which method of depreciation produced the highest net income in **2008?**
   c.   Which method of depreciation resulted in the highest total assets for Suffolk Co. at December 31, **2005?**
   d.   Which method of depreciation resulted in the highest total assets for Suffolk Co. at December 31, **2008?**

Chart for requirement 1

Year	Straight Line	Double-Declining Balance	Units of Production
2005	$	$	$
2006			
2007			
2008			

Form for requirement 2

Year	Straight-Line	Double-Declining Balance	Units of Production
2005			
Cost	$ 14,000	$ 14,000	$ 14,000
Less Accum. Depr.	_____	_____	_____
Book Value	$_____	$_____	$_____
2006			
Cost	$ 14,000	$ 14,000	$ 14,000
Less Accum. Depr.	_____	_____	_____
Book Value	$_____	$_____	$_____
2007			
Cost	$ 14,000	$ 14,000	$ 14,000
Less Accum. Depr.	_____	_____	_____
Book Value	$_____	$_____	$_____
2008			
Cost	$ 14,000	$ 14,000	$ 14,000
Less Accum. Depr.	_____	_____	_____
Book Value	$_____	$_____	$_____

Space for answering requirement 3

a.   The depreciation method that produces the highest net income in **2005** is:_____.

b.   The depreciation method that produces the highest net income in **2008** is:_____.

c.   The depreciation method that results in the highest total assets in **2005** is:_____.

d.   The depreciation method that results in the highest total assets in **2008** is:_____.

Solutions to Self-Study Problems

Articulation Problems

1.   In 2005 Ohio Co. purchased a packaging machine for $20,000 cash.

Assets	Liabilities	Equity	Revenues	Expenses	Net Income	Cash
N	N	N	N	N	N	D

Cash decreased and another asset, equipment, increased by the same amount. Thus, total assets were not affected.

2.   In 2005 Ohio Co. paid $1,000 to have the packaging machine delivered to its factory.

Assets	Liabilities	Equity	Revenues	Expenses	Net Income	Cash
N	N	N	N	N	N	D

Because the cost of having the machine delivered to its factory was a necessary cost of getting the asset ready for its intended use, this cost was recorded as a part of the cost of the equipment. Therefore, as in event (1), cash decreased and another asset, equipment, increased by the same amount.

3.   At the end of 2005 Ohio Co. recorded the first year's depreciation on the packaging machine.

Assets	Liabilities	Equity	Revenues	Expenses	Net Income	Cash
D	N	D	N	I	D	N

Because equipment does not last forever, a portion of it is removed (through the accumulated depreciation account) from assets each accounting period. Because the equipment was used to produce revenues, the portion that expired this period was recognized as an expense. The increase in expenses caused net income to decrease, which caused retained earnings, a part of equity, to decrease.

4.   During 2006 Ohio Co. paid $500 for the annual maintenance cost on the packaging machine.

Assets	Liabilities	Equity	Revenues	Expenses	Net Income	Cash
D	N	D	N	I	D	D

Routine maintenance costs do not improve the quality of the asset over its original quality, nor do they extend the life longer than its originally estimated life. Therefore, these costs are expensed as incurred. The increase in expenses reduced net income and retained earnings. Cash also decreased.

5.   During 2007 Ohio Co. paid $2,000 to have the packaging machine fitted with a computer controller. Previously the machine had been manually controlled. This new device is considered to have improved the quality of the packaging machine.

Assets	Liabilities	Equity	Revenues	Expenses	Net Income	Cash
N	N	N	N	N	N	D

Because this expenditure improved the quality of the machine, the $2,000 was added to the cost of the asset. Specifically, it was recorded as an increase in the equipment account, and another asset, cash, decreased by the same amount. Thus, total assets were not affected.

6.   During 2008 Ohio Co. spent $4,000 to replace several major parts on the packaging machine. Although these repaired parts did not increase the productive capacity of the machine, they did extend its useful life by three years.

Assets	Liabilities	Equity	Revenues	Expenses	Net Income	Cash
N	N	N	N	N	N	D

This event was not recorded as an expense because the useful life of the machine was extended. Recall that an asset represents *probable **future** economic benefits*. These major repairs clearly met the test of an asset. However, the way this amount got on the books as an asset is a bit complicated. The $4,000 was recorded as a **reduction** of accumulated depreciation, a contra asset. Because contra assets **reduce** total assets, **a reduction in contra assets will increase total assets**. At the same time, another asset, cash, is being reduced, so the net result was to not change total assets, or anything else except for cash flows.

7.   At the end of 2008 Ohio Co. sold the packaging machine for $7,000. At the time of the, sale the cost of the machine in Ohio' books was $24,000 and accumulated depreciation totaled $15,000. Thus, the book value of the machine was $9,000. Record the net effects of this sale.

Assets	Liabilities	Equity	Revenues	Expenses	Net Income	Cash
D	N	D	N	I	D	I

The book value of equipment decreased by $9,000, but another asset, cash, increased by $7,000, causing total assets to **decrease** by $2,000. Because the equipment was sold for less than its book value, a loss was incurred on the sale. Although a loss is not exactly the same as an expense, it has the same effects on net income, retained earnings, and total equity. Therefore, the solution here shows the loss as an increase in expenses.

Multiple-Choice Problems

1.   c.

Estimated Market Values	% of Total Market Value Related to Land	Cost Allocated to the Land
Land $ 80,000	$80,000 ÷ $200,000 = 40%	Total cost $180,000
Build. 90,000		Land portion .40
Equip. 30,000		Land's cost $ 72,000
Total $200,000		

2.   d.

3.   b.   **Recall that:**

Yr.	Bk. Value	Rate	Dep. Exp.
1	$25,000	.40	$10,000
2	15,000	.40	**$ 6,000**

Book Value = Cost − Accumulated Depreciation

DDB Rate =   2 x [1 ÷ life]

➔   2 x [1 ÷ 5 yrs.] = .40

4.   c.   The only effect on cash flows related to depreciation is due to taxes. Double-declining balance is **not** used for tax purposes; MACRS is used for tax purposes.

5.   a.   **Depr. Expense:** $\frac{\$26{,}000 - \$2{,}000}{10 \text{ years}}$

= **$2,400** per year

Book Value =   Cost   −   Accum. Depreciation

= $26,000   − [2 yrs. x $2,400 per year]

= **$21,200**

6.   c.   Depletion cost per ton: $1,000,000 ÷ 50,000 tons = **$20** per ton
Depletion cost for 2007: $20 per ton   x   4,000 tons = **$80,000**

7.   d.   The "half-year convention" is an explicit part of MACRS.

8.   b.   The only effect on cash flows was due to the purchase price, $15,000.

9.   b.

Step 1		**Step 2**	
Determine Bk. Value. at 12/31/2008		**Determine Revised Amount to be Depr.**	
Cost	$12,000	Bk. Value at 12/31/2008	$ 8,000
less: Accum. Depr.	4,000	add: Cost of Improvement	3,000
Bk. Value at 12/31/2008	$ 8,000	Revised Bk. Value	11,000
		less: Salvage Value	2,000
		Amount to be Depr.	$ 9,000

Step 3
Compute 2009 Depr. Expense

$9,000   ÷   6 yrs. (remaining life) = **$1,500**

10.   c.

11.   b.   The longer the period over which an asset is depreciated, the lower the amount of depreciation expense per year (regardless of the method used). If less depreciation expense is recorded, net income will be higher.

12.   d.

Step 1		**Step 2**	
Determine Fair Value of		**Calculate Goodwill**	
Bottle's Net Assets			
Cash	$100,000	Price paid for Bottle	$1,000,000
Inventory	350,000	less: Market Value of Net Assets	750,000
Equipment	500,000	Amount of Goodwill	**$ 250,000**
Total	950,000		
less: Liabilities	200,000		
Net Assets	$750,000		

13. c.   Amortization of a patent has the same effects on financial statements as does depreciation of equipment. Because a patent does not last forever, a portion of it is removed from assets each accounting period. Because the patent was used to produce revenues, the portion that expired this period was recognized as an expense. The increase in expenses caused net income to decrease, which caused retained earnings, a part of equity, to decrease.

14. a.   See articulation problem 5 for an explanation of the correct answer.

15. c.   The debt-to-assets ratio is: Total Debt ÷ Total Assets. The purchase of a truck with cash is an asset exchange. Thus, neither total debt nor total assets are affected, so the debt-to-assets ratio is not affected.

16. b.   The current ratio is: Current Assets ÷ Current Liabilities. The purchase of a truck with cash is an asset exchange. However, one of the assets, cash, is a current asset while the other, the truck, is a noncurrent asset. The current ratio decreases because its numerator, current assets, is reduced while the denominator, current liabilities, remains the same.

17. c.   The return-on-assets ratio is: Net Earnings ÷ Total Assets. The purchase of a truck with cash is an asset exchange. Thus, neither net earnings nor total assets are affected, so the return-on-assets ratio is not affected.

Multiple True-False Problems

1. a.   **True**, because the useful life of the asset was extended and the quality of the asset (improved gas mileage) was improved, the Equipment account should be increased.
    b.   **False**, because the useful life of the asset was extended, but the quality of the asset was **not** improved, the cost incurred should be capitalized by reducing the balance in accumulated depreciation, rather than increasing the Equipment account.
    c.   **True**, all of these items would be considered normal repair and maintenance.
    d.   **False**, if an asset's estimated useful life is extended, then its cost is being spread over a longer period, so each year will be charged with less expense, not more.
    e.   **True**, if the salvage value of an asset is lower, the amount that is being depreciated in total (cost – salvage value) and for each year [(cost – salvage value) ÷ estimated life] will be higher.

2. a.   **True**.
    b.   **False**, depreciation expense for 2005 should be $4,800.
          [($100,000 – $20,000) ÷ 10,000 hrs] x 600hrs. = $4,800.
    c.   **True**. [($100,000 – $20,000) ÷ 10,000 hrs] x 3,000hrs. = $24,000.
    d.   **False**, if the depreciation expense per machine hour was $9, then depreciation expense for 2009 would be $3,600. Even though the machine was used for 1,000 hours in 2009, depreciation can be recorded for only 400 of these hours. This is because the machine originally had an estimated life of 10,000 hours and 9,600 hours were used from 2005 to 2008. Unless the company officially changes the estimated life or salvage value of the machine, depreciation computations must be consistent with the original estimates, and the machine may not depreciated below its originally estimated salvage value of $20,000. If depreciation for 2009 is based on 1,000 hours rather than 400 hours, the book value will be reduced below $20,000.
    e.   **True**, the book value of the machine on the date of sale would be equal to its estimated salvage value (see the explanation of d. above). Thus, an asset with a book value of $20,000 that is sold for $17,000 causes a loss of $3,000.

3. a.   **False**, goodwill occurs when a company buys another company and pays more than the **fair market value** of its assets, not their **book value**.

b.   **False**, generally only MACRS can be used for taxes. The tax law does permit an alternate straight-line depreciation, but even this does not usually result in the same depreciation expense each year as does the straight-line method used for GAAP.

c.   **True**, GAAP sets 40 years as the maximum time over which an intangible asset may be amortized.

d.   **True**, depreciation causes the book value of assets to decrease, so the debt-to-assets ratio (total debt ÷ total assets) will increase.

e.   **True**, the cost of having a machine delivered must be added to the recorded cost of the machine. The higher the cost of a machine, the greater is its depreciation expense, other things being equal.

Exercise-Type Problem

Computations needed for requirements 1 and 2:

Straight-Line: Depreciation Expense = [$14,000 - $2,000] ÷ 4 years = **$3,000 each year.**

	2005	2006	2007	2008
Accumulated Depreciation:	$3,000	$6,000	$9,000	$12,000

Double-declining balance: Recall that:

Book Value = Cost - Accumulated Depreciation

DDB Rate = 2 x [1 ÷ life]

→ 2 x [1 ÷ 4 yrs.] = **.50**

Year	Book Value	Rate	Depr. Expense	Accumulated Depreciation
2005	$14,000	.50	$7,000	$ 7,000
2006	7,000	.50	3,500	10,500
2007	3,500	N/A[1]	1,500[1]	12,000
2008	2,000	N/A[1]	0[1]	12,000

[1] The book value cannot go below the estimated salvage value. Therefore, only $1,500 of depreciation expense can be taken in 2007 [2007's book value of $3,500, minus the salvage value of $2,000 = $1,500]. This also means that **no** depreciation is recorded in 2008, even though the automobile had a life of 4 years. This is one of the peculiarities of the double-declining balance method.

Units of production: First, compute the depreciation expense per mile:

[$14,000 − $2,000] ÷ 100,000 miles = **$.12 per mile driven.**

Year	Miles Driven	Depreciation per Mile	Depreciation Expense	Accumulated Depreciation
2005	26,000	$ .12	$3,120	$ 3,120
2006	29,000	.12	3,480	6,600
2007	23,000	.12	2,760	9,360
2008	20,000	.12	2,400	11,760[2]

[2] Note that with the units of production method the accumulated depreciation does not total $12,000 at the end of 2008. This is because the "4 year life" is irrelevant to the units of production approach. The only relevant useful life for this method is the *total units expected to be produced*, 100,000 miles in the case of Suffolk's automobile. Also be aware that the car can only be depreciated a maximum of 100,000 miles. If it is driven more than 100,000 miles, depreciation stops, at which point accumulated depreciation would total $12,000.

Solution for requirement 1

Year	Straight-Line	Double-Declining Balance	Units of Production
2005	$3,000	$7,000	$3,120
2006	3,000	3,500	3,480
2007	3,000	1,500	2,760
2008	3,000	0	2,400

Solution for requirement 2

Year		Straight-Line	Double-Declining Balance	Units of Production
2005				
	Cost	$14,000	$14,000	$14,000
	less Accum. Depr.	3,000	7,000	3,120
	Book Value	$11,000	$ 7,000	$10,880
2006				
	Cost	$14,000	$14,000	$14,000
	less Accum. Depr.	6,000	10,500	6,600
	Book Value	$ 8,000	$ 3,500	$ 7,400
2007				
	Cost	$14,000	$14,000	$14,000
	less Accum. Depr.	9,000	12,000	9,360
	Book Value	$ 5,000	$ 2,000	$ 4,640
2008				
	Cost	$14,000	$14,000	$14,000
	less Accum. Depr.	12,000	12,000	11,760
	Book Value	$ 2,000	$ 2,000	$ 2,240

Solution for requirement 3

The depreciation method that produces the highest net income in **2005** is:__Straight-line__.

*It produced the **lowest** amount of depreciation expense in 2005.*

The depreciation method that produces the highest net income in **2008** is:__Double-Declining Balance__.

*It produced the **lowest** amount of depreciation expense in 2008.*

The depreciation method that results in the highest total assets in **2005** is:__Straight-Line__.

*It is the method with the **highest book value** at the end of 2005.*

The depreciation method that results in the highest total assets in **2008** is:__Units of Production__.

*It is the method with the **highest book value** at the end of 2008.*

Chapter Ten
Accounting for Long-Term Debt

Learning Objectives for the Chapter

After completing this chapter you should be able to:

1. Show how the amortization of long-term notes affects financial statements.
2. Show how a line of credit affects financial statements.
3. Describe the different types of bonds that companies issue.
4. Explain why bonds are issued at face value, a discount, or a premium.
5. Show how bond liabilities and their related interest costs affect financial statements.
6. Explain how to account for bonds and their related interest costs.
7. Explain the advantages and disadvantages of debt financing.
8. Explain the time value of money. (Appendix)

Brief Explanation of the Learning Objectives

1.   Show how the amortization of long-term notes affects financial statements.

Term debt, not to be confused with *term bonds*, is debt for which the principal repayments **and** interest payments are made in **a series of equal, periodic payments**. As each payment is made, the remaining principal balance of the loan is reduced. Thus, each payment reduces assets (*cash*), liabilities *(notes payable)*, and *retained earnings* (because of the increase in *interest expense* on the income statement). The interest expense for each succeeding period will be *less* than it was for the previous period because the balance in notes payable was reduced. In other words, with each successive payment, a *larger* portion of the payment goes to reducing the principal of the loan and a *smaller* portion goes to interest expense. Payments on automobile loans and house loans are typically term debt type loans.

2.   Show how a line of credit affects financial statements.

A line of credit is a type of borrowing agreement that allows a company to borrow money, up to a predetermined limit, as needed. It also allows the company to repay part or the entire amount borrowed as funds are available to do so, with certain restrictions, of course. Interest on the loan usually has to be paid at regular intervals, and the interest rate on a line of credit is usually *variable* rather than *fixed*. As the balance in the line of credit increases, total liabilities increases (as will total assets due to the additional cash that was borrowed). The balance in the line of credit will determine how much interest expense a company has to record and pay.

A line of credit for a business works much the same as a credit card does for individuals.

3.   Describe the different types of bonds that companies issue.

The variety of different types of bonds that many companies may issue is almost endless. Several of the major types described in the textbook are:

- *Secured bonds* versus u*nsecured bonds* (also known as debentures).
- *Registered bonds* versus u*nregistered bonds* (also known as *bearer bonds* or *coupon bonds*).
- *Term bonds* versus *serial bonds*.
- *Convertible bonds*.
- *Callable bonds*.

4.   Explain why bonds are issued at face value, a discount, or a premium.

Bonds are issued either at *face value*, at a *discount*, or at a *premium* depending on the relationship of the bonds stated interest rate to the market rate of interest being paid on bonds of similar maturity and risk. **If the stated rate is equal** to the market rate, the bonds sell at face value, (also called "at 100" and "at par"). **If the stated rate of interest is less** than the market rate of interest, the bonds sell at a discount. **If the stated rate of interest is greater** than the market rate, the bonds sell at a premium.

The selling price of bonds is expressed in terms of their percentage relationship to face value. For example, if bonds sell at 98, this means the bonds were are being sold at 98% of their face value. These bonds are selling at a 2% discount. Bonds selling at 105 are selling at a 5% premium.

5.   Show how bond liabilities and their related interest costs affect financial statements.

When a company borrows money, assets and liabilities increase by the same amount. If the liability involved is a bond issued at a premium or discount, two separate liability accounts will be affected, but the net result will always be to increase liabilities by the same amount as assets were increased.

Interest on debt is an expense that causes net income and retained earnings to decrease. Interest costs also cause assets to decrease, sooner or later. Interest often is **paid** during the year or at the end of the year in which the interest expense is incurred, so assets decrease immediately. However, sometimes interest on debt incurred "this year" is not paid until later. In such cases companies must increase liabilities at the same time they record interest expense (at the end of this year). Later, when the interest is actually paid in cash, both assets and liabilities decrease.

6.   Explain how to account for bonds and their related interest costs.

This objective is addressed with the self-study problems. Exercise-type problem **P-1** is especially intended to cover this topic.

7.   Explain the advantages and disadvantages of debt financing.

There are two important advantages of debt financing. First, it provides the opportunity for *financial leverage*. The means that owners of a business can use borrowed money to make more money as long as the return they earn from investing the money exceeds the cost of borrowing (interest expense). The second advantage is that interest expense paid on borrowed money is *tax-deductible*.

The primary disadvantage of borrowing money (versus using money contributed by the owners) is that interest must be paid on debt whether the company is earning a profit or not. A company that fails to pay interest on borrowed money may have to forfeit some of its assets to creditors, or worse, be forced into bankruptcy.

8.   Explain the time value of money.

The concept of the time value of money means that a dollar today is worth more than a dollar in the future. This is **not** because of expected inflation. Rather, money that is possessed today can be invested, and therefore, will be worth more in the future. How much a dollar invested today will be worth in the future depends on two factors: (1) the *rate of return* the investment earns, and (2) *how long* the money will be invested. The mathematics of *future value* can be used to answer this question.

Self-Study Problems

Articulation Problems

For each situation below, indicate its effects on the accounting elements shown on the accompanying chart. Use the following letters to indicate your answer (you do not need to enter amounts):

Increase = **I**   Decrease = **D**   No effect = **N**

1.   On January 1, 2005, Sanchez Co. issued $100,000 of bonds at face value (i.e., at 100). Interest of 8% on the bonds is to be paid on January 1, of each year, beginning in 2006.

Assets	Liabilities	Equity	Revenues	Expenses	Net Income	Cash

2. On January 1, 2005, Fonseca Co., issued $100,000 of bonds at 98 (i.e., at a discount).

Assets	Liabilities	Equity	Revenues	Expenses	Net Income	Cash

3. On January 1, 2005, Kim Co. issued $100,000 bonds at 103 (i.e., at a premium).

Assets	Liabilities	Equity	Revenues	Expenses	Net Income	Cash

4. On December 31, 2005, Sanchez Co. (see event 1) accrued the interest on the bonds it had issued at the beginning of the year.

Assets	Liabilities	Equity	Revenues	Expenses	Net Income	Cash

5. On January 1, 2006, Sanchez Co. paid the interest it had accrued on December 31, 2005 (see event 4).

Assets	Liabilities	Equity	Revenues	Expenses	Net Income	Cash

6. On December 31, 2005, Fonseca Co. (see event 2) amortized part of the discount on the bonds it had issued at the beginning of the year.

Assets	Liabilities	Equity	Revenues	Expenses	Net Income	Cash

7. On December 31, 2005, Kim Co. (see event 3) amortized part of the premium on the bonds it had issued at the beginning of the year.

Assets	Liabilities	Equity	Revenues	Expenses	Net Income	Cash

8. On January 1, 2005, Kuhn Co. borrowed $50,000 from the Local Bank by issuing a 3-year term note that carried an 8% annual interest rate. Kuhn agreed to repay the loan and related interest by making annual cash payments of $19, 401.65. **Show the effects of the first year's payment.**

Assets	Liabilities	Equity	Revenues	Expenses	Net Income	Cash

Multiple-Choice Problems

1. On January 1, 2007, Sinola Co. issued bonds with a face value of $50,000 at 97. What journal entry would Sinola make on the date the bonds were issued?

   a.   Cash   50,000
        Bonds Payable   50,000

   b.   Cash   48,500
        Bonds Payable   ·   48,500

   c.   Cash   50,000
        Bonds Payable   48,500
        Discount on Bonds Payable   1,500

   d.   Cash   48,500
        Discount on Bonds Payable   1,500
          Bonds Payable   50,000

2. A bond will sell at a premium if:
   a.   The market rate of interest is equal to the bond's stated rate.
   b.   The market rate of interest is greater than the bond's stated rate.
   c.   The market rate of interest is less than the bond's stated rate.
   d.   The bond is convertible into common stock.

The following information applies to questions 3 through 6.

On January 1, 2007, Talbot Co. issued bonds with a $100,000 face value and a stated interest rate of 8%. The bonds have a 10-year term to maturity and pay interest on December 31 of each year. The bonds were issued at 98.

3. How much discount should be amortized on December 31, 2007?
    a. $ 98
    b. $ 200
    c. $ 250
    d. $2,000

4. What would be the carrying value of the bonds on the December 31, 2007, balance sheet?
    a. $100,000
    b. $ 98,000
    c. $ 98,200
    d. $ 97,800

5. What amount of interest expense should be reported on the 2007 income statement?
    a. $7,800
    b. $7,840
    c. $8,000
    d. $8,200

6. What amount of cash flow from *operating activities* should be shown on the 2007 statement of cash flows?
    a. $7,800
    b. $7,840
    c. $8,000
    d. $8,200

The following information applies to questions 7 through 9.

On January 1, 2008, Gyro Co. issued bonds with $100,000 face value and a stated interest rate of 8%. The bonds have a 10-year term to maturity and pay interest on December 31 of each year. The bonds were issued at 102.

7.   How much cash was received from issuance of the bonds?
    a. $108,000
    b. $102,000
    c. $100,000
    d. $ 98,000

8.   What would be the carrying value of the bonds on the December 31, 2008, balance sheet?
    a. $102,200
    b. $102,000
    c. $101,800
    d. $100,000

9.   What amount of interest expense should be reported on the 2008 income statement?
    a. $8,200
    b. $8,160
    c. $8,000
    d. $7,800

10.   Which of the following statements is true?
    a.   A *debenture* is a type of bond for which assets have been pledged as collateral.
    b.   *Callable bonds* may be converted into common stock of the corporation issuing the bonds.
    c.   *Term bonds* are bonds for which the principal is to be repaid in a series of payments, rather than a single payment.
    d.   *Unregistered bonds* are the same as *bearer bonds*.

11.   On January 1, 2005, Lewis Co. issued bonds with a face value of $1,000,000 and a stated interest rate of 8%. The bonds mature in 20 years and pay interest on January 1 of each year, beginning in 2006. The bonds were issued at 100. What would be the total liabilities related to these bonds on Lewis's December 31, 2005, balance sheet?
    a. $1,080,000
    b. $1,000,000
    c. $ 920,000
    d. $ 80,000

12. On January 1, 2005, Quail Co. borrowed $20,000 from the City Bank by issuing a 10%, 4-year, term note. To repay the note and related interest, Quail agreed to make equal annual payments of $6,309.42. What amount of interest expense would Quail recognize on this loan during **2006** (the 2nd year of the loan)?
    a. $2,000.00
    b. $1,569.06
    c. $1,309.42
    d. $ 630.94

13. Parker Co. has a line of credit with the Merchant's Bank. The agreement with the bank calls for Parker to pay interest on the outstanding balance of the debt at a rate equal to the 3-month Treasury Bill rate plus 4%. Any money borrowed or repaid by Parker must occur on the first day of a month. Data related to Parker's line of credit during the first three months of 2008 are shown below:

Date	Amount Borrowed or (Repaid)	Treasury Bill Rate
Jan. 1	$40,000	5%
Feb. 1	10,000	5%
Mar. 1	(20,000)	6%

Based on this data, what amount of interest expense should Parker recognize **for the first three months** of 2008?
    a. $ 750
    b. $ 925
    c. $1,125
    d. $1,800

14. Moncton Co. borrowed $100,000 from the Local Bank by issuing a one-year note with a 10% interest rate. The income taxes rate for Moncton Co. averages 30%. What is the after tax interest cost of this loan?
    a. $ 3,000
    b. $ 7,000
    c. $10,000
    d. $13,000

15. Halifax Co. issued bonds on January 1, 2005, at a discount. On December 31, 2005, Halifax amortized part of the discount on these bonds. Which of the following choices reflects how the **amortization of the discount only** would affect the company's financial statements?

	Assets	=	Liab.	+	Equity		Rev	.	Exp.	=	Net Inc.		Cash
a.	N		I		D		N		I		D		N
b.	N		D		D		N		I		D		N
c.	D		N		D		N		I		D		N
d.	D		D		N		N		N		N		D

16. Sydney Co. issued bonds on January 1, 2005, for $100,000. On December 31, 2007, the bonds were repurchased for $102,000. Which of the following choices reflects how **the repurchase of the bonds only** would affect the company's financial statements?

	Assets	=	Liab.	+	Equity		Rev	-	Exp.	=	Net Inc.		Cash
a.	D		D		I		I		N		I		D
b.	N		D		D		N		N		N		D
c.	D		D		N		N		N		N		D
d.	D		D		D		N		I		D		D

The following information applies to questions 17 through 19.

The following account balances are available for Bangor Co.:

Current Assets	$100,000	Sales	$500,000
Total Assets	400,000	Cost of Goods Sold	300,000
Current Liabilities	60,000	Operating Expenses	105,000
Total Liabilities	250,000	Interest Expense	15,000
Common Stock	25,000	Income Tax Expense	30,000
Retained Earnings	125,000	Net Earnings	50,000

17. What is Bangor's EBIT?
    a. $ 50,000
    b. $ 80,000
    c. $ 95,000
    d. $395,000

18. **Assume** Bangor's EBIT is $150,000. What is Bangor's *times interest earned* ratio?
   a.   3.3 times
   b.   5.0 times
   c.   10.0 times
   d.   33.0 times

19. **Assume** Bangor's EBIT is $80,000. What is its return-on-assets ratio (ROA) using net earnings, and using EBIT?

	ROA Using Net Earnings	ROA Using EBIT
a.	12.5%	20%
b.	12.5%	80%
c.	33.0%	20%
d.	50.0%	80%

20. The following information is available for London Co. for 2008.

Net Income	$60,000	Total Assets	$300,000
Interest Expense	10,000	Total Debt	120,000
Tax Expense	30,000		

   What was London's *times interest earned* for 2008?
   a.   6 times
   b.   9 times
   c.   10 times
   d.   12 times

21. On his 12th birthday Karl Koch's grandfather invested $10,000 in an account that promises to pay 7%, compounded annually, over the next 6 years. Karl's grandfather told him the money could be used to buy a car when Karl turns 18. Using the time value of money tables in your textbook, determine how much Karl will have to spend on his new car.
   a. $15,007
   b. $14,200
   c. $71,533
   d. $47,665

22.   To help with her college education, Iris Olsen's grandmother is considering depositing $10,000 each year for the next 6 years into an account that promises to pay 7%, compounded annually. If the money in this account is given to Iris 6 years from now, how much will she receive?
    a. $85,200
    b. $71,533
    c. $47,665
    d. $15,007

23.   On January 1, 2007, the Memphis Co. is planning to issue bonds payable with a face value of $1,000,000. The bonds have a stated interest rate of 9%, but the market rate of interest for these bonds is 10%. How much cash will Memphis receive from the sale of the bonds if they have a 10-year life and pay interest annually on December 31, of each year?
    a. $1,434,368
    b. $ 553,011
    c. $ 385,543
    d. $ 938,554

Multiple True-False Problems

1.   Indicate if each of the following statements related to the types of bonds payable a company might issue is true or false.
    a.   A **mortgage bond** is a type of secured bond.
    b.   A **debenture** is an unsecured bond.
    c.   A company that wishes to keep exact records of who owns its outstanding bonds payable so interest checks can be mailed to the bondholders should issue **coupon bonds**.
    d.   The name **serial bonds** refers to the fact that bonds are sequentially numbered for purposes of internal control.
    e.   If a company wishes to issue bonds payable that all mature on a specific date, the company would issue **term bonds**.

2.   Indicate if each of the following statements related to bonds payable is true or false.

a.   A **convertible bond** is a bond whose interest rate may be converted from a variable interest rate into a fixed interest rate.

b.   If Burbank Co. issues **callable bonds** with a 10-year term, the company can force the bondholders to sell the bonds back to it in less than 10 years.

c.   The conditions which a company issuing bonds agrees to follow are set forth in the **bond indenture**.

d.   Other things being equal, secured bonds will carry a higher interest rate than unsecured bonds.

e.   Other things being equal, convertible bonds will carry a lower interest rate than non-convertible bonds.

3.   Indicate if each of the following statement related to bonds payable are true or false.

a.   A company that issues bonds payable with a face value of $800,000 at 97 will receive $776,000 of cash when the bonds are issued.

b.   On January 1, 2005, Ventura Co. issued bonds with a face value of $500,000. On December 31, 2006, when the bonds had a carrying value of $480,000, the bonds were called at a call price of 102. Ventura Co. will have to pay $489,600 to redeem the bonds.

c.   Sandman Co. issued bonds with a face value of $1,000,000. The bonds have a stated interest rate of 10%, and were issued at face value. If Sandman has a tax rate of 40%, the after-tax interest cost on its bonds will be $40,000 per year.

d.   Beckley Co. has bonds payable outstanding that have a face value of $10,000,000. The balance in the Discount on Bonds Payable account for these bonds is $50,000. If Beckley pays $10,100,000 to redeem these bonds, it must recognize an extraordinary loss of $50,000 as a result of the redemption.

e.   If Peek Co. issued bonds with a face value of $300,000 and received cash of $306,000, the bonds were issued at 106.

Exercise-Type Problems

P-1.   Big-Box, Inc. issued $500,000 of 10-year, 6% bonds on January 1, 2007, at 97. Interest on the bonds is paid on January 1 of each year, beginning in 2008.

Required:
1.   Prepare all journal entries related to the bonds for 2007 and 2008. Use the space provided below.
2.   Post the journal entries to the appropriate T-accounts. Use the T-accounts provided.
3.   Prepare the liabilities section of the balance sheets for 2007 and 2008. Use the forms provided.

Space for answering requirement 1

Journal entries for 2007:

Jan. 1 _____

Dec. 31 _____

Journal entries for 2008:

Jan. 1 _____

Dec. 31 _____

T-accounts for requirement 2

Cash	

Bonds Payable	

Interest Payable	

Disc. On Bonds Payable	

Interest Expense	

Forms for requirement 3

Big-Box, Inc.
Balance Sheet
As of December 31, 2007

Liabilities:

Current Liabilities:
    Interest Payable $

Long-term Liabilities:
    Bonds Payable $
    Less: Discount   _____   _____

Total Liabilities $

Big-Box, Inc.
Balance Sheet
As of December 31, 2008

Liabilities:

Current Liabilities:
    Interest Payable $

Long-term Liabilities:
    Bonds Payable $
    Less: Discount   _____   _____

Total Liabilities $

P-2. On January 1, 2005, Sioux Co. borrowed $100,000 from the Thrifty Bank by issuing an 8%, 4-year note. Sioux is to repay the note by making four annual payments of $30,192.05. The payments are to be made on December 31 of each year, beginning on December 31, 2005.

Required:
1. Prepare an amortization table for the 4-year life of the note. Use the form provided below.
2. Prepare the journal entries related to this debt that Sioux should make during 2005. Use the space provided below.

Form for requirement 1

Year	Principal Balance on Jan. 1	Cash Payment on Dec. 31	Amount Applied to Interest	Amount Applied to Principal	Principal Balance After Payment
2005	$	$	$	$	$
2006					
2007					
2008					

P-2.   Space for requirement 2

Journal entries for 2005:

Jan. 1 _____   _____ _____
          _____   _____ _____

Dec. 31 _____   _____ _____
          _____   _____ _____
          _____   _____ _____

Solutions to Self-Study Problems

Articulation Problems

1.   On January 1, 2005, Sanchez Co. issued $100,000 of bonds at face value (i.e., at 100). Interest of 8% on the bonds is to be paid on January 1 of each year, beginning in 2006.

Assets	Liabilities	Equity	Revenues	Expenses	Net Income	Cash
I	I	N	N	N	N	I

Assets increased by $100,000 because cash equal to the face value of the bonds was received. Liabilities increased because the bonds must be repaid.

2.   On January 1, 2005, Fonseca Co., issued $100,000 of bonds at 98 (i.e., at a discount).

Assets	Liabilities	Equity	Revenues	Expenses	Net Income	Cash
I	I	N	N	N	N	I

Assets increased by $98,000 because cash was received equal to 98% of the face value of the bonds. Liabilities increased by the same amount as assets, $98,000, but two liability accounts were involved. First, Bonds Payable increased by $100,000, the face value of the bonds. Next, Discount on Bonds Payable increased by $2,000, 2% of the face value of the bonds. Discount on Bonds Payable is a contra liability account, so increasing it caused total liabilities to decrease. Thus, the net result of increasing Bonds Payable by $100,000 and increasing Discount on Bonds Payable by $2,000 was to increase total liabilities by $98,000.

3.   On January 1, 2005, Kim Co. issued $100,000 bonds at 103 (i.e., at a premium).

Assets	Liabilities	Equity	Revenues	Expenses	Net Income	Cash
I	I	N	N	N	N	I

Assets increased by $103,000 because cash was received equal to 103% of the face value of the bonds. Liabilities increased by the same amount as assets, $103,000, but two liability accounts were involved. First, Bonds Payable increased by $100,000, the face value of the bonds. Next, Premium on Bonds Payable increased by $3,000, which is 3% of the face value of the bonds. Premium on Bonds Payable is an adjunct liability account, so increasing it caused total liabilities to increase. Thus, the net result of increasing Bonds Payable by $100,000 and increasing Premium on Bonds Payable by $3,000 was to increase total liabilities by $103,000.

4.   On December 31, 2005, Sanchez Co. (see event 1) accrued the interest on the bonds it had issued at the beginning of the year.

Assets	Liabilities	Equity	Revenues	Expenses	Net Income	Cash
N	I	D	N	I	D	N

Because Sanchez has used the bondholders' money for one year, it has incurred a year's worth of interest expense. This increase in expenses in turn caused net income and retained earnings to decrease. Because Sanchez had not actually paid the interest to the bondholders as of December 31, 2005, Sanchez also had to increase a liability, Interest Payable.

5.   On January 1, 2006, Sanchez Co. paid the interest it had accrued on December 31, 2005 (see event 4).

Assets	Liabilities	Equity	Revenues	Expenses	Net Income	Cash
D	D	N	N	N	N	D

Cash, an asset, decreased, and Interest Payable, a liability, also decreased. Expenses were not involved because the expense was recorded on December 31, 2005.

6.   On December 31, 2005, Fonseca Co. (see event 2) amortized part of the discount on the bonds it had issued at the beginning of the year.

Assets	Liabilities	Equity	Revenues	Expenses	Net Income	Cash
N	I	D	N	I	D	N

Discount on Bonds Payable is a contra liability account. As the discount account is amortized (reduced), liabilities increase. Amortization of the discount also causes interest expense for a given period to be higher than the cash interest that the company paid. Thus, as liabilities increased, expenses also increased, which caused net income and retained earnings to decrease.

7.   On December 31, 2005, Kim Co. (see event 3) amortized part of the premium on the bonds it had issued at the beginning of the year.

Assets	Liabilities	Equity	Revenues	Expenses	Net Income	Cash
N	D	I	N	D	I	N

Premium on Bonds Payable is an adjunct liability account. As the premium account is amortized (reduced), liabilities decreased. Amortization of the premium also caused interest expense for a given period to be lower than the cash interest the company paid. Thus, as liabilities decreased, expenses decreased from what the cash interest would have been, which caused net income and retained earnings to be greater than they otherwise would have been.

8.   On January 1, 2005, Kuhn Co. borrowed $50,000 from the Local Bank by issuing a 3-year term note that carried an 8% annual interest rate. Kuhn agreed to repay the loan and related interest by making annual cash payments of $19, 401.65. **Show the effects of the first year's payment.**

Assets	Liabilities	Equity	Revenues	Expenses	Net Income	Cash
D	D	D	N	I	D	D

Cash, an asset, decreased. The periodic cash payments of term-debt are for interest expense **and** repayment of principal. The reduction of principal reduced liabilities, while the interest expense caused net income and retained earnings to decrease.

Multiple-Choice Problems

1.   d.

2.   c.

3.   b.   Total discount: $100,000 x [100% - 98%] = **$2,000**
          Discount amortized per year: $2,000 ÷ 10 years = **$200**

4.   c.   Carrying Value = Face Value - Unamortized Discount
          Unamortized Discount: $2,000 - $200 = $1,800
          Carrying Value: $100,000 - $1,800 = **$98,200**

5.   d.   Interest Expense = Stated Interest + Discount Amortized [or - Premium Amortized]
          Stated Interest: $100,000 x 8% = $8,000
          Interest Expense: $8,000 + $200 = **$8,200**

6.   c.   Because the stated interest must be paid on December 31 of each year, Talbot paid $8,000 of interest during 2007. The portion of interest expense related to the discount amortized is a noncash expense, so it does not affect the statement of cash flows. The $100,000 of cash that was received from issuance of the bonds is disclosed in the *financing* section of the statement of cash flows.

7.   b. $100,000 x 102% = $102,000

8.   c.   Carrying Value = Face Value + Unamortized Premium
          Unamortized Premium: $2,000 - $200 = $1,800
          Carrying Value: $100,000 + $1,800 = **$101,800**

9.   d.   Interest Expense = Stated Interest - Premium Amortized [or + Discount Amortized]
          Stated Interest: $100,000 x 8% = $8,000
          Interest Expense: $8,000 - $200 = **$7,800**

10. d.   Do not to confuse the nature of a **term loan** with that of **term bonds** (choice c). Although the names are almost identical, they have very different meanings.

11. a.   Liabilities on Lewis's balance sheet would include the bonds payable of $1,000,000 **and** the accrued interest on the bonds of $80,000 that must be paid on January 1, 2006.

12. b.

Year	Principal Balance on Jan.	Cash Payment on Dec. 31	Amount Applied to Interest	Amount Applied to Principal	Principal Balance After Payment
2005	$20,000.00	$6,309.42	$2,000.00	$4,309.42	$15,690.58
2006	$15,690.58	$6,309.42	**$1,569.06**	$4,740.36	$10,950.22

13. b.

Month	Outstanding Balance	Annual Interest Rate Divided by 12 Months	Interest Expense for the Month
Jan.	$40,000	0.0075 [(5% + 4%) ÷ 12]	$300
Feb.	50,000	0.0075 [(5% + 4%) ÷ 12]	375
Mar.	30,000	0.0083 [(6% + 4%) ÷ 12]	250
			$925

14. b. **Interest Expense x (1.0 - Tax Rate)**
$10,000   x (1.0 -   .30)   = **$7,000**

[Interest Expense = $100,000 x 10% = $10,000]

15. a. See articulation problem 6 for an explanation of the correct answer.

16. d. The repurchase of the bonds payable required the payment of cash, which decreased assets. Because the bonds are no longer outstanding, liabilities decreased. Sydney paid an amount greater than the carrying value of the bonds to repurchase and retire them, resulting in an *extraordinary loss* on the retirement. For the purpose of these problems, extraordinary losses are recorded like expenses. Expenses reduce net earnings, which in turn, cause retained earnings to decrease.

17. c. **Net Earnings +   Interest Expense +   Tax Expense   =   EBIT**
$50,000   + $15,000   + $30,000   =   **$95,000**

18. c. **EBIT   ÷   Interest Expense   =   Ratio**
$150,000   ÷ $15,000   =   **10 times**

19. a. ROA using net earnings: **Net Earnings   ÷   Total Assets   =   %**
$50,000   ÷ $400,000   =   **12.5%**

ROA using EBIT: **EBIT   ÷   Total Assets   =   %**
$80,000   ÷ $400,000   =   **20.0%**

20. c. First, compute EBIT: **Net Earnings +   Interest Expense +   Tax Expense   =   EBIT**
$60,000   + $10,000   + $30,000   =   **$100,000**

EBIT   ÷   Interest Expense   =   Ratio
Next, compute times interest earned: $100,000 ÷ $10,000   =   **10 times**

21. a. $10,000 x 1.500730 [Table I] = **$15,007**

22. b. $10,000 x 7.153291[Table III] = **$71,533**

23. d. Present value of the principle: $1,000,000
[Table II; n = 10, i = 10%]   x 0.385543
$385,543

Present value of the annual interest payments: 90,000
[Table IV; n = 10, i = 10%]   x 6.144567
553,011

Proceeds received from issuing the bonds   **$938,554**

Multiple True-False Problems

1.   a.   **True.**
      b.   **True.**
      c.   **False,** a company that wishes to send interest checks directly to bondholders would issue **registered bonds,** not coupon bonds or bearer bonds.
      d.   **False,** serial bonds are a set, or "series," of bonds whose principal will be repaid at varying maturity dates, as opposed to term bonds, which are repaid all at one time.
      e.   **True,** see "d." above.

2.   a.   **False,** convertible bonds are bonds that can be converted into another type of financial security, usually shares of common stock.
      b.   **True.**
      c.   **True.**
      d.   **False,** other things being equal, secured bonds will carry a lower rate of interest than unsecured bonds. This is because the collateral that supports the secured bonds lowers the risk that the bondholder will not get their cash back if the company defaults on payment.
      e.   **True,** investors who purchase nonconvertible bonds get only interest payments and a return of principal as a reward for their investment. Investors who buy convertible bonds also get interest and the return of their principal if the bonds are not converted. However, through conversion, they may get the chance to acquire common stock of the company that issued the bonds at a price that is lower than market price.

3.   a.   **True.** ($800,000 x .97 = $776,000.)
      b.   **False,** the redemption price of callable bonds is based on their face value, not their book value. Ventura would have to pay $510,000 to call these bonds. ($500,000 x 1.02 = $510,000)
      c.   **False,** the after-tax interest cost on Sandman's bonds would be $60,000.
        [$1,000,000 x .10 x (1.0 − .40) = $60,000]
      d.   **False,** the gain or loss on the early redemption of bonds is computed by comparing the purchase price of the bonds to the book value (also called carrying value) of the bonds. In this case the loss on early redemption would be $150,000, computed as follows:

Face value of the bonds	$10,000,000
Less: balance in the Discount account	50,000
Book value of the bonds	9,950,000
Less: cost to redeem the bonds	10,100,000
Extraordinary loss on early redemption	$ 150,000

      e.   **False,** the bonds were issued at 102. ($306,000 ÷ $300,000 = 1.02 = 102%)

Exercise-Type Problems

P-1.   **Solution for requirement 1**

Journal entries for 2007:

Jan. 1	Cash ($500,000 x .97)		485,000	
	Discount on Bonds Payable		15,000	
	Bonds Payable			500,000
Dec. 31	Interest Expense		31,500	
	Discount on Bonds Payable	($15,000 ÷ 10 years)		1,500
	Interest Payable	($500,000 x .06)		30,000

Journal entries for 2008:

Jan. 1	Interest Payable	30,000	
	Cash		30,000
Dec. 31	Interest Expense	31,500	
	Discount on Bonds Payable		1,500
	Interest Payable		30,000

Solutions for requirement 2

Cash	
1/07 485,000	
	30,000 1/08

Bonds Payable	
	500,000 1/07

Interest Payable	
	30,000 12/07
1/08 30,000	
	30,000 12/08

Disc. On Bonds Payable	
1/07 15,000	
	1,500 12/07
Bal. 13,500	
	1,500 12/08
Bal. 12,000	

Interest Expense	
12/07 31,500	
12/08 31,500	

Solutions for requirement 3

Big-Box, Inc.
Balance Sheet
As of December 31, 2007

Liabilities:
Current Liabilities:

Interest Payable		$ 30,000
Long-term Liabilities:		
Bonds Payable	$500,000	
Less: Discount	13,500	486,500
Total Liabilities		$516,500

Big-Box, Inc.
Balance Sheet
As of December 31, 2008

Liabilities:

Current Liabilities:
    Interest Payable $ 30,000

Long-term Liabilities:
    Bonds Payable $500,000
    Less: Discount   12,000   488,000

Total Liabilities $518,000

P-2.   Solution for requirement 1

Amortization Table

Year	Principal Balance on Jan. 1	Cash Payment on Dec. 31	Amount Applied to Interest	Amount Applied to Principal	Principal Balance After Payment
2005	$100,000.00	$30,192.05	$8,000.00 [1]	$22,192.05 [2]	$77,807.95
2006	77,807.95	30,192.05	6,224.64	23,967.41	53,840.54
2007	53,840.54	30,192.05	4,307.24	25,884.81	27,955.73
2008	27,955.73	30,192.05	2,236.32 [3]	27,955.73 [3]	0

[1]   Amount Applied to Interest = Principal Balance on Jan. 1 x 8%.

[2]   Amount Applied to Principal = Payment − Amount Applied to Interest.

[3]   These numbers are plugged to make the ending principal balance equal $0.

Solution for requirement 2

Journal Entries for 2005

Jan. 1	Cash		100,000.00	
	Note Payable			100,000.00
Dec.31	Interest Expense (from amortization. table)		8,000.00	
	Note Payable (from amortization table)		22,192.05	
	Cash			30,192.05

Chapter Eleven
Accounting for Equity Transactions

Learning Objectives for the Chapter

After completing this chapter you should be able to:

1. Identify the primary characteristics of sole proprietorships, partnerships, and corporations.
2. Analyze financial statements to identify the different types of business organizations.
3. Explain the characteristics of major types of stock issued by corporations.
4. Explain how to account for different types of stock issued by corporations.
5. Show how treasury stock transactions affect a company's financial statements.
6. Explain the effects of declaring and paying cash dividends on a company's financial statements.
7. Explain the effects of stock dividends and stock splits on a company's financial statements.
8. Show how the appropriation of retained earnings affects financial statements.
9. Explain some uses of accounting information in making stock investment decisions.
10. Explain accounting for not-for-profit entities and governmental organizations. (Appendix)

Brief Explanation of the Learning Objectives

1. **Identify the primary characteristics of sole proprietorships, partnerships, and corporations.**

There are three major forms of business enterprises: sole proprietorships, partnerships, and corporations. Some of the primary advantages and disadvantages of each include:

Sole Proprietorships: *Advantages* include ease of formation, due to less regulation than a corporation, and avoidance of double taxation.
Disadvantages include unlimited liability for the owner and the difficulty of raising capital.

Partnerships: *Advantages* include the ability to raise capital easier than for sole proprietorships and avoidance of double taxation.
Disadvantages include unlimited liability (it is worse than for sole proprietorships because each partner may be able to create liabilities for other partners). Lack of easy continuity of the entity can also be a problem.

Corporations: *Advantages* include limited liability, easy transfer of ownership, and greater ability to raise capital.
Disadvantages include the potential of double taxation, greater regulation, and more complex management structure.

2.   **Analyze financial statements to identify the different types of business organizations.**

The **equity section** of the balance sheet usually reveals the type of business organization to which the statements relate. The equity section of a **corporation** is usually called *shareholders' equity* or *stockholders' equity* and it will list one or more categories of stock. The equity section of the balance sheet for a **sole proprietorship** is usually called [*name of owner's*] *capital*, and there will be only one owner. Like sole proprietorships, **partnerships** also use the term *capital*, along with the names of the owners, to describe the equity section of the balance sheet. Unlike a sole proprietorship, partnerships have more than one owner, and, thus, more than one capital account.

3.   **Explain the major types of stock issued by corporations and their disclosure on the balance sheet.**

There are two major classes of stock that a corporation might issue, common and preferred. **Common stock** is the primary stock of most corporations. Common shareholders usually have the most power to run the corporation because they can vote for the board of directors. Common stock can have a *par value*, *stated value* or be *no-par stock*.

Owners of **preferred stock** usually get preferred treatment on one or more ways. Should the corporation liquidate, the preferred stockholders may get their share of any available assets before owners of common stock. Preferred stock usually has a preference to dividends over common stock. This means that in some situations preferred shareholders will get a dividend while common stockholders will not.

Preferred stock usually has a par value on which a stated dividend is calculated. Stated dividends on preferred stock are often stated as a percentage of the stock's par value, but the stated dividend can be an absolute dollar amount per share. Stated dividends do not have to be paid, but they usually are. Furthermore, if the stated dividend on preferred stock is not paid, no dividend may be paid to common stockholders. The stated dividends on preferred stock may also be *cumulative* in the event they are not paid in any given year or years.

Both preferred stock and common stock are shown in the stockholders' equity section of the balance sheet. Preferred stock is usually listed before common stock.

4.   **Explain how to account for different types of stock issued by corporations.**

The accounting treatment of stock depends on whether or not it has a par value. When stock with a par value is issued, cash is increased for the full issue price. but the Common Stock or Preferred Stock account is increased only for the total par value of the stock (par value per share multiplied by the number of shares issued). The difference between the total issue price of the stock and its total par value is recorded in a stockholders' account titled *Paid-in Capital in*

Excess of Par. The sum of the balances in the Common Stock account, Preferred Stock account, and their related Paid-in Excess of Par accounts is often referred to as simply, *paid-in capital.*

5.   Show how treasury stock transactions affect a company's financial statements.

When a company buys its own previously issued stock, that stock is called treasury stock. The purchase of treasury stock causes assets, specifically cash, to decrease. This event also causes equity to decrease. The way in which equity decreases is unusual. Treasury stock is **not** considered a reduction of common stock or retained earnings. Rather, treasury stock is a separate, negative category of equity. The treasury stock account is **not** a contra account in the technical sense, but it behaves much like a contra account.

When a company sells treasury stock, its assets increase, and the negative equity account, treasury stock, decreases. Decreasing a negative equity account causes total equity to increase. Treasury stock may be sold for more or less than the amount the corporation paid for it, but **the difference is not a gain or loss**. A business cannot recognize a gain or loss on capital exchanges. Any difference between the purchase and selling price of treasury stock will affect paid-in capital (and in some cases, retained earnings).

6.   Explain the effects of declaring and paying cash dividends on a company's financial statements.

Cash dividends are distributions of retained earnings; they are not expenses. Dividends are typically *declared* on one date and paid at a later date that was designated at the time of declaration. On the date of declaration retained earnings will be reduced, and liabilities will be increased. Even though the dividend is being paid to the owners of the business, it is a legal obligation of the business. On the date the dividend is actually paid, cash will be decreased and the liability that was established on the date of declaration will be removed from the books. Thus, the net effect on the financial statements is to reduce assets and retained earnings.

7.   Explain the effects of stock dividends and stock splits on a company's financial statements.

There are few, if any, substantive effects of a stock dividend or split on the financial statements of a business. Stock dividends result in numbers, not real dollars, being transferred from the retained earnings account (an equity account) to the paid-in capital accounts (other equity accounts). Stock splits do even less. They simply reduce the par value (if one exists) of the company's stock. The balance in paid-in capital and retained earnings will be the same before and after a stock split. **Stock dividends and splits do** have a significant **effect** on the **market price** of the stock involved; generally, the price of the stock will go down in proportion to the percentage of additional shares being issued in the split or dividend.

8.   Show how the appropriation of retained earnings affects financial statements.

The appropriation of retained earnings does not change total assets, liabilities, or equity. It simply separates the balance of total retained earnings into two accounts. After the appropriation, there will be one account for *unappropriated retained earnings* and a separate account for *appropriated retained earnings*.

9.   Explain some uses of accounting information in making stock investment decisions.

The financial statements alone do not provide enough information to make a well-informed decision about stock investments. However, financial statements, along with other accounting information, can help. For example, accounting information can help the reader assess a company's financial position (from the balance sheet), and determine what it has been doing to generate and use cash (from the statement of cash flows). Although most accounting information is historical in perspective, the MD&A section of the annual report provides some information about how management views future prospects of the company. A company's *P/E ratio* gives an indication about how the market views future prospects of the company.

10.   Explain accounting for not-for-profit entities and governmental organizations.

Many of the accounting procedures used at not-for-profit (NFP) entities are the same as those used by profit-oriented entities. The major differences are caused by the fact that NFP entities do not have a profit motive. Unlike commercial enterprises, their primary strategy is not to spend money to make money. Nevertheless they do prepare financial statements that are similar in appearance and informational content to those prepared by businesses.

Self-Study Problems

Articulation Problems

For each situation below, indicate its effects on the accounting elements shown on the accompanying chart. Use the following letters to indicate your answer (you do not need to enter amounts):

Increase = **I**   Decrease = **D**   No effect = **N**

1.   On January 1, 2006, Macon Co. issued 100,000 shares of no-par common stock for $12 per share.

Assets	Liabilities	Equity	Revenues	Expenses	Net Income	Cash

2.   On January 1, 2007, Albany Co. issued 20,000 shares of 8% preferred stock that has a $100 par value per share.

Assets	Liabilities	Equity	Revenues	Expenses	Net Income	Cash

3.   On December 31, 2006, Macon Co. declared a $.50 per share cash dividend on common stock. The dividend will be paid on February 1, 2007. Record the effects of the declaration.

Assets	Liabilities	Equity	Revenues	Expenses	Net Income	Cash

4.   On February 1, 2007, Macon Co. paid the cash dividend that had been declared on December 31, 2006.

Assets	Liabilities	Equity	Revenues	Expenses	Net Income	Cash

5.   On November 30, 2007, Dawson Co. declared and issued a 10% stock dividend.

Assets	Liabilities	Equity	Revenues	Expenses	Net Income	Cash

6.   On December 15, 2006, Savannah Co. issued a 2-for-1 stock split.

Assets	Liabilities	Equity	Revenues	Expenses	Net Income	Cash

7.   On June 20, 2007, Pocatello Co. purchased 1,000 shares of its own common stock. Pocatello Co. paid $15 per share for the treasury stock.

Assets	Liabilities	Equity	Revenues	Expenses	Net Income	Cash

8.   On October 15, 2007, Pocatello Co. sold 500 shares of the treasury stock it had purchased on June 20, (see event 7). Pocatello sold the stock for $17 per share.

Assets	Liabilities	Equity	Revenues	Expenses	Net Income	Cash

9.   On December 15, 2007, Pocatello Co. sold the remaining 500 shares of the treasury stock it had purchased on June 20 (see event 7). Pocatello sold these shares for $12 per share.

Assets	Liabilities	Equity	Revenues	Expenses	Net Income	Cash

Multiple-Choice Problems

1.   Which of the following is <u>not</u> an advantage of the corporate form of business organization?
   a.   Amount of regulation
   b.   Continuity of life
   c.   Limited liability
   d.   Transfer of ownership

2.   As of December 31, 2009, Butte Co. has the following outstanding stock:

   Common Stock: 200,000 shares of $10 par value.
   Preferred Stock: 10,000 shares of 5%, $100 par value, cumulative.

   Butte Co. did not pay any dividends in 2007 or 2008. In December of 2009 Butte declared $300,000 of cash dividends. How much dividend will be paid on each share of preferred stock?
   a. $ 5
   b. $10
   c. $15
   d. $30

3. Peoria Co. had 10,000 shares of common stock outstanding. The stock, which had a par value of $2, was originally issued for $5 per share. At a time when the stock had a market value of $15 per share, Peoria issued a 10% stock dividend. Which of the following statements regarding this stock dividend is true?
   a. Issuing the stock dividend caused total assets to decrease.
   b. Issuing the stock dividend caused the par value of the stock to decrease.
   c. Issuing the stock dividend caused net income to decrease.
   d. Issuing the stock dividend caused retained earnings to decrease.

4. Decatur Co. issued 5,000 shares of common stock for $8 per share. The stock has a par value of $5 per share. How should this event be recorded?

   a.   Cash   40,000
              Common Stock   40,000

   b.   Cash   40,000
              Common Stock   25,000
              Paid-in Capital in Excess of Par Value   15,000

   c.   Cash   40,000
              Common Stock   15,000
              Paid-in Capital in Excess of Par Value   25,000

   d.   Cash   40,000
              Common Stock   25,000
              Retained Earnings   15,000

The following information applies to questions 5 through 7.

The following information was available for Hilltop Co. as of July 1, 2006:

Total Assets	$1,000,000
Total Liabilities	400,000
Common Stock ($10 par value, 5,000 shares outstanding)	50,000
Paid-in Capital in Excess of Par Value	200,000
Retained Earnings	350,000

5. On July 15, 2006, Hilltop purchased 100 shares of treasury stock for $70 per share. What will be the amount of total stockholders' equity after this transaction?
   a. $600,000
   b. $593,000
   c. $250,000
   d. $243,000

6.   On September 20, 2006, Hilltop sold 50 shares of the treasury stock for $75 per share. (This is the same stock that had been purchased for $70 per share on July 15.) Which of the following statements is true regarding this sale of treasury stock?
  a.   Assets were increased by $250.
  b.   Equity was increased by $3,750.
  c.   Equity was increased by $250.
  d.   The sale had no effect on total assets or total equity.

7.   On November 1, 2006, Hilltop sold the remaining 50 shares of the treasury stock for $60 per share. (This is the same stock that had been purchased for $70 per share on July 15.) Which of the following statements is true regarding this sale of treasury stock?
  a.   Assets increased by $3,000.
  b.   Assets decreased by $500.
  c.   Equity increased by $500.
  d.   Equity decreased by $3,000.

8.   At a time when Yazoo Co. had 50,000 shares of $20 par value common stock outstanding, it issued a 10% stock dividend. Immediately prior to the issuance of the dividend Yazoo's stock was selling for $30 per share. Which of the following journal entries correctly records the issuance of this stock dividend?

  a.   Cash   150,000
              Common Stock   100,000
              Paid-in Capital in Excess of Par Value   50,000

  b.   Common Stock   100,000
          Paid-in Capital in Excess of Par Value   50,000
              Dividend Payable   150,000

  c.   Dividend Payable   150,000
              Common Stock   100,000
              Paid-in Capital in Excess of Par Value   50,000

  d.   Retained Earnings   150,000
              Common Stock   100,000
              Paid-in Capital in Excess of Par Value   50,000

9.   Chicago Co. had 100,000 shares of $10 par value common stock outstanding. If Chicago issued a 2-for-1 stock split, which of the following statements is false?
  a.   The stock split will reduce the par value of common stock to $5 per share.
  b.   After the split, 200,000 shares of common stock will be outstanding.
  c.   The split will double the **total** market value of each stockholder's stock.
  d.   The stock split will have no effect on Chicago's current ratio.

10.   At December 31, 2007, Marion Co. had the following stock outstanding:

     10,000 shares of 8%, $50 par value preferred stock.
     90,000 shares of $5 par value common stock.

If the board of directors declares cash dividends of $150,000, what amount of dividends would each class of stockholders receive?

	Preferred Stockholders	Common Stockholders
a.	$15,000	$135,000
b.	$75,000	$ 75,000
c.	$40,000	$110,000
d.	$80,000	$ 70,000

11.   The following information is available for Greensburg Co. as of December 31, 2008.

Cash	$ 10,000	Common Stock ($10 par value)	$20,000
Total Assets	100,000	Paid-in Capital in Excess of Par	26,000
Total Liabilities	30,000	Retained Earnings	54,000

What was the sales price per share of the original stock issue?
a. $10
b. $23
c. $35
d. $50

12.   Port Co. declared and paid a cash dividend. Which of the following choices reflects how this event would affect the company's financial statements?

	Assets	=	Liab.	+	Equity	Rev	−	Exp.	=	Net Inc.	Cash
a.	D		N		D	N		N		N	D
b.	N		D		D	N		N		N	N
c.	D		N		D	N		I		D	D
d.	N		N		N	N		N		N	D

13.   Warterloo Co. issued a stock dividend. Which of the following choices reflects how this event would affect the company's financial statements?

	Assets	=	Liab.	+	Equity	Rev	–	Exp.	=	Net Inc.	Cash
a.	D		N		D	N		N		N	D
b.	N		I		D	N		N		N	N
c.	N		I		D	N		I		D	N
d.	N		N		N	N		N		N	N

14.   Tulsa Co. repurchased 200 shares of its own stock for $25 per share. The stock was issued originally at $20 per share. Which of the following choices reflects how this event would affect the company's financial statements?

	Assets	=	Liab.	+	Equity	Rev	–	Exp.	=	Net Inc.	Cash
a.	D		N		D	N		N		N	D
b.	N		N		N	N		N		N	N
c.	D		N		D	N		I		D	D
d.	I		N		I	N		N		N	I

15.   Topeka Co. had net income of $1,000,000 in 2008. Throughout the year Topeka had 200,000 shares of $10 par value common stock outstanding. At December 31, 2008, Topeka's stock was selling in the market at $60 per share. What was the P/E ratio of Topeka's stock?
   a.   12
   b.   6
   c.   5
   d.   2

16.   The following account balances are available for Colby Co. **before** it purchased a new truck:

Total Assets	$150,000	Net Earnings	$ 5,000
Common Stock	20,000	Dividends per share	2.50
Retained Earnings	30,000	Selling price/share of stock	7.50
Sales	100,000	Shares of stock outstanding	10,000

   What is Colby's P/E ratio?
   a.   3
   b.   15
   c.   20
   d.   30

17. Which of the following companies would probably have the <u>highest</u> P/E ratio?
     a. A company that had relatively low earnings in the last year, and is not expected to show much improvement in the near future.
     b. A company that had relatively high earnings in the last year, and is expected to have earnings in the near future that are neither higher nor lower than those of the last year.
     c. A company that had relatively low earnings in the last year, but is expected to have higher earnings in the near future.
     d. A company that had relatively high earnings in the last year, but is expected to have lower earnings in the near future.

Multiple True-False Problems

1. Indicate if each of the following statements regarding the advantages and disadvantages of different forms of business organizations is true or false.
    a. One advantage of a sole proprietorship over a partnership is that sole proprietorships are not subject to double taxation, but partnerships are.
    b. One advantage of a corporation over a sole proprietorship is that owners of corporations have limited liability, but the owner of a sole proprietorship does not.
    c. One advantage of a partnership over a corporation is that transfer of ownership is easier at a partnership.
    d. A disadvantage of a corporation compared to a partnership is that corporations are subject to greater regulation
    e. Double taxation, one potential disadvantage of a corporation, is not a problem for an "S corporation."

2. Indicate if each of the following statements related to capital stock and capital stock transactions is true or false.
    a. When a company issues common stock, its paid-in capital will increase by the same amount whether the stock has a par value, a stated value, or has neither.
    b. The number of shares of outstanding stock that a company has can never be less than the number of shares it has issued.
    c. The higher the par value of a company's common stock, the higher its market value will be.
    d. A person planning to invest in preferred stock would prefer preferred stock that is cumulative to stock that is noncumulative.
    e. A person who is going to receive 200 shares of 6% preferred stock as a gift would not care if the stock had a $50 par value or a $100 par value.

3.   Presented below is the Stockholders' Equity section of Alexandra Company's balance sheet.

Paid-in Capital
    Preferred Stock, $100 par value, 7% noncumulative, 20,000
        shares authorized, 10,000 shares issued, and ??? shares outstanding $1,000,000
    Common Stock, ?? par value, 500,000 shares authorized, 100,000
        shares issued and outstanding   1,500,000
    Paid-in-capital in Excess of Par - Preferred   20,000
    Paid-in-capital in Excess of Par - Common   2,500,000
Total Paid-in Capital $5,020,000
Retained earnings   1,780,000

Less: Treasury Stock, 3,000 shares of Preferred Stock purchased at $90 per share   ???,???
Total Stockholders' Equity $?,???,???

Indicate if each of the following statements related to Alexandra Company's stockholders' equity is true or false.

a.   Alexandra has 7,000 shares of preferred stock outstanding.
b.   The total stockholders' equity of Alexandra is $6,530,000
c.   The par value of Alexandra's common stock is $3 per share.
d.   Alexandra's preferred stock was issued originally at an average price of $100 per share.
e.   If Alexandra sells the preferred stock it now holds as treasury stock for $80 per share, its total stockholders' equity would increase.

Exercise-Type Problem

P-1.   The following events occurred during the first two years of operations at the Old Town Co.

Date	Event
2006	
Jan. 10	Issued 20,000 shares of $1 par value common stock, at $5 per share.
Feb. 1	Issued 1,000 shares of $100 par value, 8% preferred stock, at $110 per share.
July 1	Issued 10,000 shares of $1 par value common stock, at $6 per share.
Dec. 31	Closed the revenue and expense accounts to retained earnings. The revenue account had a balance of $100,000. Balances in the expense accounts totaled $70,000.
Dec. 31	Declared cash dividends of $11,000; this includes the dividends on preferred stock. Dividends will be paid on February 15, 2007, to stockholders of record on January 15, 2007.
Dec. 31	Closed the dividends account to retained earnings.

P-1 (continued)

2007

Feb. 15	Paid the dividends that were declared on December 31, 2006.
Apr. 30	Purchased 500 shares of common stock (treasury stock) for $7 per share.
Sep. 20	Sold 200 shares of the treasury stock for $8 per share.
Dec. 31	Closed the revenue and expense accounts to retained earnings. The revenue account had a balance of $150,000. Balances in the expense accounts totaled $100,000.
Dec. 31	Declared dividends on the preferred stock. No dividend was declared on the common stock. Dividends will be paid on February 15, 2006, to stockholders of record on January 15, 2006.
Dec. 31	Closed dividends account to retained earnings.

Required:
1. Prepare the journal entries to record the events described above. Use the space provided on the following page.
2. Prepare the stockholders' equity sections of the 2006 and 2007 balance sheets. Use the forms provided. (Note: You may find it helpful to post the journal entries to T-accounts before trying to prepare the balance sheet disclosures.)

P-1.   Space for answering requirement 1   Journal entries for 2006:

Jan. 10 _____   _____ _____
        _____   _____ _____
        _____   _____ _____

Feb. 1 _____   _____ _____
        _____   _____ _____
        _____   _____ _____

July 1 _____   _____ _____
        _____   _____ _____
        _____   _____ _____

Dec. 31 _____   _____ _____
        _____   _____ _____
        _____   _____ _____

Dec. 31 _____   _____ _____
        _____   _____ _____

Dec. 31 _____   _____ _____
        _____   _____ _____

Jan. 1 _____   _____ _____
        _____   _____ _____
        _____   _____ _____

Journal entries for 2007:

Feb. 15 _____   _____ _____
        _____   _____ _____

April 30 _____   _____ _____
        _____   _____ _____

Sep. 20 _____   _____ _____
        _____   _____ _____
        _____   _____ _____

Dec. 31 _____   _____ _____
        _____   _____ _____
        _____   _____ _____

Dec. 31 _____   _____ _____
        _____   _____ _____

Dec. 31 _____   _____ _____
        _____   _____ _____

Forms for requirement 2

Old Town Company
Balance Sheet
As of December 31, 2006

Stockholders' Equity:

Preferred Stock, $_____ par value, __%, cumulative,
_____ shares issued and outstanding $

Common Stock, $____ par value, _____ shares
   issued and outstanding

Paid-in Capital in Excess of Par - Preferred

Paid-in Capital in Excess of Par - Common   _____

   Total Paid-in Capital $

Retained Earnings   _____

   Total Stockholders' Equity $_____

Old Town Company
Balance Sheet
As of December 31, 2007

Stockholders' Equity:

Preferred Stock, $_____ par value, __%, cumulative,
_____ shares issued and outstanding $

Common Stock, $____ par value, _____ shares
   issued and _____ shares outstanding

Paid-in Capital in Excess of Par - Preferred

Paid-in Capital in Excess of Par - Common

Paid-in Capital in Excess of Cost of Treasury Stock   _____

   Total Paid-in Capital $

Retained Earnings

Less: Treasury Stock, _____ shares at $___ per share   _____

   Total Stockholders' Equity $_____

Solutions to Self-Study Problems

Articulation Problems

1. On January 1, 2006, Macon Co. issued 100,000 shares of no-par common stock for $12 per share.

Assets	Liabilities	Equity	Revenues	Expenses	Net Income	Cash
I	N	I	N	N	N	I

Assets increased because cash was received. Equity, specifically paid-in capital, increased because the owners invested money in the business through the purchase of stock.

2. On January 1, 2007, Albany Co. issued 20,000 shares of 8% preferred stock that has a $100 par value per share.

Assets	Liabilities	Equity	Revenues	Expenses	Net Income	Cash
I	N	I	N	N	N	I

Assets increased because cash was received. Equity, specifically paid-in capital, increased because owners invested money in the business through the purchase of stock. Notice that the results are the same whether common or preferred stock was issued.

3. On December 31, 2006, Macon Co. declared a $.50 per share cash dividend on common stock. The dividend will be paid on February 1, 2007. Record the effects of the declaration.

Assets	Liabilities	Equity	Revenues	Expenses	Net Income	Cash
N	I	D	N	N	N	N

Liabilities increased because the company is obligated to make a payment in the future. The liability involved was Dividends Payable, a current liability. Equity decreased because dividends represent a distribution of the retained earnings of the business.

4. On February 1, 2007, Macon Co. paid the cash dividend that had been declared on December 31, 2006.

Assets	Liabilities	Equity	Revenues	Expenses	Net Income	Cash
D	D	N	N	N	N	D

Assets decreased because cash was paid to stockholders. Because the promised dividends have now been paid, the company no longer owes the Dividends Payable. Thus, liabilities were decreased.

5. On November 30, 2007, Dawson Co. declared and issued a 10% stock dividend.

Assets	Liabilities	Equity	Revenues	Expenses	Net Income	Cash
N	N	N	N	N	N	N

Stock dividends cause numbers, not cash, to be transferred from one category of equity, retained earnings, to another category of equity, paid-in capital. Total equity was not affected.

6.   On December 15, 2006, Savannah Co. issued a 2-for-1 stock split.

Assets	Liabilities	Equity	Revenues	Expenses	Net Income	Cash
N	N	N	N	N	N	N

This has no effect on anything on the financial statements except to double the number of outstanding shares of common stock (and reduce the par value per share by 50% if the stock has a par value). The price of the stock in the stock market would decrease, but this does not affect the financial statements.

7.   On June 20, 2007, Pocatello Co. purchased 1,000 shares of its own common stock. Pocatello Co. paid $15 per share for the treasury stock.

Assets	Liabilities	Equity	Revenues	Expenses	Net Income	Cash
D	N	D	N	N	N	D

Assets decreased because cash was spent to acquire the treasury stock. Equity decreased because the balance in the treasury stock account increased, and it is a **negative** equity account.

8.   On October 15, 2007, Pocatello Co. sold 500 shares of the treasury stock it had purchased on June 20 (see event 7). Pocatello sold the stock for $17 per share.

Assets	Liabilities	Equity	Revenues	Expenses	Net Income	Cash
I	N	I	N	N	N	I

Assets increased because the company received cash. Equity increased because treasury stock, a negative equity account, was reduced.

9.   On December 15, 2007, Pocatello Co. sold the remaining 500 shares of the treasury stock it had purchased on June 20 (see event 7). Pocatello sold these shares for $12 per share.

Assets	Liabilities	Equity	Revenues	Expenses	Net Income	Cash
I	N	I	N	N	N	I

Assets increased because the company received cash. Equity increased because treasury stock, a negative equity account, was reduced. Notice that the effects were the same whether treasury stock was sold for more than its original purchase price, (event 8), or less than its original purchase price, (event 9). Gains and losses are not recognized on treasury stock transactions.

Multiple-Choice Problems

1.   a.

2.   c.

Par value per share	$100
x Dividend percentage	5%
x Years of dividends to be paid	3 years
	$ 15

3.   d.

4. b.

5. b.

Common Stock	$ 50,000
Paid in Capital in Excess of Par Value	200,000
Retained Earnings	350,000
Less: Treasury Stock (100 shares @ $70)	(7,000)
Total Stockholders' Equity	**$593,000**

6. b.

Increase in Equity due to
        decrease in Treasury Stock: (50 shares @ $70) $3,500
Increase in Equity due to
        sale of Treasury Stock in excess of cost: (50 shares x ($75 – $70)   250
Total increase in Equity   **$3,750**

7. a.   Assets increased by the amount of cash received: (50 shares @ $60)   **$3,000**

8. d.   **First**, compute the number of new shares issued:

Shares outstanding	50,000
Percentage of stock dividend	10%
New shares issued	**5,000**

Next, compute the Market Value, Total Par Value, and Paid-in Capital in Excess of Par Value on the new shares issued:

Market Value (5,000 shares @ $30) [**Decrease** in Retained Earnings] **$150,000**
Total Par Value (5,000 shares @ $20) [**Increase** in Common Stock] **$100,000**
Paid-in Capital in Excess of Par Value [5,000 shares @ ($30 – $20)] **$ 50,000**

9. c.

10. c.

Preferred Stockholders			**Common Stockholders**	
Shares outstanding	10,000 shares		Total dividends declared	$150,000
x Par Value per share	$ 50		less: Div. on Preferred Stock	40,000
x Dividend percentage	8%		Dividends on Common Stock	**$110,000**
Div. on Preferred Stock	**$40,000**			

11.   b.   **First**, compute the total amount received from the sale of Common Stock:
Common Stock $20,000
+ Paid-in Capital in Excess of Par Value   26,000
Total received from issuance of common stock $46,000

Next, compute the total number of shares that were issued:
Total par value of common stock ÷ Par value per share = Number of shares issued
            $20,000   ÷ $10   =   2,000 shares

Finally, compute the sales price per share:
Total from sale of common stock ÷ Number of shares issued = Sales price per share
            $46,000   ÷   2,000 shares   = $23 per share

12.   a.   Assets decreased because cash was paid to stockholders. Equity decreased because dividends represent a distribution of the retained earnings of the business.

13.   d.   See articulation problem 5 for an explanation of the correct answer.

14.   a.   See articulation problem 7 for an explanation of the correct answer.

15.   a.   First, compute earnings per share (EPS):   **Net Income ÷ Shares Outstanding = EPS**
                                                          $1,000,000 ÷   200,000   = $5

Next, compute the P/E Ratio: **Price per Share ÷ EPS = P/E Ratio**
                                                              $60   ÷ $5 =   12

16.   b.   First, compute earnings per share (EPS):

Net Earnings   ÷   Shares Outstanding   =   EPS
   $5,000   ÷   10,000   = $.50

Then, compute the P/E ratio:

Price per Share ÷   EPS   =   P/E Ratio
    $7.50   ÷ $.50   =   15 times

17.   c.   The stock of a company whose earnings are expected to rise in the future usually has a higher selling price than a company whose future earnings are expected to be flat or falling. A higher price in the numerator of the P/E ratio causes it to be higher. Furthermore, the lower a company's EPS, the smaller the denominator in the P/E ratio, which also causes the P/E ratio to be higher.

Multiple True-False Problems

1. a.   **False**, partnerships are not subject to double taxation.
    b.   **True**.
    c.   **False**, because the stock of corporations can be traded easily, in the absence of restrictive covenants, ownership is more easily transferred in corporations than in partnerships.
    d.   **True**.
    e.   **True**.

2. a.   **True**, if the stock does not have a par value or stated value, the Common Stock account is increased for the entire amount received from issuing the stock. If the stock has a par value or stated value, the Paid-in Capital in Excess of Par (or Stated) Value account is increased for a portion of the issuance price, but, like the Common Stock account, this account is a paid-in capital account.
    b.   **False**, the number of shares outstanding can be less than the total number of shares issued, because some of the shares issued may have been repurchased. These repurchased shares are recorded in the Treasury Stock account. Even though the shares are not considered to be "outstanding," they are still considered to be "issued."
    c.   **False**, the par value of common stock is not related to its market value.
    d.   **True**.
    e.   **False**, "6% preferred stock" indicates that the stock is expected to pay an annual dividend that is equal to 6% of the stock's par value. Thus, it would be better to own preferred stock with a $100 par value than with a $50 par value.

3. a.   **True**, Alexandra issued 10,000 shares of preferred stock, but there are 3,000 shares being held as treasury stock. Thus, 7,000 shares are outstanding.
    b.   **True**. First, the balance in the Treasury Stock account must be computed. It is a negative $270,000 (3,000 shares x $90). Then the amount of total stockholders' equity can be computed. ($5,020,000 + $1,780,000 – $270,000 = $6,530,000)
    c.   **False**, the par value of common stock is $15 per share. ($1,500,000 ÷ 100,000 shares issued = 15)
    d.   **False**, the preferred stock was issued at an average price of $102 per share, computed as follows:

Total par value of the preferred stock	$1,000,000
Plus, the balance in paid-in capital in excess of par - preferred	20,000
Total issue price of the preferred stock	1,020,000
Divided by total shared of preferred stock issued	÷ 10,000 shares
Average issues price per share	$ 102

    e.   **True**, even if the preferred stock being held as treasury stock is sold for less than the price for which it was purchased, total stockholders' equity will increase when it is sold. When treasury stock is sold, the balance in the Treasury Stock account decreases. Because the Treasury Stock account is a negative equity account, a decrease in its balance causes total equity to increase.

Solution to Exercise-Type Problem

Solution to requirement 1

Journal Entries for 2006:

Jan. 10	Cash (20,000 shares x $5)	100,000	
	Common Stock (20,000 shares x $1 par value)		20,000
	Paid-in Capital in Excess of Par Value - Common Stock		80,000
Feb. 1	Cash (1,000 shares x $110)	110,000	
	Preferred Stock (1,000 shares x $100 par value)		100,000
	Paid-in Capital in Excess of Par Value - Preferred Stock		10,000
July 1	Cash (10,000 shares x $6)	60,000	
	Common Stock (10,000 shares x $1 par value)		10,000
	Paid-in Capital in Excess of Par Value - Common Stock		50,000
Dec. 31	Revenue	100,000	
	Expenses		70,000
	Retained Earnings		30,000
Dec. 31	Dividends	11,000	
	Dividends Payable		11,000
Dec. 31	Retained Earnings	11,000	
	Dividends		11,000

Journal Entries for 2007:

Feb. 15	Dividends Payable	11,000	
	Cash		11,000
Apr. 30	Treasury Stock (500 shares x $7)	3,500	
	Cash		3,500
Sep. 20	Cash (200 shares x $8)	1,600	
	Treasury Stock (200 shares x $7)		1,400
	Paid-in Capital in Excess of Cost of Treasury Stock		200
Dec. 31	Revenue	150,000	
	Expenses		100,000
	Retained Earnings		50,000
Dec. 31	Dividends (1,000 shares x $100 par value x 8%)	8,000	
	Dividends Payable		8,000
Dec. 31	Retained Earnings	8,000	
	Dividends		8,000

Solution to requirement 2

Old Town Company
Balance Sheet
As of December 31, 2006

Stockholders' Equity:

Preferred Stock, $100 par value, 8%, cumulative;		
1,000 shares issued and outstanding	$100,000	
Common Stock, $1 par value; 30,000 shares		
issued and outstanding	30,000	
Paid-in Capital in Excess of Par - Preferred	10,000	
Paid-in Capital in Excess of Par - Common	130,000	
Total Paid-in Capital		$270,000
Retained Earnings		19,000
Total Stockholders' Equity		$289,000

Old Town Company
Balance Sheet
As of December 31, 2007

Stockholders' Equity:

Preferred Stock, $100 par value, 8%, cumulative;		
1,000 shares issued and outstanding	$100,000	
Common Stock, $1 par value; 30,000 shares		
issued and 29,700 shares outstanding	30,000	
Paid-in Capital in Excess of Par - Preferred	10,000	
Paid-in Capital in Excess of Par - Common	130,000	
Paid-in Capital in Excess of Cost of Treasury Stock	200	
Total Paid-in Capital		$270,200
Retained Earnings		61,000
Less: Treasury Stock, 300 shares at $7 per share		(2,100)
Total Stockholders' Equity		$329,100

Chapter Twelve
Statement of Cash Flows

Learning Objectives for the Chapter

After completing this chapter you should be able to:

1. Identify the types of business events that are reported in the three sections of the statement of cash flows.
2. Convert an accrual account balance to cash.
3. Use the T-account method to prepare a statement of cash flows.
4. Explain how the indirect method differs flow from the direct method in reporting cash flow from operating activities.
5. Explain how the statement of cash flows could mislead decision makers if not interpreted with care.

Brief Explanation of the Learning Objectives

1. Identify the types of business events that are reported in the three sections of the statement of cash flows.

There are three sections of the statement of cash flows: operating, investing, and financing. The following general rules describe the types of events that usually go in each section. There are exceptions to these rules, but they are beyond the scope of this course.

The *operating section* includes events that typically affect net income; these are mostly related to revenues and expenses. The official pronouncement from the FASB says that anything that is not an investing or financing activity is an operating activity, but the general rule given in the previous sentence usually works.

The *investing section* includes cash activities related to the acquisition and disposal of assets **not** directly related to period expenses (for example, prepaid rent is related to rent expense). Usually, but not always, this means cash activity related to long-term assets is reported as an investing activity.

The *financing section* includes cash flow activity related to obtaining and repaying the financial resources of the business. This includes the borrowing and the repaying of most debt, issuing stock, treasury stock transactions, and the payment of cash dividends. Interest paid on debt goes in the *operating* section.

Significant events that do not involve cash are disclosed in the footnotes to the statement of cash flows, **not** on the statement itself. An example would be if a company acquires land by giving the owner a 5-year note payable.

2.   Convert an accrual account balance to cash.

Usually, revenues and expenses on the income statement do not represent the amount of cash actually received or paid during that accounting period. To convert the accrual-based amounts on the income statement into their cash equivalents usually involves analyzing activity in a related balance sheet account. For example, to determine the amount of cash received due to sales, it is necessary to adjust the *sales* figure appearing on the income statement for the change that occurred in *the accounts receivable* accounts that appear on the current period's and the prior period's balance sheets. This objective is covered in detail with the self-study problems.

3.   Use the T-account method to prepare a statement of cash flows.

Exercise-type problem P-3 is intended to cover this learning objective.

4.   Explain how the indirect method differs flow from the direct method in reporting cash flow from operating activities.

Most companies use the ***indirect method*** to report net cash flow from operating activities (CFO). To determine CFO, this method begins with a company's net earnings, or more precisely, its operating earnings, and this amount is adjusted to determine CFO. The adjustments involved are due to business events that affected net earnings, which is an accrual-based measurement, differently than they affected cash flows. Most of the events that cause adjustments relate to items affecting current assets and current liabilities. However, the largest single adjustment usually is due to depreciation expense.

The ***direct method***, in essence, determines CFO by preparing a cash-based earnings statement. All cash revenues are listed, and all cash expenses are subtracted from the cash revenues. Rather than refer to cash revenues minus cash expenses as cash net earnings, it is called CFO.

5.   Explain how the statement of cash flows could mislead decision makers if not interpreted with care.

The statement of cash flows is divided into three categories: *operating activities*, *investing activities*, and *financing activities*. The classification of several different events might provide misleading information to decision makers, but the two that follow are common occurrences.

If a company builds a new retail store, the cash spent to acquire the long-term assets (land, building, and equipment) are reported as *investing activities*. However, the cash paid to purchase inventory for the new store is reported as an *operating activity*, even though the new inventory is just as much an investment in the new store as the building itself.

If a company replaces an old machine with a new machine, this cash outflow is reported as an *investing activity*. Thus, the company's statement of cash flows gives the impression that the company is expanding when, in fact, its productive capacity is basically unchanged. The statement of cash flows does not give readers a way to distinguish cash expenditures that **expand** a company's capacity from those that merely **maintain** its existing capacity.

Self-Study Problems

Matching Problem

Listed below are 20 business events. In the space provided at the end of each description, indicate which section of the statement of cash flows, if any, would be affected by that event. If an event involves more than one type of activity, indicate all activities involved. Assume the *indirect method* was used. Use the following letters to indicate your answer:

Operating Activities = **O**
Investing Activities = **I**
Financing Activities = **F**
Not on the SCF = **N**

1. The monthly electricity bill was paid with cash.
2. Purchased inventory for cash.
3. Purchased equipment for cash.
4. Issued common stock for cash.
5. Recorded depreciation expense.
6. Purchased equipment using a note payable.
7. Issued a term note for cash.
8. Paid cash for three months rent in advance.
9. Recognized that one month's prepaid rent had expired.
10. Paid cash interest on bonds payable.
11. Purchased treasury stock with cash.
12. Sold treasury stock for more that it's original cost; received cash.
13. Sold, for cash, an old piece of equipment. The equipment was sold for an amount equal to its book value.
14. Sold, for cash, an old piece of equipment. The equipment was sold for an amount less than its book value (i.e., at a loss).
15. Made the annual cash payment for principal and interest on a term loan.
16. Recorded amortization on a patent.
17. Made cash sales.
18. Collected cash from accounts receivable.
19. Paid cash dividends.
20. Issued a stock dividend.

Multiple-Choice Problems

1. Derek Co. reported sales of $50,000 in 2007. Derek's balance sheets for 2006 and 2007 showed the following:

	2006	2007
Accounts Receivable	$10,000	$12,000
Accounts Payable	7,000	10,000

    Based on this information, how much cash did Derek collect from sales during 2007?
    a. $53,000
    b. $52,000
    c. $48,000
    d. $47,000

2. Gordon Co. reported utilities expense of $15,000 in 2007. Utilities Payable was $4,000 on January 1, 2007, and $3,000 on December 31, 2007. How much cash did Gordon pay for utilities during 2007?
    a. $15,000
    b. $16,000
    c. $17,000
    d. $19,000

3. In what sections of the statement of cash flows should companies report cash dividends paid and cash dividends received?

	Dividends Paid	Dividends Received
a.	Financing	Operating
b.	Financing	Investing
c.	Operating	Financing
d.	Operating	Operating

4. In what sections of the statement of cash flows should companies report cash borrowed with a note payable and interest paid on the note payable?

	Cash Borrowed with Note Payable	Interest Paid on Note Payable
a.	Financing	Financing
b.	Investing	Operating
c.	Financing	Operating
d.	Operating	Financing

5. Which of the following would be a cash inflow from investing activities?
    a.   Borrowed cash by issuing bonds payable.
    b.   Sold inventory for cash.
    c.   Exchanged land for common stock of another company.
    d.   Sold used equipment at a loss.

6. Jensen Co. reported $20,000 of rent expense on its 2006 income statement. The balance in Prepaid Rent was $6,000 on December 31, 2005, and $4,000 on December 31, 2006. How much cash did Jensen Co. pay for rent during 2006?
    a. $16,000
    b. $18,000
    c. $22,000
    d. $26,000

7. For 2007 Lane Co. reported *net income* of $750,000 and *net cash flows from operating activities* of $1,000,000. Which of the following could <u>not</u> have been a reason that Lane's net cash flows from operating activities were **greater** than its net income?
    a.   Depreciation expense.
    b.   Loss on sale of equipment.
    c.   Decrease in inventory from the beginning of the year to the end of the year.
    d.   Decrease in wages payable from the beginning of the year to the end of the year.

8. Consider the following events that occurred at Lewis Co. during 2008:

    Jan. 1   Issued bonds for $100,000.
    Jan. 20 Used cash from the sale of bonds to purchase equipment for $80,000.
    Oct. 1   Sold used equipment for $15,000. This equipment had been acquired in 2005, and was sold at a $5,000 loss.
    Dec. 31 Paid interest of $8,000 on the bonds.

    Based only on the facts above, what would be Lewis' *net cash flow from investing activities* for 2008?
    a. $95,000 decrease
    b. $65,000 decrease
    c. $10,000 increase
    d. $ 5,000 increase

9. On July 1, 2006, Neptune Co. sold a building for $100,000. The building had cost Neptune $300,000 fifteen years earlier, and had accumulated depreciation of $230,000 at the time of sale. What were the effects of this event on Neptune's net income and cash flows?

	Net Income	Cash Flows
a.	$200,000 decrease	$130,000 increase
b.	$ 30,000 increase	$ 70,000 increase
c.	$ 30,000 increase	$100,000 increase
d.	$ 70,000 increase	$100,000 increase

10. The following account balances are available for Perez Co.:

	December 31, 2006	December 31, 2007
Equipment	$500,000	$600,000
Accumulated Depreciation	200,000	240,000

    During 2007 Perez Co. sold equipment for $65,000 that had originally cost $80,000. At the time of the sale this equipment had accumulated depreciation of $30,000. How much equipment did Perez **purchase** during 2007?
    a. $110,000
    b. $140,000
    c. $150,000
    d. $180,000

11. In 2007 the Shark Co. had net income of $50,000. Depreciation expense for 2007 was $8,000. Listed below are net changes in selected account balances at Shark, for 2007:

	Net Increase or (Decrease)		Net Increase or (Decrease)
Cash	$(10,000)	Accounts Payable	$(11,000)
Accounts Receivable	13,000	Wages Payable	14,000
Inventory	(12,000)	Long-term Liabilities	12,000
Long-term Assets (net)	15,000		

    How much was Shark's *net cash flow from operating activities* for 2007?
    a. $60,000
    b. $63,000
    c. $70,000
    d. $73,000

Multiple True-False Problems

1. Indicate if each of the following statements regarding the statement of cash flows is true or false.

    a. If a company that operates a chain of retail stores is closing some of its stores, its positive cash flow from **investing** activities will probably be higher than those of a company in the same industry that is opening new stores.

    b. If a company that operates a chain of retail stores is opening new stores, its positive cash flow from **financing** activities will probably be higher than those of a company in the same industry that is neither opening new stores nor closing existing stores.

    c. If a company that operates a chain of retail stores is opening new stores, its positive cash flow from **operating** activities will probably be higher than those of a company in the same industry that is neither opening new stores nor closing existing stores.

    d. Assume a company only buys new equipment to replace old equipment that is being retired. The net cash flow from **investing** activities for this company will probably be neither significantly negative nor significantly positive.

    e. Over its lifetime, a company's cash flows from **operating** activities will probably exceed significantly its net earnings.

2. Consider the following events that occurred at the Yeager Co.

    Event 1
    On January 1, 2005, Yeager borrowed $100,000 from the City Bank and immediately used the cash to purchase land from Linda Lott.

    Event 2
    On January 1, 2005, Yeager bought land valued at $100,000 from Fred Farmer by agreeing to pay Fred the $100,000 plus accrued interest, in 10 equal installments over the next 10 years. Based on an interest rate of 6%, each payment will be $13,587.

    Event 3
    On July 15, 2007, Yeager sold the land it purchased from Linda Lott for $105,000, cash.

    Based on the three events described above, indicate if each of the following statements is true or false.

    a. As a result of Event 1, Yeager should show a $100,000 cash inflow from **financing** activities during 2005.

    b. As a result of Event 2, Yeager should show a $100,000 cash inflow from **financing** activities during 2005.

    c. As a result of Event 2, Yeager should show a $100,000 cash outflow from **investing** activities during 2005.

    d. As a result of Event 3, Yeager should show a $5,000 cash inflow from **operating** activities during 2007.

    e. As a result of Event 3, Yeager should show a $105,000 cash inflow from **investing** activities during 2007.

Exercise-Type Problems

P-1   The following account balances are available for the Abacus Co. for 2006 and 2007.

	December 31, 2006	December 31, 2007
Accounts Receivable	$70,000	$65,000
Prepaid Rent	10,000	14,000
Wages Payable	18,000	17,000
Interest Payable	12,000	15,000

Also available for 2007:

Sales	$900,000
Rent Expense	25,000
Wages Expense	107,000
Interest Expense	13,000

Required:

Based on the information above, prepare schedules or T-accounts to answer the following questions:

1. How much cash did Abacus collect from accounts receivable during 2007? Assume all sales were initially made on account.
2. How much cash did Abacus pay for rent during 2007?
3. How much cash did Abacus pay for wages during 2007?
4. How much cash did Abacus pay for interest during 2007?

Note: Partially completed schedules and T-accounts are provided for you to use in answering these questions, but you do not need to complete both. Some students understand the T-account method best; others prefer the scheduling technique.

Forms for answering P-1.

Schedule for Question 1

Sales	$
Beginning Accts. Rec.	_____
Max. that could have been collected	
Ending Accts. Rec.	_____
Cash collected	$ _____

T-Account for Question 1

Accounts Receivable		
Beg. Bal.	70,000	
Sales		
		Collected
End. Bal.	65,000	

Schedule for Question 2

Rent Expense $

Ending Prepaid Rent _____

Max. that could
  have been paid

Beg. Prepaid Rent _____

Cash Paid $ _____

T-Account for Question 2

Prepaid Rent

Beg. Bal.	10,000	
		Rent Exp.
Cash Paid		
End Bal.	14,000	

Schedule for Question 3

Wages Expense $

Beg. Wages Payable _____

Max. that could
  have been paid

End. Wages Payable _____

Cash Paid $ _____

T-Account for Question 3

Wages Payable

	18,000	Beg. Bal.
		Wages Exp.
Cash Paid		
	17,000	End. Bal.

Schedule for Question 4

Interest Expense $

Beg. Interest Payable _____

Max. that could
  have been paid

End. Interest Payable _____

Cash Paid $ _____

T-Account for Question 4

Interest Payable

	12,000	Beg. Bal.
		Wages Exp.
Cash Paid		
	15,000	End. Bal.

P-2   This problem is based on the same information presented in problem **P-1** with additional information provided. The information is presented here in a slightly different format; net increases and decreases are given rather than beginning and ending balances. There are several different ways to approach problems related to the statement of cash flows. The problems in this study guide deliberately present information in different ways to expose you to different problem-solving styles. Once you determine the way that works best for you, that method can be used to solve most SCF problems.

The following information is available for Abacus Co. for 2007:

Account:	Net Increase or (Decrease)
Accounts Receivable	$ (5,000)
Inventory	18,000
Prepaid Rent	4,000
Accounts Payable	(5,000)
Wages Payable	(1,000)
Interest Payable	3,000

Net Income for 2007 was $63,000.
Depreciation Expense for 2007 was $55,000.

Required:

Compute the *Net Cash Flow from Operating Activities* for Abacus Co. for the year ended December 31, 2007, using the indirect method. A partially completed schedule is provided below, but you must decide whether to add or subtract each item.

P-2.   Form for partial Statement of Cash Flows

Abacus Company
Statement of Cash Flows
(Operating Section Only)
For the Year Ended December 31, 2007

Net Income $ 63,000
   Add or (subtract) the following:
     Decrease in Accounts Receivable
     Increase in Inventory
     Increase in Prepaid Rent
     Decrease in Accounts Payable
     Decrease in Wages Payable
     Increase in Interest Payable
     Depreciation Expense
Net Cash Flow from Operating Activities $

P-3   *This problem is based on the same information presented in problems P-1 and P-2 with additional information provided.*
The following information is available for Abacus Co. at the end of 2007:

	December 31, 2006	December 31, 2007
Assets:		
Cash	$ 20,000	$ 28,000
Accounts Receivable	70,000	65,000
Inventory	100,000	118,000
Prepaid Rent	10,000	14,000
Equipment	500,000	580,000
Accumulated Depreciation	(100,000)	(155,000)
Total Assets	$ 600,000	$ 650,000
Liabilities and Equity:		
Accounts Payable	$ 60,000	$ 55,000
Wages Payable	18,000	17,000
Interest Payable	12,000	15,000
Bonds Payable	150,000	200,000
Common Stock	300,000	300,000
Retained Earnings	60,000	103,000
Treasury Stock	0	(40,000)
Total Liabilities and Equity	$ 600,000	$ 650,000
Sales		$ 900,000
Cost of Goods Sold		637,000
Gross Margin		263,000
Wages Expense	$ 107,000	
Rent Expense	25,000	
Depreciation Expense	55,000	
Interest Expense	13,000	200,000
Net Income		$ 63,000

Additional information:

Equipment was purchased during the year for cash. The cost of the equipment was $80,000. Cash dividends of $20,000 were declared and paid. Assume that all sales were made on account and that Accounts Payable relates to inventory purchases.

Required:

Prepare the Statement of Cash Flows for Abacus Co. for the year ended December 31, 2007. Assume Abacus uses the direct method. Use the T-account method. Partially completed T-accounts are provided on the following page. A partially completed Statement of Cash Flows is also presented on a following page.

P-3. T-accounts for preparing Statement of Cash Flows

Cash	
Bal. 20,000	
Operating Activities	
Investing Activities	
Financing Activities	
Bal. 28,000	

Accounts Payable	
	60,000 Bal.
	55,000 Bal.

Common Stock	
	300,000 Bal.
	300,000 Bal.

Wages Payable	
	18,000 Bal.
	17,000 Bal.

Treasury Stock	
Bal. 0	
Bal. 40,000	

Accounts Receivable	
Bal. 70,000	
Bal. 65,000	

Interest Payable	
	12,000 Bal.
	15,000 Bal.

Retained Earnings	
	60,000 Bal.
	103,000 Bal.

Inventory	
Bal. 100,000	
Bal. 118,000	

Bonds Payable	
	150,000 Bal.
	200,000 Bal.

Prepaid Rent	
Bal. 10,000	
Bal. 14,000	

Equipment	
Bal. 500,000	
Bal. 580,000	

Accumulated Depreciation	
	100,000 Bal.
	155,000 Bal.

P-3.   Form for Statement of Cash Flows

Abacus Company
Statement of Cash Flows
For the Year Ended December 31, 2007

Cash Flows from Operating Activities
Cash Receipts from:
     Sales $

Cash Payments for:
     Inventory Purchases $(   )
     Wages   (   )
     Rent   (   )
     Interest   (   )
Total Cash Outflows   (   )
Net Cash Flows from Operating Activities $

Cash Flows from Investing Activities
     Outflow to Purchase Equipment   (   )
Net Cash Flows from Investing Activities   (   )

Cash Flows from Financing Activities
     Inflow from Issuance of Bonds

     Outflow to Purchase Treasury Stock   (   )
     Outflow to Pay Dividends   (   )
Net Cash Flows from Financing Activities   (   )
 Net Increase in Cash
     Add: Cash Balance, January 1, 2007
Cash Balance, December 31, 2007 $

Solutions to Self-Study Problems

Matching Problem

1. The monthly electricity bill was paid with cash __O__
2. Purchased inventory for cash. __O__
3. Purchased equipment for cash. __I__
4. Issued common stock for cash. __F__
5. Recorded depreciation expense. __O__

    Depreciation expense is a noncash expense, but it is usually shown as an adjustment to net income in the *operating section* of the SCF. This adjustment is necessary to convert accrual-based net income to cash flows from operating activities.

6. Purchased equipment using a note payable. __N__

    Because the note payable was exchanged directly for the equipment, no cash was involved in this transaction. This noncash transaction would be disclosed in a separate schedule or in the footnotes to the financial statements if the amount is material.

7. Issued a term note for cash. __F__
8. Paid cash for three months rent in advance. __O__
9. Recognized that one month's prepaid rent had expired. __O__

    Recognizing that one month's rent has expired does not involve cash. However, the change in prepaid rent from the beginning of the year to the end of the year is usually shown as an adjustment to net income in the operating section of the SCF. This adjustment is necessary to convert accrual-based net income to cash flows from operating activities.

10. Paid cash interest on bonds payable. __O__
11. Purchased treasury stock with cash. __F__
12. Sold treasury stock for more that its original cost; received cash. __F__

    Purchasing and selling treasury stock is always a financing activity. It does not matter whether the treasury stock was sold for an amount more, less, or equal to its original purchase price.

13. Sold, for cash, an old piece of equipment. The equipment was sold for an amount equal to its book value. __I__

14. Sold, for cash, an old piece of equipment. The equipment was sold for an amount less than its book value (i.e., at a loss). __I, O__

    The cash received from the **sale** of long-term assets, such as equipment, is a cash inflow in the **investing** section of the SCF whether the sale produced a gain, loss, or neither. The **loss** on the sale causes an adjustment to be needed in the **operating** section of the SCF. The loss on the sale reduced net income but did <u>not</u> reduce cash, so an adjustment is necessary to convert net income to cash flows from operating activities.

15. Made the annual cash payment for principal and interest on a term loan. __F, O__

    The portion of the payment on term debt that reduced **principal** would be shown in the **financing** section. The portion that was for **interest** expense would affect **operating** activities.

16. Recorded amortization on a patent. __O__

    Amortization expense, like depreciation, is a noncash expense, but it is usually shown as an adjustment to net income in the operating section of the SCF. This adjustment is necessary to convert accrual-based net income to cash flows from operating activities.

17. Made cash sales. __O__

18.   Collected cash from accounts receivable. __O__
19.   Paid cash dividends. __F__
20.   Issued a stock dividend. __N__

Stock dividends do not affect cash. This event would be disclosed in the footnotes to the financial statements, however. The same answer would apply if a stock split had been issued rather than a stock dividend.

Multiple-Choice Problems

1.   c.

		OR		
Sales	$50,000		Accounts Receivable	
- Incr. in Acct. Rec.	2,000			
Cash Coll. from Sales	**$48,000**	Beg. Bal.	10,000	
		Sales	50,000	
				? Collections
		End. Bal.	12,000	

2.   b.

		OR		
Utilities Expense	$15,000		Utilities Payable	
+ Decr. in Utl. Payable	1,000			
Cash Paid for Utilities	**$16,000**			4,000 Beg. Bal.
				15,000 Utility Exp
		Cash Paid	?	
				3,000 End. Bal.

3.   a.

4.   c.

5.   d.   Cash received from selling the equipment would be a cash inflow in the *investing* activities section of the SCF. However, the loss on the sale caused net income to decrease, but this loss did not consume cash. Therefore, such losses are usually shown as an adjustment to net income in the *operating section* of the SCF. This adjustment is necessary to convert accrual-based net income to cash flows from operating activities.

6.   b.

		OR		
Rent Expense	$20,000		Prepaid Rent	
- Decr. in Prepaid Rent	2,000			
Cash Paid for Rent	**$18,000**	Beg. Bal.	6,000	
				20,000 Rent Exp.
		Cash Paid	?	
		End. Bal.	4,000	

7.   d.

8.   b.   Only the events occurring on January 20, and October 20, were investing activities.

Purchase of equipment	$(80,000)
Sale of equipment	15,000
Net decrease from investing activities	**$(65,000)**

9. c.

Effect on Net Income		
Proceeds from sale		$100,000
less Book value: Original cost	$300,000	
Accum. Depr.	230,000	70,000
Gain on sale (increased Net Income)		**$ 30,000**

The only effect on cash flows was the increase in cash from the proceeds, **$100,000**.

10. d.

Ending Balance in Equipment		$600,000
Beginning Balance in Equipment	$500,000	
– Equipment sold	80,000	420,000
Equipment Purchased		**$180,000**

OR

Equipment

Beg. Bal.	500,000		
		80,000	Equipment Sold
Equipment Pur.	?		
End. Bal.	600,000		

11. a.

Net Income	$ 50,000
+ Depreciation Expense	8,000
– Increase in Accounts Receivable	(13,000)
+ Decrease in Inventory	12,000
– Decrease in Accounts Payable	(11,000)
+ Increase in Wages Payable	14,000
Net Cash Flow from Operating Activities	**$ 60,000**

Multiple True-False Problems

1. a. **True**, a company that is closing existing stores will probably sell some of the property, plant and equipment from the stores being closed. Any cash received from the sale of these assets would be reported as a cash inflow from investing activities.

b. **True**, a company that is opening new stores must get the cash needed to purchase the land, buildings, equipment, and inventory needed to establish these stores. Since a rapidly expanding company would probably not be able to finance the new stores entirely from cash generated by existing stores, it would need to issue new stock or long-term debt. The cash inflows from the issuance of stock or long-term debt would be reported as cash flows from financing activities.

c. **False**, a company opening new stores would be spending significant amounts of cash to purchase inventory for the new stores. Cash paid for inventory is reported as a cash **outflow** (negative, not positive) from operating activities.

d. **False**, cash paid for the new equipment is reported as an outflow (negative) from investing activities. Although any cash received from the sale of old equipment is reported as a cash inflow (positive) from investing activities, the cost of the new equipment almost certainly exceeds the salvage value of the old.

e. **True**, depreciation expense, which is significant at most companies, decreases net income, but does not decrease cash flows from operating activities. While cash is decreased when depreciable assets are purchased, this cash outflow is reported as an **investing** activity, not as an operating activity.

2.   a.   **True**, the cash received from the bank loan would be reported as a cash inflow from financing activities.

b.   **False**, <u>Event 2</u> did not involve cash flows, since Yeager did not receive or pay cash immediately as a result of its transaction with Fred Farmer. This event would probably be reported as a significant non-cash event in the footnotes to the statement of cash flows, but it would not be reported on the statement itself.

c.   **False**, see "b." above for an explanation.

d.   **False**, cash received from the sale of long-term operational assets should be reported as investing activities, not as operating activities, even if the assets are sold at a gain.

e.   **True.**

Exercise-Type Problems

P-1.   Solutions for P-1

Schedule for Question 1

Sales	$900,000
+ Beginning Accts. Rec.	70,000
Max. that could	
have been collected	970,000
– Ending Accts Rec.	65,000
Cash collected	$905,000

T-Account for Question 1

Accounts Receivable

Beg. Bal.	70,000	
Sales	900,000	
		905,000 Collected
End. Bal.	65,000	

Schedule for Question 2

Rent Expense	$ 25,000
Ending Prepaid Rent	14,000
Max. that could	
have been paid	39,000
Beg. Prepaid Rent	10,000
Cash Paid	$ 29,000

T-Account for Question 2

Prepaid Rent

Beg. Bal.	10,000	
		25,000 Rent Exp.
Cash Paid	**29,000**	
End Bal.	14,000	

Schedule for Question 3

Wages Expense	$107,000
Beg. Wages Payable	18,000
Max. that could	
have been paid	125,000
End. Wages Payable	17,000
Cash Paid	$108,000

T-Account for Question 3

Wages Payable

		18,000	Beg. Bal.
		107,000	Wages Exp.
Cash Paid	**108,000**		
		17,000	End. Bal.

Schedule for Question 4

Interest Expense	$ 13,000
Beg. Interest Payable	12,000
Max. that could have been paid	25,000
End. Interest Payable	15,000
Cash Paid	$ 10,000

T-Account for Question 4

Interest Payable

		12,000	Beg. Bal.
		13,000	Wages Exp.
Cash Paid	10,000		
		15,000	End. Bal.

P-2.   Solution for partial Statement of Cash Flows

Abacus Company
Statement of Cash Flows
(Operating Section Only)
For the Year Ended December 31, 2007

Net Income	$ 63,000
Add or (subtract) the following:	
+ Decrease in Accounts Receivable	5,000
− Increase in Inventory	(18,000)
− Increase in Prepaid Rent	(4,000)
− Decrease in Accounts Payable	(5,000)
− Decrease in Wages Payable	(1,000)
+ Increase in Interest Payable	3,000
+ Depreciation Expense	55,000
Net Cash Flow From Operating Activities	$ 98,000

P-3.   T-accounts for solution

Cash

Bal.	20,000		
Operating Activities			
(a2)	905,000	660,000	(b3)
		108,000	(d2)
		29,000	(e2)
		10,000	(f2)
Investing Activities			
		80,000	(g1)
Financing Activities			
(h1)	50,000	40,000	(i1)
		20,000	(j1)
Bal.	28,000		

Accounts Receivable

Bal.	70,000		
(a1)	900,000	**905,000**	**(a2)**
Bal.	65,000		

Inventory

Bal.	100,000		
(b2)	**655,000**	637,000	(b1)
Bal.	118,000		

Prepaid Rent

Bal.	10,000		
(e2)	**29,000**	25,000	(e1)
Bal.	14,000		

Equipment

Bal.	500,000		
(g1)	80,000		
Bal.	580,000		

Accumulated Depreciation

		100,000	Bal.
		55,000	(c1)
		155,000	Bal.

Accounts Payable

		60,000	Bal.
(b3)	660,000	655,000	(b2)
		55,000	Bal.

Wages Payable

		18,000	Bal.
(d2)	108,000	107,000	(d1)
		17,000	Bal.

Interest Payable

		12,000	Bal.
(f2)	**10,000**	13,000	(f1)
		15,000	Bal.

Bonds Payable

		150,000	Bal.
		50,000	**(h1)**
		200,000	Bal.

Common Stock

		300,000	Bal.
		300,000	Bal.

Treasury Stock

Bal.	0		
(i1)	**40,000**		
Bal.	40,000		

Retained Earnings

		60,000	Bal.
		900,000	(a1)
(b1)	637,000		
(c1)	55,000		
(d1)	107,000		
(e1)	25,000		
(f1)	13,000		
(j1)	20,000		
		103,000	Bal.

NOTE

Amounts shown in **bold** type were plugged to be the amounts needed to make the T-accounts balance.

Solution for Statement of Cash Flows

Abacus Company
Statement of Cash Flows
For the Year Ended December 31, 2007

Cash Flows from Operating Activities
Cash Receipts from:

Sales		$905,000	

Cash Payments for:

Inventory Purchases	$(660,000)		
Wages	(108,000)		
Rent	(29,000)		
Interest	(10,000)		
Total Cash Outflows		(807,000)	
Net Cash Flow from Operating Activities			$98,000

Cash Flows from Investing Activities

Outflow to Purchase Equipment		(80,000)	
Net Cash Flow from Investing Activities			(80,000)

Cash Flows from Financing Activities

Inflow from Issuance of Bonds		50,000	
Outflow to Purchase Treasury Stock		(40,000)	
Outflow to Pay Dividends		(20,000)	
Net Cash Flow from Financing Activities			(10,000)
Net Increase in Cash			8,000
Add: Cash Balance, January 1, 2007			20,000
Cash Balance, December 31, 2007			$28,000

Appendix
Summary of Financial Ratios

Chapter	Ratios

Chapter   **Ratios**

1   **Price-Earnings** $$\frac{\text{Selling price of one share of stock}}{\text{Earnings per share}}$$

3   **Return-on-Assets** $$\frac{\text{Net income}}{\text{Total assets}}$$

         Debt-to-Assets $$\frac{\text{Total debt}}{\text{Total assets}}$$

         Return-on-Equity $$\frac{\text{Net income}}{\text{Equity}}$$

5   **Gross Profit Percentage** $$\frac{\text{Gross margin}}{\text{Sales}}$$

         Return-on-Sales $$\frac{\text{Net income}}{\text{Sales}}$$

6   **Inventory Turnover** $$\frac{\text{Cost of goods sold}}{\text{Inventory}}$$

         Average Days to Sell Inventory $$\frac{365 \text{ days}}{\text{Inventory turnover}}$$

Chapter		Ratios
7	**Current**	$\dfrac{\text{Current assets}}{\text{Current liabilities}}$
8	**Accounts Receivable Turnover**	$\dfrac{\text{Sales}}{\text{Accounts receivable}}$
	Average Days to Collect Accounts Receivable	$\dfrac{365 \text{ days}}{\text{Accounts receivable turnover}}$
10	**Times Interest Earned**	$\dfrac{\text{EBIT}}{\text{Interest expense}}$
	Return-on-Assets (redefined)	$\dfrac{\text{EBIT}}{\text{Total assets}}$
11	**Earnings Per Share (repeated)**	$\dfrac{\text{Net income for the year}}{\text{Outstanding shares of common stock}}$
	Price-Earnings	$\dfrac{\text{Selling price of one share of stock}}{\text{Earnings per share}}$